THE TIGHTROPE WALKER

SASAN HABIBVAND

This edition published 2025
Copyright © Sasan Habibvand 2025

First published in Australia by Aurora House (http://aurorahouse.com.au)

Cover design: Donika Mishineva (www.artofdonika.com)
Typesetting and e-book design: Amit Dey (amitdey2528@gmail.com)

The right of Sasan Habibvand to be identified as Author of the Work has been asserted in accordance with the Copyright, Designs and Patents Act 1988.

ISBN number: 978-1-923298-78-1 (paperback)

All rights reserved. No part of this publication may be reproduced, stored in a retrieval system, or transmitted, in any form or by any means without the prior written permission of the publisher, nor be otherwise circulated in any form of binding or cover other than that in which it is published and without a similar condition being imposed on the subsequent purchaser.

 A catalogue record for this book is available from the National Library of Australia

DEDICATION

For Isa and Ryan, whose love, light, and laughter brighten my days and whose presence brings meaning to every page.

*"What are you about, circle of the blind?
Seek a sighted guide, so the path you find."*

(Rumi)

A WORD WITH YOU

It took long years of craving for that true happiness — not a fake one — to discover that invaluable truth. Thirsty and weary, I begged at every door and wandered countless roads, only to find, as Rumi cautioned, that the treasure I sought was right at home, and the spring I longed for was within reach all along.

A simple truth: that I already had what I was looking for right here, with me, in me! And you can guess how exciting this was, a revolution in the way I looked at myself and the world.

In the wake of that monumental discovery, I realised the main root of pain and sorrow — for everyone — lies within, rather than without, as does the source of joy and happiness. Only then did I appreciate what Rumi meant when he made almost the same statement centuries ago:

> *The road to happiness lies within, not without.*
> *It is foolish to seek palaces and castles.*
> *See this one, happy and cheerful in the corner of a mosque.*
> *Watch the other sitting in a palace, sad and disheartened.*

I understood that to live in peace and happiness, instead of running after a mirage, you only need to delve into yourself to discover the root of your sorrow. This book will share what I have found so far on this fascinating journey, to help you get to know yourself.

Self-awareness is a road whose traveller wakes up from a disturbing nightmare and opens their eyes to a happy, tranquil world. So this simple story aims to offer vivid, convincing answers to many important questions regarding the meaning of life, liberation from pain, the true nature of ego, and more.

Among other things, you may be interested to see what really happens in a matter of a few years to turn an innocent, loveable baby into an anxious person or a spiteful adult. Above all, you'll see how you can get relief from grief and stress to live in harmony and tranquillity.

If what I have shared interests you so far, I invite you to read on.

ABOUT THE TIGHTROPE WALKER

Liberation from inner pain has been a central concern for humanity throughout history. For thousands of years, thinkers and philosophers have grappled with this issue in various ways, hoping to alleviate human suffering.

This book is motivated by the belief that internal difficulties are not separate problems or disconnected entities. Instead, they are different manifestations of the same underlying issue.

In my view, we face one fundamental problem, while issues such as anxiety, aggression, and depression are merely its symptoms. The same applies to a lack of self-confidence, self-esteem, and human flourishing. These are but colourful leaves and branches of a sinister tree I call *Fundamental Humiliation*. This deep-rooted humiliation largely stems from society's unjust treatment of individuals and from their eventual surrender to this pervasive abuse. Such surrender is often driven by a lack of awareness, a lack of confidence, and a learned complacency.

Humans are profoundly and extensively humiliated regarding their rights, abilities, and worth. Tragically, they have internalised this humiliation and taken it for granted. The imposition of an illusory, exploitative worldview and self-perception is a key part of this condition. Naturally, as long as such vast mistreatment persists, mental, existential, and psychological afflictions are unavoidable.

As such this book is an effort to present a theory of the human condition, tracing the roots of our individual emotional and behavioural problems back to social, historical, and biological origins. It also aims to offer possible solutions to this collective dilemma.

In summary, a few points could characterise this work.

The first relates both to the approach and the form. On the one hand, this work aims to explain what the ego is and to analyse what it implies; on the other hand, it aims to present all of this in the form of a simple but sincere story.

Most available works emphasise the necessity of knowing the self and, or from ones's ego. Surprisingly, few works offer convincing answers to the question of what the natures of the self and the ego are.

Eastern philosophy almost invariably advises that to be freed from sorrow and live a painless life, it's necessary to know yourself and recognise the false self, called ego—perfectly wise advice. But few scholars have tried to show clearly what that self is and how that ego comes into being. There are still a myriad of debates on the nature of ego, its roots, and how it functions, with many vague, disparate ideas shared.

This book focuses on that essential question. Here, you'll witness the birth and growth of the entity named *ego* as a living, dynamic organism inside your being. You'll see how your consciousness reacts to this intruder, how it causes your emotional suffering, and what implications it has on your life.

Here, along with this story's characters on their journey to life, you'll make amazing discoveries and experience great joy from what you learn. You'll watch these characters emerge into society and see how they are treated by the ethical, cultural, and educational system. You'll see how worry and suffering are born, and you'll notice how happy lives are soon afflicted by pain and anxiety. Finally, you'll understand how these characters can regain their freedom.

And then you'll realise that these characters are me and you!

We will see a structured exploration of self-awareness and self-knowledge here. Knowing ourselves involves both discovering our true self and recognising the plagues and impurities imposed upon it. I've aimed to outline this not as a collection of scattered reflections but as a coherent and unified body of thought. The topics explored here—including happiness, ego (self and I), identity, conditioning, and what I call the *Outward I*—are approached as inherently interconnected aspects of the inner journey. A comprehensive list of key concepts appears in the keyword list at the end of the book. These ideas are presented not in isolation but as parts of a larger system of understanding. That is what this book seeks to uncover.

If you often ask yourself, *What is self-knowledge anyway?*, I hope you find your answer here.

The other point relates to the book's philosophical approach, which I find essential and indispensable. Don't worry! You won't have to grapple with complex philosophical notions. Rather, the core idea is that confusion and suffering mainly arise from vague, imposed, and contradictory philosophies of life.

So often, humans seek unfeasible and illusory goals. Their wants and ideas are plagued by conflicts and ambiguities, the main cause of distress and bewilderment.

Once you revisit and reform your philosophy of life, your mental and emotional tensions will fade away. But that requires defining your values and principles consciously and independently.

In this story, we'll explore mysticism and spirituality but will not endorse any particular kind of faith or school of thought. Similarly, the more modern disciplines of linguistics and psychology will be surveyed without you needing to study these subjects for their own sake.

The characters in this story, Shabe and Soren, find themselves lost in a wilderness, thirsty and hungry, looking for their beloved home. Like them, you have some crucial questions. Who am I? What is the purpose of life? What is the right and what is the wrong thing to do? And what's the way to enduring happiness, if any?

To find answers, you may seek advice from any kind of likely knowledge. As an enthusiastic, diligent seeker, you may listen to anyone who will share a clue, but you won't stay in any one spot for too long. You'll be impatient to find your way back to your own familiar, cosy home. Only there will you find true peace and happiness.

Like me, you might also believe that true change and liberation don't come from mere knowledge but from insight or seeing. Knowledge is a collection of data in the memory, which is not of essential value by itself. However, insight is the ability to discern and decide.

I call the approach here *logical self-awareness* because it is founded on clear, reason-based views and analyses of the issues it addresses, rather than on vague, reason-evading methods. The same method is applied to spirituality and mysticism, the teachings of which we will use in a reasoned, practical way, rather than relying on vague mottos or dubious claims.

You can also call this book's approach an intuitional or realistic one. Here, instead of delving into theoretical debates or resorting to different hypotheses, you can look directly inside yourself and observe your own attitudes, feelings, and states to see what's going on.

And this will be an exciting discovery because it is *you* who sees and feels, not this psychologist or that philosopher. This is the only method where confidence and autonomy replace doubt and reliance. When you've read this book, what you'll believe will be what you yourself have seen, not what you've been told.

Everyone dislikes dishonesty, violence, and prejudice and expects kindness, honesty, and justness. Yet rarely does anyone bother to deal with the causes of such difficulties—another topic this book will attend to.

Across the story, I have taken advantage of sayings and quoted excerpts from the beautiful and insightful poetry of Rumi, a 13th-century Persian philosopher and poet. You'll be glad to know that, contrary to many inaccurate and misleading materials circulating around, all excerpts here are my own authentic, firsthand translations from the Persian originals. I have also retold parables from *Masnavi Ma'navi*, Rumi's brilliant and highly celebrated work. That doesn't mean we must fanatically believe any idea simply because it's been endorsed by Rumi, unique as his insight and understanding are.

Instead of deifying Rumi as an infallible superhuman, we shall strive to put his message to practical use, hearing all the sorts of "Ohs!" and "Heys!" he utters to capture our attention to the moving truths he perceives—truths that many cannot see.

Place two fingers upon your eyes
Do you see the world? Answer honestly.
If you can't see the world, it isn't non-existent.
The problem is the fingers of the sinister ego.
Hey, you! Lift your fingers from your eyes.
Then see everything clearly.

If you read *The Masnavi*, or anything else to know yourself and your world, you'll find your eyes opening to new horizons of truth. One such truth is that person-worship is simply another type of idol-worship. Never compromise your wisdom because that's your only true freedom.

Now, a few tips.

First, the view taken in this book may seem slightly different from the familiar, usual way you look at life, which is quite normal with the self-knowledge approach, at least in the genuine sense of the term. Self-knowledge means discovering yourself, and discovery, of course, takes a new, fresh outlook. Many of the issues might sound new-fangled. Many familiar questions have also been answered with a novel approach.

Just be patient and read on until things become clear. As new things are explored, previously unclear topics will be clarified. Presumption is the enemy of discovery.

CONTENTS

A Word with You	vii
About The Tightrope Walker	ix

Chapter One: Dizziness — 1

Here, you set off on your journey with a story from Rumi's *Masnavi* and begin to see the ways society tries to control you.

The Donkey's Gone! (a parable from the *Masnavi*)	8
"Seek Thirst, Not Water!"	16

Chapter Two: The Wildlife — 25

This looks at the historical and natural backgrounds of the human condition. It shows how society devises a *false language* along with a set of *pseudo-values* to manipulate and subdue the individual.

The False Language	29
The Label	38

Chapter Three: The Cross-eyed Servant — 53

This chapter explains the contradictory nature of the *pseudo-values* and how they impose various problems onto humans.

Two but Nothing	58
Blurry Lenses	62
Superman	67

Blind Traditions	71
Advertisement	74
The Sunglasses	78

Chapter Four: Behind the Mask — **91**

This is the birth of a second self, which we will call the *outward I*. We'll discuss the numerous pains in the struggle for this imposed identity as an unattainable ideal and how the psyche reacts to this unwelcome entity.

A Destination Not to Reach!	96
The Mind and the Burden of Identity	102
The Outward I and the Inner Mechanisms	109
Fear	115
Anger	119
Jealousy	124
Pride	124
Self-Deceit	133
Identification	135
Self-Blame	141

Chapter Five: The Office — **147**

Here, we discuss the various tricks used to indoctrinate the *outward I* as an imposed identity.

The Tale of the Mud-Eating Man	150
The Fundamental Humiliation	153
Comparison	158
Blame	159
Insult	162
Praise and Admiration	166
The Village of the Slaves	168

Chapter Six: The Circus   173

We present the consequences of the imposition of the ego or the *outward I* on the psyche.

The Society Within	176
The Reed Moans	185
Self-Alienation	188
Conflict	189
Fear and Insecurity	199
Ignorance	200
The Remote Control	201
Projection	203
Running for a Mirage	205
The Doubled Pains	209
Conditioning	211
On the Bolting Horse	218
The Treadmill	221

Chapter Seven: The Reclining Chair   231

We watch the self through the magnifying glass and discuss ways to be liberated from the anguished ego.

Who Is I?	233
The Opium	256
What is the Truth?	280
The Chance to Be Present	288

And your journey ends here. However, this could be the beginning of a new road towards joy and marvels.

Acknowledgments	295
About The Author	297
The Keyword List	299

CHAPTER ONE

DIZZINESS

Soren was dazed. He had no idea what had just happened. He could only see two shadows quickly disappearing. His head was spinning, and his cheek throbbed with pain.

He remembered then. Hans and Daniel tearing off. Daniel had punched Soren's face hard, and Hans had landed a few agonising blows to his back and hips. Now they were gone.

The pain was harder to ignore now. He felt something flowing down his nose. Mucus? He wiped his nose with the back of his hand and saw blood. As he fumbled around in his pocket for a tissue, he found himself surrounded by three looming figures. From his prone position, their tall bodies resembled the three gigantic, unsightly buildings that had sprouted up like mushrooms around the park next to his home a few years ago. This park had been the setting for many of Soren's pleasant and carefree childhood games.

The buildings cast dark shadows almost completely over the park. Whenever he peered up at them, Soren imagined they'd collapse on top of him, burying him alive. Soren wished he could give a loud shout at the selfish people who had left those ugly things there and vanished.

The first of the shapes to speak was Steve, the butcher. He glowered down at Soren. "What a gutless kid!" he bellowed in a high, nasally voice that hardly matched his large figure. He shook his head. "You just stood there like a statue and did nothing while they were beating you up! If it were my son, Mike, he would've taught them a good lesson!"

The next shadow to speak was Mrs Grant, the local dressmaker. She pushed her round glasses down to the tip of her long, thin nose and peered down at Soren sympathetically, then glared at the butcher. "Oh no, Steve! Soren deserves praise for being so restrained. Well done, son. Fighting is never a good thing." She shook her head. "No, no, no."

"They're all savages! All three of them should be punished," Joe the carpenter gruffed, frowning, his long, khaki overalls making him look even taller. He would have seen the whole commotion from his shop only a few metres away. "If I was their parent, I'd give them all a good hiding so they don't get into any more fights."

They muttered among themselves for a while longer and then drifted away. Head swimming, Soren clambered unsteadily to his feet and readjusted his clothes. He was still sore all over. Cradling his face where it had been punched, he sat down on the kerb.

He'd confronted Hans and Daniel in the past for their bullying. They often mocked his short height and called him a dwarf. Today, they'd made fun of his dad's old car, calling it "the heap" and his dad "Captain Heap".

After ages of torment and ridicule, this had been the last straw. As they were leaving school, Soren called them out. "Just leave me alone! You fools!"

They'd simply laughed at him hysterically.

That was when Soren cracked and punched Hans on the chin. Ms Grant obviously hadn't seen that part, which Soren was thankful for.

Lost in his thoughts, he wheeled around when he felt something touch his shoulder, his fists at the ready. He was relieved to find it was Mr Ashton, his favourite teacher, smiling warmly as he always did in class. His white shirt, dark trousers, and checkered jacket, plus his light-brown wavy hair, medium height, and slim build made him easily recognisable. Just like in the classroom, Mr Ashton's kind black eyes gazed penetratingly at Soren.

"Hi, Soren. I saw what happened. Are you all right?" Mr Ashton said.

Soren, embarrassed, his mind racing, wondered what Mr Ashton would have to say about the fight if he'd seen it, yet he felt his teacher would understand. He wasn't the type to blame or reproach. And regardless, Soren was relieved to see him.

"Yeah, I'm okay. Thanks, sir," Soren answered, peering down at his now-dusty white sneakers.

Mr Ashton was different from other teachers. He spoke confidently and clearly and answered every student's question in a kind and considerate manner. Soren had never seen him lose his temper or get angry, not even with the most difficult students. He'd taken a strong liking to him ever since he'd started teaching philosophy at their school a few months before. Everyone felt the same way about him. His lessons were popular among students.

Mr Ashton's demeanour was often considered unusual in their small town. Soren's mother, Sally, had also become intrigued by Mr Ashton soon after his arrival. He was different from other teachers she'd worked with.

"They ran away, didn't they? Are you hurt?" The teacher's brows furrowed in concern.

"It doesn't matter." Soren's voice broke as a sob began to form in his chest. He sat back down on the kerb and stared off into the distance, stifling the sob.

"Are you sure?"

"Yes."

Soren lifted his head and looked at Mr Ashton, catching his trademark penetrating gaze from behind his thick glasses. His large blue eyes radiated a particular kind of curiosity. A slight, not-too-serious frown gave his face a thoughtful and appealing expression.

"Then why are you so upset?" Mr Ashton asked.

"I'm feeling more dizzy than upset."

"Oh, dear! Do you need to see a doctor?"

Soren's smile was bitter. "No, it's not that, Mr Ashton. I'm just … I don't know. I'm feeling awfully confused."

"Well, that's understandable. I saw you copped a few hits."

"No, not that. After Hans and Daniel ran away, Steve, the butcher, Ms Grant, the dressmaker, and Joe, the carpenter, all approached me and said some things."

"What did they say?"

"Well, Steve called me timid and a wimp. Ms Grant thought I was well-behaved for not fighting back …"

"Oh, I see."

"Yes, and then Joe said we were savages who should all be punished."

"Really? And which part are you confused about?" asked Mr Ashton.

"All of it," Soren said. "Is fighting the same as savagery? Or is it a sort of self-defence? Everybody says something different. Am I a savage or gutless?" Soren let out a long sigh. "What's the right thing to do? What should I have done? They were making fun of my dad and insulting me! Shouldn't I have said something or fought back? Or should I have ignored it? Shouldn't I have defended myself? What's the right thing to do, sir?"

Mr Ashton put his bag down. He sat beside Soren on the kerb and tilted his head back thoughtfully. "You have every right to be puzzled."

"And you know what's funny? Some kids at school call me a dwarf, while others call me Professor Soren."

"Ah, yes. That's because you like to read books and know things they don't. And I agree with them."

"Agree with who?" Soren wondered.

"With the second group. You're a bright young man. You consider things deeply and ask interesting questions. And you're a talented writer too! I still remember the story you wrote for class, *The Lion Who Turned into a Mouse*. It was insightful and creative."

Ah, yes. Soren recalled he'd written the story around the time when Mr Ashton had first joined their school. It was about a sly fox's hatred of a strong, fearsome lion.

Once upon a time, a cunning fox lived in the jungle. The fox was jealous and afraid of the mighty lion, whose strength made the fox feel small and insignificant. So he hatched a cunning plan to strip the king of the jungle of his greatness.

One day, the fox approached the lion and said, "Sir, why waste your energy chasing after prey when you could use tricks and lies to catch them easily?"

The lion, liking the easier way, agreed to the fox's suggestion. He began setting traps and disguising his voice to trick animals into coming close, no longer needing to hunt them down.

As time went on, however, the lion grew lazy. He rarely left his den, and his once-powerful muscles became weak and frail. His voice, after many disguises, turned high-pitched and squeaky, losing the fierce roar he was known for. With each passing day, the lion became smaller and weaker, while the fox watched from the shadows, happy and satisfied that his plan was working.

Eventually, the lion became so weak and scrawny that he was even smaller than the fox. Seeing his chance, the fox pounced on the once-mighty lion and devoured him in one swift bite. And so the fox stripped the king of the jungle of his power and took his place.

Soren's mother had enjoyed the story and had had it published in the local *Weekly*, where she wrote as a columnist. It had received good feedback from many readers.

"I'm glad you liked it." Soren smiled. "I'd like to write more."

"I'll look forward to reading more of your stories. Anyway, congratulations, Professor Soren!" Mr Ashton grinned.

"For what?" Soren tilted his head.

"First, for the thoughtful questions you ask. And second, for actually looking for answers."

"Really?" Soren looked up at his teacher.

"You know, not all questions are useful. Some people ask stupid questions and waste their time. And many others do have good questions but aren't really serious about looking for their answers." He patted Soren on the shoulder. "But you have both valuable questions and a serious heart to learn."

"Thanks!" Soren felt happier now. "So what's the answer, Mr Ashton?"

"Please, Soren, call me Shabe. And what sort of answer art thou seeking, oh wise one?" Shabe asked, gesturing dramatically.

Soren let out a small laugh. "What do you mean, Mr — I mean, Shabe?"

"Well, a question can be answered in two ways: an instant, brief, often superficial answer or a well-reasoned one. Now, which one are you after?"

"Obviously, the well-reasoned answer," Soren said. *It's called well-reasoned, after all*, he thought.

"I thought you'd choose that answer! You know, incomplete or superficial answers can be misleading. Sometimes even dangerous."

Soren's eyes widened. "What do you mean?"

Pointing at the large, grey car parked on the roadside, Shabe said, "Take this car. If you asked me, 'What is this object here?' and I said, 'This is a thing you drive and move around in,' that answer would be incomplete and even harmful."

"Oh," Soren nodded. "You mean I should also know about traffic rules and things?"

"Yes, and how to drive safely. Otherwise, it could lead to tragedies."

Glad I chose the well-reasoned answer, then, Soren thought.

"Well, ladies and gent — uh." He glanced at Soren. "Well, I mean, the only gentleman."

Soren looked up at Shabe, now standing with his bag in one hand and the other outstretched theatrically, his eyes gleaming.

Soren stared at him, amused and bewildered. He'd often witnessed glimpses of Shabe's acting talent shining through in class. He could have made a great career for himself as a performer.

"I bear great news! You are now honourably invited to embark on a fresh and unprecedented journey!" Shabe announced.

"A journey?" Soren was intrigued. "Where?"

"A journey to the world!"

Soren stared at Shabe. "The world? We're already in the world, aren't we?"

"Well —"

"I think I understand," Soren interrupted. "You mean a journey to the world of stories and myths or something like that?"

"You couldn't be more mistaken! I mean this very world, the world we're in right now."

"Oh."

"Do you think we've travelled or explored this world and we've learnt enough?"

"Hmm." Soren thought for a moment. "I'm not too sure. Probably not."

"Do you know what a true journey is like? One where you keep your eyes open from beginning to end, learn throughout, and enjoy everything?"

"I think so," Soren said. "You should be looking everywhere and at everything closely to discover new things and understand what they are and what they mean. And it's also important to have adequate tools and stuff on you, like a compass, binoculars, a tent, and a backpack. Like the journeys of Miguel Hans, Christopher Columbus, or Maurice Maeterlinck, or even like the *Journey to the Moon*."

"That's right, Soren."

"You told us before that you've been on lots of trips all over the world. I enjoy the stories you share in class about your journeys to Africa, Greece, Egypt, and Iran. I thought your trip to India was particularly interesting."

"Yes, and I recall you said you also loved travelling?" asked Shabe.

"Yes, I do love travelling," Soren replied, his mind wandering to his bucket-list of destinations. "Yet I can't really make sense of what you mean by a journey to the world."

"Well, in this particular journey, we'd take a tour to our own world, this very world. The only difference is that what we'd see on this journey has always been in front of us, before our eyes. But perhaps we've never looked carefully. In this journey, we'd want to see everything closely, with curious eyes, to discover as many new things as we can, including the very question you have right now. That way, we'd learn who we really are and what we're like. Who determines what we ought to be like? Is the world really how we see it? Are we all really who we thought we were? Of course, we'd answer many other questions, which I'm sure would be very interesting to an inquisitive boy like you. So would you like to join me?"

Soren nodded enthusiastically.

Shabe stood and dusted the back of his pants before reaching his hand out to Soren. "Well, then. Let's go."

Soren took his hand, and Shabe pulled him to his feet. The pain had subsided, he noticed. "Where?"

"We're going to my house."

"But ..."

"Don't worry; we'll call your mum to let her know where you are. Let's go. We can talk more on the way."

Soren glanced down at his watch. Still plenty of time before he was due home for dinner. "Okay. Let's go."

As Shabe led the way, turning from the main road onto a crooked woody street, Soren began to wonder what equipment they'd need for this so-called journey. Knowing Shabe, he guessed books would be involved.

Like a mind-reader, Shabe declared, "Our travel equipment includes some books — old and new. Makes no difference."

Knew it, Soren thought.

"There'll be some other items as well that I'm sure will interest you."

The Donkey's Gone!

They passed through the white wooden gate, into the bushy garden, and through the old front door. A large, brightly painted hall greeted Soren. A beautiful, handwoven carpet with an Oriental pattern of birds and flowers ran through. Colourful vases adorned each corner of the house. To their left, Soren noticed a tidy kitchen beside the living room, which was furnished like the hall. Soren liked the cheerful feel of Shabe's home.

He then noticed a large bookcase to his right, with shelves full of books, small and large, old and new, all neatly sorted.

Soren hadn't even seen Shabe leave until he returned a few minutes later, carrying a tray of coffee and cake. He set the tray on the coffee table in the living room, gesturing for Soren to take a seat.

"What's your mum's number?" he asked, then rang her from the next room. "Good afternoon, Mrs Dustin. It's Shabe Ashton, Soren's teacher."

"Oh, hello, Mr Ashton. How are you going?"

"Very well, thank you. I'm just calling to let you know I have Soren with me now, at my home. We're going to be together for a few hours today. We wanted a chance to do some reading and talk. We're just calling so you don't worry."

"Oh, that's fine." Sally sounded pleased. "I'm happy you're spending time with Soren."

"I'm happy too. Oh, by the way —"

"Yes?"

"Soren and I may need to see each other a few more times, depending on our talks. I hope you don't mind?"

"No, that's fine," said Sally. "Today is the beginning of the holidays, and Soren has little else to do. Besides, he takes a special interest in you and your lessons, as I'm sure you have realised."

Shabe smiled to himself. "Thank you. I appreciate intelligent and curious young men like him. That's why I wanted us to talk together and learn from each other. Well, so long, Mrs Dustin."

"Bye."

Shabe returned to Soren carrying a large brown leather bag, quite old and worn. He sat down beside Soren. "Our travel kit mostly consists of books. We'll also rely on this bag — actually, not the bag so much as what's in it." Shabe opened it and removed a white mask with a smile on it. He held it in front of his face, making it look like he was smiling behind the mask. Shabe tilted his head. "Well, am I happy or sad?"

Soren chuckled. "Happy!"

"How do you know?"

"Because you're laughing."

Shabe took the mask off, glowering.

Soren was taken aback. In a moment, a dark grey mask had replaced the white one, this time with a frown.

"Am I happy or sad?"

"Sa — I don't know," Soren said.

"Uh-huh. The first mask misled you, and you thought you knew, but then you realised you didn't. This is the very point where any learning starts: questioning what we *think* we know." Shabe put the masks aside, and his usual smile reappeared.

"I'd like to know what else you've got in there," Soren said.

"You'll see in time. Most of it is memorabilia from shows I've been in." As if reading Soren's thoughts, Shabe added, "I used to work in a circus."

Soren was stunned. "Really? What did you do?"

"I was a clown," Shabe said.

Soren's jaw dropped this time. "You're kidding! I'd never have guessed that!" *So he was a performer after all.*

"Well, you can learn many things in a circus, as in anywhere else."

"I thought the circus was just a place to make you laugh!"

"Perhaps," Shabe agreed. "But the whole world is full of lessons! Anyone who likes to learn finds out many new things every day."

"So why did you change your job?"

"Because I wanted to live a free life. But you can't do that while you're in the circus. There, you're always the same: a showman with a couple of fixed roles. I decided that if I wanted to be myself, I had to get out. Once I did, everything changed. The world was the same, but *everything* was different. It was fascinating! And I wanted to share all that experience with others. That's why I quit the circus and became a teacher."

Soren nodded. "Teaching philosophy."

"Exactly. The only way to truth is in knowledge and reason." Shabe took a large sip of coffee. "I'm currently writing a book about what

I've learnt so far. This book will accompany us through our journey. Or you could say that our journey *is* reading this book, as well as discussing it. Parts of this book come from my notes and diaries from my days in the circus."

"Must be very interesting, then. What's the name of the book?" asked Soren.

"I haven't chosen a title yet, but our journey through the world takes place over the course of seven chapters. Like any explorer, we will visit a new place in each chapter until, gradually, our picture of this land becomes complete. We can stop wherever we wish and comment on the scenery or ask questions and share what we see."

"Okay. So what's this story about?"

"You could say this is the story of your life and mine," said Shabe.

"Hey, cool!"

"I'm glad to hear that." Shabe stood up and went to the bookcase, selecting a rather thick book from the top shelf. He sat back down and opened a page. "Let's start our journey with a beautiful parable …"

"Um, what's a parable?" Soren asked.

"An old story, yet new and fresh at the same time. The original story is a poem, but I have quoted it in prose. It's called *The Donkey's Gone*."

Soren's eyes glinted. "Sounds great."

"The person who wrote it was Rumi."

"Who is he? Or perhaps she?"

"Rumi was a 13th-century Persian poet," said Shabe. "He wrote many interesting and insightful parables in his book *The Masnavi*. This one bears a lot of meaning to me."

"I'm all ears," Soren said, shifting in his seat.

"He says, in the old days, there was a poor, naïve Sufi …"

Soren interrupted, curiosity lighting up his eyes. "Wait. What is a Sufi?"

Shabe smiled. "A Sufi is like a monk but in the Muslim context. They are people who live piously and simply to get closer to a spiritual truth. They are also often called *dervishes*, referring to their modest way of life and simple hearts."

Soren nodded slowly. "So they're kind of like spiritual people who meditate or something?"

"Exactly! And they perform other practices, such as prayers and fasting, to achieve unity with God and find inner peace."

Soren blinked. "That's interesting, isn't it?"

Shabe nodded. "It is, and that's what Rumi himself did and what his followers still do today," he added, noting Soren's careful attention.

"I'd really like to see these people."

Shabe nodded, a knowing smile on his face. "You will one day. I'm sure. Well, this Sufi man only had a donkey, on which he travelled from town to town, performing shows for the public on the streets and earning a modest living," Shabe went on.

"On one journey, this dervish found himself in a new town. He made his way to the town's caravanserai—an inn, in ancient times—to stay for a while. He approached the innkeeper to ask about the town and its people.

"'It's not a bad place,' the innkeeper said. 'There are many things to see and do. But like anywhere else, we have both good and nasty people. And I'd warn you, there are many thieves and muggers in this town. So as a newcomer, be very careful about your belongings. They may easily trick you out of your money or rob you.'

"'Thank God I don't have much to worry about,' the traveller said. Then he left his donkey with a stablehand and headed to his room to rest.

"He'd barely stepped outside when he found himself surrounded by a group of strangers, greeting him warmly. They asked him where he came from, where he was going, and why he was there. When they discovered the dervish was travelling alone, they persuaded him to stay the night at their place. The simple-minded man agreed.

"After a while, the guest faced a table set with a colourful variety of delicious food, drinks, fruits, and refreshments. Weary and famished, he tasted some of each dish and drank to his heart's content.

"During the meal, musicians began playing cheerful music, so his new friends stood up to dance drunkenly and merrily while singing:

Joy is here, worry's gone!
The donkey's gone! The donkey's gone!'

"Meanwhile, as the dervish was enjoying their food and company, one of the new friends went to the stables to untie the donkey, then rode off with it.

"The stablehand, having seen the warm and cordial friendship between the dervish and his hosts, assumed the owner must have permitted them to borrow his donkey.

"Eventually, influenced by the heady atmosphere of the party, not to mention the charming music and delicious drinks, the Sufi also got up to dance. He even sang, loudly, 'The donkey's gone; the donkey's gone …'

"The celebrations went on until dawn. Late next morning, when the man woke up, he thanked his hosts sincerely for all their warm hospitality and told them he'd be on his way.

"'Hey! Think nothing of it. We enjoyed having your company for the night, dervish!' the bandits said.

"However, when the man went to collect his donkey, he found its spot empty. Bewildered, he asked, 'Where's my donkey?'

"The stablehand answered, 'Didn't you come yesterday to take it away?'

"The dervish's jaw dropped. 'I came to take it?'

"'Well, *you* didn't, but your friend did. And I gave it to him because I saw you were both so chummy.'

"The Sufi, astounded, left to confront the bandits. 'Why did you take my donkey away? What did you do with it?'

"'Well, clearly, we sold it!' the chief bandit answered calmly.

"The dervish couldn't believe his ears.

"'You did what?! Sold it! Why? Who the hell let you do that?' he shouted.

"'Oh, you idiot! Didn't you wonder why there was so much food and drink? Who paid for that fruit, the sweets, the music?'

"The man was speechless, bewildered.

"'For God's sake, what had you done for us to expect so much in return?' The chief bandit went on. 'How could you be so stupid? Don't you remember? You *yourself* joined our dance and sang the loudest: *The donkey's gone, the donkey's gone.* Didn't you?'

"For a while, the poor man was totally silent. At last, he understood the bitter truth: his entire wealth had gone with the wind. He cried out in anguish, cursing himself for his stupidity."

Shabe glanced at Soren. When he saw that the boy looked deeply immersed in the tale, he continued. "And he shouted in remorse and sorrow.

*'I was gone with the wind of imitation.
A hundred times, damn this imitation.'*"

Shabe closed the book and took another sip of coffee. "Well, what do you think?"

"Oh, it's a great story. Thought-provoking. Which book did you say it was from?"

"It's from *Masnavi Ma'navi*. As I said, it's a book of poetry by Jalal Aldin Rumi, a 13th-century Persian mystic and philosopher. It's been translated into many other languages since then.

"This book is not only stories or artful poetry; it's enlightening and educational. I've learnt a lot of lessons from Rumi. He's had considerable influence on many authors and thinkers across the world. We'll read more from him through our journey. What did you make of this parable?"

Soren frowned. "Um ... that you shouldn't follow others blindly. And to be careful others don't trick you out of your belongings. But what do you think?"

"I agree." Shabe nodded. "But I think there's much more to this story — things that are very important. My interpretation ..." Shabe opened the book again. "To me, the story of the dervish with his donkey symbolises an individual and how society treats him. The caravanserai represents the world, which is a passing thing. Everyone comes to it, only to leave, sooner or later.

"The bandits are a symbol of society, which can be cunning and manipulative. The wandering dervish, on the other hand, symbolises the naïve human stepping into the world with the wealth of life, energy, and potential, oblivious to the traps and tricks in their way. And the donkey, which is his vehicle for moving and growth, is a symbol of these assets."

Soren leaned back with a hint of a smile. "Maybe we give many precious things away without even knowing it. But how do we know when it's happening?"

"Great question. Do you remember the innkeeper?" Shabe went on before Soren could answer. "In *The Donkey's Gone*, the man thoughtlessly steps into a deceptive, exploitative world. Despite warnings from his own common sense, the innkeeper, he's enticed by society to follow its models and suggestions blindly. So when the man gets drunk and joins their dancing, this refers to the human tendency to recklessly follow others and the loss of reasoning and authenticity.

"Once he sobers up, he realises he's only gained a passing childish pleasure in return for his priceless belongings. Perhaps the saddest part of the story is that the the individual stupidly dances to society's music, while losing his life's assets at the party that is held for him."

Soren slapped his knee. "That's a great interpretation! Really thought-provoking. Is the whole book about this story?"

"Sort of, but you can find the answer to many questions if you look closely at this short story. Would you like to continue?"

"Yes! How much have you written?"

"The book is nearly done. In fact, Soren, the only thing missing has been an enthusiastic audience." Shabe grinned. "But my book will be complete if you'd like to go to the end with me."

Soren felt thrilled. He could see how much this meant to his teacher. "Of course, Shabe. I'm especially keen to see how your book answers my questions."

"Great. Then let's get on with our journey. Oh, and before I forget, let's make an agreement."

"What sort of agreement?" Soren asked.

"First, that you'll tell me whenever something doesn't make sense to you. We won't go on until everything is clear."

"Okay. I agree. What else?"

"Second, don't jump to conclusions," said Shabe. "Asking is necessary and useful to clarify something, but prejudgement is a mistake, especially about ideas that are new to you."

"Okay. I promise." Soren raised his right hand and shut his eyes, as if he was taking an oath.

Shabe laughed.

Seek Thirst, Not Water!

Shabe cleared his throat and flicked to the next page. "Humans are social beings. We're born into society. We grow in it and need its help for survival and development. Many aspects of society's relationship with us are of a useful and constructive nature.

"Suppose other people and social institutes weren't there. Think about it! Life might not be impossible, but it'd surely be challenging and very primitive in shape. As you know, society helps each person to meet their basic needs for food, clothing, and shelter. What else do you think society does for us?" Shabe looked up from his book.

"Well, I'd guess we learn many things from other people, like language or reading, even how to help and care for others," Soren said.

"Right! In fact, much of human potential takes shape and flourishes within society." Shabe returned his gaze to the book. "But unfortunately, the ties society forms with an individual aren't always helpful or constructive. As an established and powerful entity, society sometimes treats the newly arrived and vulnerable individual in ways that can be destructive and exploitative."

Soren furrowed his brow, thinking. "I get what you mean. Society helps us grow, but sometimes, it's like it just wants us to fit in, even if it's not always good for us."

"That's true. And when relationships are not fair or constructive, this can cause numerous problems for the individual, as well as society. So you can see it's essential to properly understand this aspect of the issue to find a solution to human suffering. Without this, any effort will fail, both practically and theoretically."

Soren bit his lip, then asked, "You mean, if we don't really get how things work, we'll just keep having the same problems?"

"We might even create new problems," Shabe answered with a smile. "Before we start our discussion, I want you to understand an important point. Physical problems, such as pain from a decayed tooth, or problems like financial hardship, need action to be solved. But mental and behavioural problems often only need a diagnosis. Very often, the solution is the same as the diagnosis."

"Pardon me, Shabe. I can't understand how diagnosing can be the same as resolving," said Soren.

Shabe half-smiled. "Good work, Soren!"

"Why?"

"You're sticking to our agreement. To answer your question, this is because of the nature of the issue. Suppose you're standing at the edge of a steep cliff and are scared you'll plunge to your death. Now, if someone was going to help you, what would they do?"

"Obviously, they'd help me get off the cliff."

"That's right. Now imagine you're standing in a big, open field with nothing to worry about, yet you kept fearing you'll fall off. What would a sensible person do to help you? Still keep you off the cliff?"

"No. I'd want them to convince me there were no cliffs, that there wasn't anything to worry about. I think if they did that, I'd automatically calm down," Soren said.

"Exactly! If you understand the nature of your problem, that it comes from a false impression, it will disappear, and you'll relax again."

"Okay. I see."

"It's the same with many mental and emotional issues. Often, my problem as a human being is simply that my mind is cluttered with stale suggestions, and my thoughts are infected with all sorts of misperceptions. Then the only thing I need to eliminate my pain is to realise my thoughts are just false impressions. If I do that, I can be free of them and can be happy and healthy again.

"That's what the wise teachers who understand the true nature of human suffering have always recommended," said Shabe. "'Pull aside the curtains of ignorance and illusion!' they say. So does Rumi when he warns those who resort to external, unhelpful things to reach inner peace.

'Your treasure lies within yourself.
All these outward things are plagues to your being.'

"That means that when the pain is rooted in your own misconceptions, any sort of outer search is like running towards a mirage. Rumi says, again:

'Do not seek water; seek thirst instead.
So water will flow from behind and ahead.'"

Soren's eyebrows rose. He thought, *I can't see the point. Become thirstier if you want to be quenched? If I hadn't promised not to jump to conclusions, I'd object to that.*

Shabe glanced at Soren. "Well, the subject still needs a lot of explanation and discussion. I know you have a lot of questions too. But first, let's see what the problem is and what having a captivating tie between society and an individual means."

"I'm all ears," Soren said.

"Like we said, when a human being is born, they're a newcomer confronted with a vast, powerful entity called society. This entity, or rather, structure, has already been there for millennia, with a complex system of rules, values, and relations. Naturally, the individual is supposed to learn the rules and play their role in it.

"The one thing society expects from a newly arrived member is conformity. Just as a family's adults expect their child to heed what they say and abide by the house rules without rebellion or defiance. No parents want to have an unruly child, do they?"

Soren shook his head.

"And if that expectation is not met, measures are taken to ensure the child behaves in the desired way. These measures generally include rewards to encourage good behaviour and punishment to discourage bad behaviour."

"Shabe?"

"Yes?"

"This is where I have my first question. What do *good* and *bad* actually mean here?"

"That's an important question. We'll attend to that later, I promise, but for now, let's say that, generally, the standard of *good* and *bad* is decided by the parents and society. So this is how the child gradually learns to obey society and its authorities or face punishment."

"And who are the authorities?"

"They are the different kinds of ruling powers, such as parents, leaders, and the law, as well as culture and traditions. Many of the teachings by parents and society are useful, aren't they?"

Soren thought about his own mother's rules: homework after dinner, brush your teeth twice a day, take the rubbish out weekly, no vulgar language, and more. But he understood the reasons behind them. "Yes, like looking after your health, traffic rules, and respecting others' rights," he said.

"You're right, and many more things. It goes without saying that a person should follow the rules of any group or system they're part of and cooperate with it — provided it's a good and fair system," Shabe said.

Soren asked, "And if it isn't? I mean, if it's unjust or foolish?"

Shabe replied, "Obviously, you shouldn't follow anything that doesn't align with reason and ethics."

"So we should oppose it? We should fight?"

"Right. But opposition or fighting is itself a science and an art that must be learnt, understood, and practised. Otherwise, instead of fixing things, our struggle may lead to more misery and destruction," said Shabe.

Scratching his head, Soren said with a laugh, "Things just got complicated."

Shabe replied, "I understand, but I'm sure that as we continue our discussions, things will become clearer to you."

"Fair enough!" Soren said.

'Now, among other things, language is an important tool of reward and punishment. A parent's first reaction to any right or wrong behaviour from their child is usually verbal. If a child accidentally breaks a plate, the father may grumble, 'You're such a sloppy kid!' Or a mother might react to seeing her daughter's poor marks with, 'That's not good enough.' If the child achieves some goal, they could say, 'Well done!' or 'Oh, darling, we're so proud of you!'"

Soren thought of his own situation. He was sometimes called clumsy for dropping cutlery in the middle of dinner, but this was usually followed by a chuckle. As for his marks at school, his parents were always pleased.

"Such reactions, delivered in a tone of praise or reproach, tell the child that their actions — good or bad — will always be followed by a judgement about their personality or about who they are. It seems that what upsets or delights the parents is not breaking a plate or getting good or bad marks. This is the way they frame the child's character as being stupid or clever."

Soren raised his hand.

"Yes, Soren?" asked Shabe.

"How do we know the parents are sad or happy about the child's character? I mean, what about the incident itself?"

"Well, they could have simply told the child to take more care with objects or discussed their recent class lessons with them without bringing up matters like clumsiness, intelligence, or pride. That is, they could've paid attention to the issue itself, rather than describing the child's personality."

"I guess so."

"On the other hand, adults are in charge of protecting the child, caring for them and securing their needs," Shabe said. "They're also the main sources of mental and emotional security for the child. Thus, naturally, grownups' judgements and opinions are of particular importance to an innocent and receptive child. As a result, the child knows that if they want to live in peace and safety, there's no choice but to keep grownups happy."

"That's true," Soren agreed. "It happened to me today! When those people came over to me after the fight, nobody asked how I was feeling. Instead, one said, 'You're good.' And the other said, 'You're bad.' No one cared about my injuries, let alone my questions. Except you, of course."

Shabe gave Soren a reassuring smile. "As we know, there's an instinct in human beings, and in other animals, called fear. It's responsible for warning them about danger in order to save their lives, either by defending themselves or escaping from the situation. But fear plays a more vital role in a child, due to their limited knowledge and weaker physical capacities. That is why children are more vulnerable to fear and threats than grownups.

"Adults know this all too well. They often use fear to control children's behaviour and keep them in line with expectations. They do so by using verbal warnings, such as 'Shame on you!' or 'You're all thumbs!' Seeing grownups unhappy or annoyed, the child tries to avoid doing things that can cause a negative feeling towards them."

"Understandably," Soren said.

"Meanwhile, the child comes to understand things as good or bad based on others' reactions, and they remember this. Hence, a frown or a smile can make the child avoid repeating an undesirable behaviour and try to earn satisfaction and approval instead."

Shabe closed the book and picked up a slice of cake.

Soren was still in deep thought. A couple of minutes passed without a word. Finally, Soren broke the silence. "Now I can see why adults say, 'What a clumsy child' or 'Good boy.' And why everyone said something different to me after the fight happened. I'm glad we're reading this together. Still, there are many things I don't really get."

"Like what?"

"Why do people have so many contradictory ideas on things? Aren't good and evil clear to everyone?"

"Sort of. But like I said, if you are patient enough, many things will be clarified soon, perhaps even things you hadn't thought of," Shabe said.

Soren nodded, reminding himself to be patient. He had so many questions, but Shabe was right.

"Well, now, would you like to watch a few scenes of *The Wildlife* together?" Shabe asked.

Soren grinned. "My mind could use a break. And I do enjoy wildlife films but —"

"I promise it's relevant," Shabe said. He picked up the remote control and switched on the television. He put a cassette into the machine, and in a minute, a montage of animals flashed on the screen.

A large grey eagle rapidly dived to hunt a brown hare, but the swift creature fled into a bush. The bird retreated to the sky in search of other prey.

Next, a tiny snail crawled slowly and silently along a green leaf, leaving a slimy, shiny trail of mucus. A shadow loomed over the creature as a child's hand appeared, getting closer to the snail before touching one of its telescopic eyes. The snail's eyes recoiled, followed by its soft, slimy body disappearing into its shell.

Then a fox with a large, fluffy tail and slender muzzle bolted towards a hole, a colourful bird between its teeth. As the scene changed, a fight erupted between a black snake and a badger. Soren was surprised to see the small animal defeat the powerful snake, strangling it to death.

They watched a few more action scenes: a bulbous frog hunting a fly with its long lash-like tongue. The capture took a millisecond. That fascinated Soren. The speed was unexpected from such a fat, lazy-looking creature.

Another scene showed a bright, colourful butterfly whose futile struggle only entangled its delicate wings more firmly in the spider's web. The host could be seen waiting patiently for its dinner to be fully ready.

But the last scene was the most interesting one. Shabe himself appeared in front of the camera.

"Well, this is the secret of survival in nature: Kill to Live! The secret behind which is a mysterious power named instinct."

CHAPTER TWO

THE WILDLIFE

"Wow!" Soren exclaimed. "Where did you do this? And you filmed all these scenes yourself?"

"Not all of them. A few are mine. I like to get out and into nature as often as I can," said Shabe.

"Interesting!" Soren paused. "But I can't wait to see how all this is related."

"Well, on to the next part." Shabe returned to the notebook, flicking through the pages until he reached *Chapter Two: The Wildlife*.

"To better understand issues such as judgement, language, and what I'd call *false values* as important tools for suggestion, we should research their historical, natural, and psychological backgrounds," Shabe read. "That way, we can get a clearer picture."

He glanced at Soren to make sure he was following before he went on. "In the 19th century, the British naturalist Charles Darwin introduced the theory of natural selection to the world, along with the principles of the struggle for existence and survival of the fittest. This theory brought about massive changes in the fields of science and philosophy, including a new perspective on humans and their nature and attributes.

"Among other things, it was discovered that humans, at least from a biological point of view, are just another type of animal, their primary advantages being their higher intelligence and stronger reasoning, thanks to a more sophisticated brain structure. As a result, human activities generally resemble those of other animals in their nature but are more advanced and complicated in form and shape.

"For example, animals may try to attract the opposite sex with particular movements and behaviour, to mate and produce offspring. They meet their nourishment needs by looking for food or hunting other animals. Similarly, women attract men with clothing or perfume, and men attempt to flatter women through words. In order to meet their vital needs, humans marry, start families, get jobs and maintain households or run business activities, all of which are advanced forms of mating, hunting and gathering."

"So humans are just … smarter animals. Doesn't it make us a bit … arrogant to think we're so different?" Soren said.

"Maybe it does sound arrogant," Shabe replied. "But it's not just intelligence that sets us apart. It's how we use it. Unlike other animals, we create art, build societies and question our existence. We're not just surviving; we're searching for meaning."

"But isn't survival still at the core of it all?" Soren asked.

"It is, and it isn't. We shall see." Shabe went on. "The battle between animals and humans is very similar, as clarified by the struggle for existence. Animals fight with their claws, paws and fangs, while humans fight using weapons, guns, bombs and rockets. Animals deceive or frighten outsiders to stop them from approaching or attacking. For instance, the lion roars, the dog barks and the cat scratches. The mouse runs into its hole. The snake bites, and the chameleon changes colours. All of these are forms of deceit, attack and escape. These tactics aim to repel the enemy or to secure a better chance of surviving.

"Likewise, making use of their exceptionally high intelligence, people also confront their enemies by wielding money, designing and producing weapons and the like, to remove or subdue their foes.

"But thanks to their sophisticated intelligence and power of thought, humans have created a phenomenon called civilisation to organise their vital activities within its framework. For instance, you could think of sales or advertisements as advanced forms of traps laid to catch prey. Just as animals try to trick other creatures, humans try to attract their peers using sophisticated methods, such as film and television productions, and they use advertising and marketing to persuade audiences to buy particular products and services. All these activities are part of the struggle for existence, the hope for an increased chance of survival and a better life."

Soren narrowed his eyes. "How interesting! I'd read about the struggle for existence and stuff like that. I remember you discussing it in class as well, but I'd never thought of it this way."

Shabe nodded. "The first principle of survival is called self-preservation. Have you heard of it?"

"Um, self-preservation … That reminds me of those rumours about celebrities! You know, the ones who have their bodies frozen to come back to life hundreds of years later." Soren grinned. "Isn't that mind-blowing?"

Shabe chuckled. "As you know, self-preservation is about protecting oneself and one's life. Every living being naturally defends its life and its loved ones. It's instinctive. That's the key to survival."

"I see."

"But the desire for living also prompts human beings to make every effort to expand their power and control over vital resources. This inevitably involves striving to overcome competing powers, including other human beings.

"However, humans' other advantage is their ability to communicate through a sophisticated language. Thanks to their complex brain and higher intelligence, humans invented language as a natural instrument. This is their main vehicle of communication. What is significant about language is that is hasn't simply been an outcome of human evolution; it's been a driving factor, and it continues to play that role."

Shabe paused to look at Soren and asked, "Any questions so far?"

Soren eyed the horizon thoughtfully before replying. "Is language that important? Because I've always thought of language simply as a means of communication."

"Yes, very important." Shabe nodded. "Linguists believe language has played such an essential role in the growth and development of humanity that one can claim we owe our entire culture and civilisation to the phenomenon of language. It's impossible to think or reason, unless in a very simple and primitive form, without language.

"It's language that has given humans the power of thought and imagination and, consequently, the ability to write and preserve their thoughts, findings and intellectual treasures in various fields, such as art, technology, philosophy and science," said Shabe. "You can even argue that language and thought are so interwoven that it's virtually impossible to define a clear boundary between the two. By means of language, humans express their joy or hatred or talk about their hunger or thirst. They warn, teach, demand and so on."

"I'd always thought of traffic lights and street signs or when motorists honk their horns and use indicators as a form of talking to each other," Soren said.

"Right! We should keep in mind that *language* doesn't just refer to using words or generating sentences. It's a term that covers all means of communication, including poses and gestures, known as body language, as well as the tone of speech that can convey, distort or shape a message."

"Interesting! I just came to that conclusion myself."

"Very good!" Shabe exclaimed. "And here's a supporting idea. Unlike other creatures, humans use language for purposes of defence, attack and deceit. The noteworthy point is that due to such a power, a unique phenomenon has emerged in human relationships, which I'd call the *false language*."

Shabe glanced at Soren and went on. "Well, we'll finish chapter two together, and we can pick up where we leave off tomorrow if you're interested. You're welcome to come over."

Soren scratched his head as he often did when hesitating. "Can't we read one more chapter today?"

"I don't think it's a good idea, you know. We should give ourselves a bit of a break to think about what we've learned before moving to the next part. What we're learning now forms the foundation of our next discussions. There isn't much use in reading without adequate thinking. Do you ever eat lunch while your stomach is still digesting your breakfast?"

Soren smiled. "No, I guess not. Except maybe a snack."

"Well, a little snack would be a great idea, actually. You're right!" said Shabe.

The False Language

Shabe returned from the kitchen and put a bowl of popcorn on the table. The appetising smell of the popcorn stimulated Soren to grab a handful and start chewing.

So did Shabe, and when he'd swallowed, he went ahead. "So far, we've learned that according to the struggle for existence, every living being tries to get as many vital resources as possible to achieve a better life and survival rate. The natural outcome of such an effort is the outbreak of rivalry and fighting among living beings. In animals, this struggle has a primitive and instinctive form, while in humans, it has expanded itself to the instrument that is language."

"So what does that mean, exactly?" Soren asked.

"It means that, in addition to arms and weapons used in physical wars, humans also use language as a tool in the struggle. They do use it to communicate friendship, care and cooperation, but they also often utilise it to fight and hurt each other. You could say that weapons are the hardware of war, and language is the software," Shabe explained.

"Oh, I'd never thought of it like that! The tool of language …" Soren laughed. "I've got this image of a tongue like a wrench! Or a gun with a pipe that shoots words instead of bullets." Soren thought of Hans and Daniel's tools. *Stupid. Mouth-breather. Captain Heap.* He shuddered.

Shabe smiled. "Quite an imagination you've got! And that reminds me, language has not only given human beings the ability to convey real ideas but unreal things too, like fantasy or suggesting imaginary ideas to others. This abstract capacity of language lets humans make up fictional stories and talk about make-believe things like fairies, unicorns or dragons. They can also talk about the past, which is no longer here, and the future, which doesn't exist yet."

"Wait. So you're saying language can be used to show reality but also to manipulate it? How do we know when it's real or just words?" Soren said.

"A great question, Soren," Shabe said. "That's what we want to see here." He nodded thoughtfully. "The tricky part is that language shapes how we understand the world. And words can distort reality just as much as they reveal it. It's like looking through a lens. Sometimes, it brings things into focus, and other times, it can blur the image or even create illusions. Recognising this is the first step in figuring out what's real and what's just a story."

"Right. Please go on."

"By the same token, language means humans can lie and deceive each other," Shabe said. "They do this to inflict fear on others and make false claims or pretend to be stronger than they are. Think of fraud, deceit, cheating, fallacy and demagogy. They're all different manifestations of this abstract power of language."

"So language can really be a weapon of war?" asked Soren.

"Yes, and a powerful one, indeed. People invented false ideas to use them as a tool for threats, trickery and overcoming rivalry."

"That ability is limited to humans, isn't it?" Soren asked.

"Well, most creatures use a form of language for communication, but they don't have the sophisticated level of thought that humans do," replied Shabe.

"And what you refer to as false ideas are like the legends and myths of fairies and dragons? They don't exist in the real world?"

"We'll talk about false ideas, and particularly *false values*, soon. In detail! For now, I hope the following answers that question."

Shabe grabbed another handful of popcorn and began eating. After a minute, he continued. "Calling some values false doesn't mean that such values don't exist. They do, but they're not part of many things that we often assume they are. In other words, a false value is a quality that we wrongly attach to something that is, in fact, empty of that quality, whether it's positive or negative."

"Sorry, Shabe. I think you've lost me," Soren admitted.

Shabe chuckled. "Well, what produces such value is interpretation and attribution. Thanks to our power of abstraction, we can attribute various values, like shameful or honourable, to things that aren't actually that, and seeing them as such is merely the product of our own imagination."

"Ah." Soren nodded.

"By error or by deceit or lying, humans can associate things with differing values, like greatness, meanness, positivity, cruelty, power, weakness, beauty or ugliness. This is similar to what primitive humans used to do when they interpreted thunder as the gods' wrath and rain as tears. They made sculptures and claimed they possessed mysterious, ominous powers and threw them at their enemies. Some people claimed to be magicians, spiritual healers and the like, with mysterious powers. They sang nonsense slogans, alleging they were healing or harming. In this way, they manipulated people to extort money, gain other benefits or attain social or charismatic power …"

"Oh, I see."

Shabe went on. "In other words, human language has developed two functions or uses: a genuine use and a fake one. In genuine use, humans apply language to refer to real notions and entities. Can you think of any examples?"

"Yes," said Soren. "Physical things like a tree and a house, and mental things, like mathematics or art."

"You're on the right track! Also, emotional things, like love and hunger. Moral things, like honesty and kindness. Even arbitrary things, like size and weight. All these refer either to something real or to something agreed by both the speaker and the listener."

"For instance …?" prompted Soren.

"We all know such concepts as weight, size, distance and scale are relative and conventional. This awareness prevents delusions or misunderstandings in how we think of them."

"Clear. Thanks."

"But the second use of language is judgement and interpretation," said Shabe. "As I'll explain later, we should distinguish between realistic or logical interpretations and baseless, false ones. For example, saying that lying is a wrong thing to do points out that lying has a harmful nature, which is a reality, a truth."

"What about telling a white lie?"

"That's what I'm trying to say here," said Shabe. "Putting a label on something cannot change its reality. A wrong label can only obscure facts and cloud our understanding."

"I see." Soren hummed. "You were saying?"

"In false interpretations, things can be associated with properties that are not part of them and are utterly wrong. It's a false description to say that an ordinary, low-paid job is humiliating or embarrassing work. It may bring little income or impose challenging conditions, but humility and embarrassment are not part of it. It's the mind, deluded by social influences, that attaches a value to that job by the use of language. In a nutshell, our minds accept such properties about a job, simply through the wrong use of language."

"Makes perfect sense now!" said Soren.

"False values are produced by the imagination. But an individual often accepts them as actual features. These big lies cause most of the ignorance and suffering in the world. They turn harmony into hatred and misunderstanding. You can see why I call this type of communication false language," said Shabe.

"Rumi sees this as humans being painted with colours of disunity and discord, the superficial differences that turn friendship into hatred and war. He believes that if these colours faded, humans would regain their initial peace and friendship:

> *As colourlessness was captivated by colours,*
> *One Moses fought the other Moses.*
> *When you return to colourlessness,*
> *Moses and Pharaoh will go back to peace.'"*

"Excuse me," Soren said, perplexed. "What does he mean by 'one Moses fought the other Moses'? Why are there two Moseses? In the Bible, Moses fights the Pharaoh, doesn't he? So why Moses and Moses?"

"Yes, you're right. But what Rumi says is that, at their cores, humans are all the same. They all hold a godly, pure being, like Moses. But when colour, or the veils of appearances, taint people's beings, one becomes the Pharaoh and the other Moses, and that's when hatred and fighting breaks out. However, if the illusive veils were to be removed, disunity would cease, and each would realise that they are both Moses. Does that make sense?" asked Shabe.

"It does." After some thought, Soren asked, "By the way, does this language come with a dictionary, or is it taught at any institute?" He grinned.

Shabe chuckled. "Jokes aside, false language is not a different or independent language; it's the same language that we use in everyday speaking. Its falsehood lies in its false use. Where we learn it, sadly, is the institution of society, to answer that part of your question, Soren."

"So is this false language only used in our society or in other places too?"

"The false language isn't confined to any particular country, region or tribe. It's a language for communicating untrue ideas, used to mock, humiliate or pretend with the aim to deceive, dominate, exploit or torment. As such, the false language is a universal one. And when we talk about society, Soren, let's remain aware that society is not something other than us. Society is me and you, and as long as we have not grown aware of ourselves as the role players of this network, this system will continue to work just the same way it always has, unless we stop to think and start to change."

"Makes sense."

Shabe pressed on. "Rumi says,

> *'People fight because of names.*
> *When they dig through to meanings,*
> *Enmity is gone.'"*

"Names are labels, aren't they?" asked Soren.

"They are. And see how, taking a deep look into people's relationships, Hafiz also beautifully depicts our struggles,

*'Tell the tradesmen of the world of delusions.
Lessen your merchandise, as profit and loss are the same.'"*

Soren smiled.

"What's so amusing?" Shabe asked.

"I just remembered a scene from a pantomime where two men had a tug-of-war."

"Oh, did they?"

"Yes. Each man tried to pull an imaginary rope towards himself. After a lot of fighting and struggling, both men collapsed to the floor. Then they got up and threw invisible sticks and stones at each other. In the end, they both collapsed, wounded and unconscious."

"Well, that sounds interesting. I must add that to the book. Is that okay?" asked Shabe.

"Of course. Please do. I can't claim copyright for that!" Soren smiled.

Shabe chuckled, removing a pencil from his shirt pocket and writing down a few words in the book. Then he went on. "Rumi's emphasis on the issue of names is one of his most treasurable pieces of advice. Elsewhere, he warns:

*'Move beyond names; look into properties.
So that properties lead you to the essence.
To be obsessed with images is idolatry,
So leave the appearance and look into the meaning.'*

"Well, we've had a good look at the question of language, and now I'd like to return to the subject of a child's birth and growth in society. But let's do that tomorrow." Shabe closed the book and rested it beside the now-empty bowl of popcorn. "Let's think about what we read today, and if you have any questions, ask me tomorrow."

Soren thanked Shabe as they said their farewells. They decided Shabe would call for the next session. As Soren walked home, he thought, *The false language is like a false gun with false bullets* ...

Soren's home sat on the bank of a broad, deep, blue river, running through the city, creating many lakes and ponds across it and dividing it in two. It drifted past Soren's house with a slight curve and ran past many houses, lands and fields to eventually meet the ocean. A mass of tall, dense trees surrounding the house cast broad shadows. Close by was a small park with a playground, shelters and a few benches and tables. This had been the setting of many joyful and carefree times in Soren's childhood, days of fun and play when the world had seemed thrillingly mysterious to his curious eyes.

The white-painted house occupied a large block of land, and its stone driveway led to the main road. Consistent rain had made the lawn luscious and green. In the backyard, an oversized garage stored a mass of old furniture, tools and sundries that had piled up over the years. Soren's father had always intended to tidy it up and get rid of the unwanted items, but he was a procrastinator—though he himself disagreed!

As Soren turned into the yard, he spotted Melody, his little sister, riding her rocking horse. Mum watched from the kitchen window while she cooked.

Catching sight of him, Melody leapt from her horse and ran into Soren's arms to kiss him.

Hugging and kissing Melody back, Soren pondered his readings with Shabe. *Can the way we treat this innocent child affect her whole future? Is it just us who build children's lives?* Then he answered himself. *No, surely not. There must be many other influences, like friends, school, books and teachers. Like Shabe. Meeting him has made a great difference. Maybe he'll be a good teacher for Melody too.*

Following that last thought, Soren took Melody's hand and led her inside. He thought, *I want to leave a good impression on her. I want to be a good role model.*

"Hi, Mum."

"Hi, Soren. How was your day?"

"Good. Great actually!" Soren told his mum about the fight with Hans and Daniel. It wasn't an easy topic to discuss, but Soren had never kept anything from his mother. He then told her about the three people spookily appearing out of the blue, all saying something different, and how this had prompted some persistent questions in his mind.

Despite the worry evident in her expression, Sally waited until he'd finished. "Let me see what's happened," she said, leaning towards Soren. As she spotted one button that had almost come off his collar, she rolled up Soren's shirt, looking for signs of injury. There was only a slight bruise on his back, near his hip. "Oh, dear!" She touched it gently, but Soren seemed calm. "Does it hurt?" she asked, looking up at him.

"No. Don't worry, Mum," Soren said, sorry to see his mother so upset.

Taking a deep breath, Sally stood back. Putting one hand on her hip, she paused for a moment, looking Soren in the eyes. "Well, first of all, how long have they been doing this?"

Soren was silent, avoiding her eyes.

"Bullying is a serious matter, and you know that well. It must be thoroughly looked into."

"A little while," Soren admitted. "But, Mum, please give me a bit more time."

"For you or them?" Sally huffed.

"If we tell the school, they'll be in trouble, but so will I. After all, I was the one who went at them first. I don't want to sort it out like that anymore. I did at first, to be honest, but after talking to Shabe …"

"*Shabe?*"

"Yes, he asked me to call him that. After we talked, I had second thoughts. We discussed the questions I had, and now I feel that I can finally answer them."

"Are you crazy? What are you on about? You could have injured each other! I should call their parents and—" Sally exclaimed.

"Mum, please! I'm sorry. I promise it won't happen again, but for now, stop. I'll—"

"You'll what? Let them do whatever the hell they want? Or make more trouble by getting into another fight?"

Soren sighed. "I promise I won't fight anymore, Mum. But I don't know. I want to find myself. I want to know why they do these things. I started a lesson with Shabe today, and I'm finding some answers. I feel I'm getting answers to so many unanswered questions."

"You're using such big words lately, Soren. It seems your teacher has you getting very idealistic. Are you sure you're okay? We don't need to see the doctor?"

"Yes. I'm okay, Mum. Don't worry. I'm fine".

Sally ran her fingers through her hair. "Okay. I'll think about it."

"Thank you, Mum." Soren smiled, relieved.

"Well, now, tell me. What did you talk about with Shabe today? Seems he's made quite an impression on you."

Soren sat at the dining table and excitedly told his mother about the book Shabe was writing. She nodded along as she returned to cooking, stopping every now and then to ask him a question about the wildlife footage, the *false values* and other ideas he'd come to understand. They also had a long conversation about Rumi's *The Donkey's Gone* parable and the profound meaning that a simple story could carry.

"Very interesting," Sally said. "I've always thought of Shabe as someone who's more than a schoolteacher. I'd like to hear the rest of the story."

Soren was thrilled to see how curious his mother was.

"Of course, Mum. We're going to continue tomorrow, and I'll tell you what I learn."

In Soren's room sat a small hazelwood bookshelf filled with an array of books. Some were fiction, like *A Captain at Fifteen* by Jules Verne or *The Man Who Laughs* by Victor Hugo. There were works by Dostoyevsky, Tolstoy and Charles Dickens, along with science fiction by Isaac Asimov and travelogues like Miguel Hans's *Voyages* and *Gulliver's Travels*. And there were some philosophical and religious books, including the Bible and a few language books and dictionaries.

To the right sat Soren's matching wooden desk, housing a computer and a globe. The wall next to it was adorned with a puzzle world map and a few pictures of his family, as well as scenes of nature and animals.

Soren remembered travelling the world in his imagination when he was younger, tracing his finger on the plastic light-up globe, moving it across the countries and oceans. He often joined heroes in their adventures across lands and seas in historical and fiction stories, which was likely why he was so good at geography. Beside the bed, the window looked out at the river and passing boats.

Soren, sitting in bed with a book on his lap, found his current thoughts too interesting to open it. *The world is a guesthouse. Was that traveller in the story also tricked by the false language?*

He pondered the thought for a while before giving up on the book and placing it on the bedside table. "The donkey's gone. The donkey's gone …" he whispered to himself as he switched his reading lamp off. In the dark, he smiled and went to sleep.

The Label

"Hello. Soren speaking,"

"Hi, Soren. Shabe. How's it going? Just calling to say we can meet today at five, if that suits you?"

"Oh, yes, thanks. See you then, Shabe!"

Half an hour later, Soren turned into a leafy street that wound through a forest and finished by the seaside. Even on a sunny afternoon, the path was shaded by a thick canopy of trees, all competing for their share of sunlight. A squirrel on a low branch caught sight of Soren, gave him a curious look for a moment, then scurried up the trunk and disappeared. At the beach, a panorama of colourful boats floated just offshore, with dense, white clouds dotting the sky above them, while squawking seagulls hovered overhead. *Quite the scene*, Soren thought.

Shabe's house overlooked the ocean. The scents of grass, wood and forest combined with the flowers blooming in Shabe's garden.

Soren drew in a deep breath, filling his lungs with fresh air. "Good evening, Shabe," Soren greeted him as he watered the flowers.

"Soren, hello. Would you care to sit outside?"

Soren nodded, a bit in awe of his surroundings. He took a seat in the outdoor setting while Shabe retrieved a tray of tea and biscuits, put it on the table, then sat down to pour them both a cup of tea.

Soren looked around at the manicured grass and the kaleidoscope of colours in the garden. "I like your garden. It's delightful."

"Thank you. I do enjoy gardening. I planted all these flowers myself. They're like my children. Oh, and this is my dog, Tara." Shabe gestured to the small white dog approaching through the gate. The dog trotted over and, after a little fidgeting, settled beside them, staring at Shabe as she wagged her tail.

"Oh, so cute! Can I pat her?"

"Of course. Tara is very sociable."

Soren left his chair and went to the dog. As he stroked Tara's fluffy coat, he said, "My mum really liked your book. She says she'd like to know the rest. Is it okay if I share our discussions with her?"

"Of course. Why not? But give her my advice too, about jumping to conclusions, especially holding an objective and a clear outlook."

"I did! I told her about other things as well, like the fight after school and what Steve and the others said."

Shabe sipped his tea. "I know. I'm glad you did."

"You know. How?" Soren asked.

"We spoke on the phone."

"Really? And—"

"Don't worry. It was a pleasant conversation. We reached some conclusions too. You know about their situations, don't you? I mean Hans and Daniel?"

Soren nodded.

Shabe smiled. "But we can talk about it later," he said. "Now, have your tea so we can start."

"Okay."

Shabe glanced down at the book. "Yesterday, we said a child learns from their parents' judgements that they need to be wary of others' opinions and always try to appease authority figures. They learn good values through expected behaviour."

Soren nodded.

"Right here, a wide gap emerges between the reality of each thing and the social value attached to it, particularly because a child can notice that the conventional values of things often matter more than their realities," said Shabe.

"Interesting. The pieces of the puzzle are coming together!" Soren said.

"Absolutely. Another significant turning point is what can be called becoming *comment-bound* or *society-bound*. This means that because a child believes whatever is said about them is now a part of their identity, they may become increasingly dependent on others' likes and fearful of their dislikes."

"So we start worrying more about what others think of us than about who we really are," said Soren. "In other words, we end up chasing labels instead of being true to ourselves."

"Exactly, Soren! And this view can become so engraved in a child's mind that, even as an adult, well into the age of autonomy and self-sufficiency, they can remain sensitive to external judgements. In such a situation, although they may not need to depend on others, they still feel that people's opinions of them is important. They feel they must always keep others satisfied, even at the cost of their own interests and peace of mind."

"But, Shabe, there have always been exceptions to that, right? I mean, there are people who think independently and have their own values."

"Yes, you're right. And we need to learn from and be inspired by them."

"It's not easy, though."

"I agree. It can be difficult at times, and entails costs. However, living a dependant, worried and, as Socrates calls it, an *unexamined* life also has costs, pains and troubles," said Shabe.

"I agree."

Shabe scribbled something in his book and then went on. "The more a child is influenced by comments and judgements, the more sensitive they become to people's opinions. In such circumstances, an individual gradually loses their authenticity—that is, their freedom of thought and action—and turns into a dependent, anxious follower.

"We could say that the most fundamental turn is that, for the misled individual, the joy of living gives way to a concern for approval and conformity. This is the point at which society's domination over the individual's thoughts takes root, and social exploitation starts."

"When you say *conformity*, you don't mean conforming to sensible rules, I suppose," Soren said.

"No! We are talking about thoughtless following."

"Sure. Makes sense."

Shabe went on. "One inevitable outcome of this process is increased mental pressure on the person, followed by their self-alienation, egoism and misery."

"What do you mean by egoism?" Soren asked.

"By egoism, we refer to the birth of an alien entity in human beings, known as the ego. *Ego* and *egoism* may have different meanings elsewhere, but that's what we mean by them here. In this process, this foreign entity settles in us and gradually takes control of our thoughts and feelings. In fact, the ego is the greatest human affliction! You can also call it the *imposed identity* or *the outward I*."

"Shabe, I have a question."

"Yes?"

"As I understand it, you can use the word *egoism* to mean selfishness or paying too much attention to yourself. Is that right?"

"Yes."

"At the same time, you say humans become society-bound, which means we pay too much attention to society's opinions. Yes?" asked Soren.

"Well done! Sensible question!"

Soren smiled and bowed a little.

"Well, let's see what ego is, precisely. The problem is that society installs a foreign representative in our minds. So ego is an *alien self* in our being. That's why I've named it the *outward I*. Therefore, egoism is the result of obsession with pleasing society or slavishly following society, hence the term *society-bound*.

"In other words, egoism means you're constantly concerned about a puppet self, a puppet that is appointed by society. That's how being *sel*f*ish* and being society-bound are interrelated. Am I clear?"

"Fully clear, thanks. But what's the relationship between being society-bound, as you say, and being selfish, caring little about others?"

"Oh, okay. In order to gain approval, you need to conform to society's expectations and show you possess all the properties expected. So you have to prove—even to yourself—that you are indeed who you're supposed to be," said Shabe.

"Yes."

"All this will turn you into someone who is perpetually concerned about your social popularity and how others grade you, instead of striving to build constructive, fruitful relationships. Thus, ironically, being dependent on others means being selfish and insensitive to their needs and emotions. What it means is in an egotistical relationship, each person is concerned about whether the other grants them the values they are after, rather than about learning from them, helping them grow or caring about what they are going through. Why? Because ego is a mask, and in such a relationship, it is masks that talk and communicate, not real, genuine people. So the stronger the ego, the less space for caring for others in one's mind and heart."

"Okay. I see. But what's the substance of this ego? Is it thought, spirit or something else?"

"We'll talk about the nature of this entity later, in detail, but for now, we should discuss the difficulties of the *pseudo-values* and what problems they bring to an individual's life."

"Okay, Shabe."

"Let's move to the next part. I think you'll find it particularly interesting."

"Can't wait!"

"The first problem with the labels people use is their essential conflict; this conflict forces a person into a vicious cycle and leaves them grappling with an unsolvable question for the rest of their life. Here's an example. Suppose Jack fights with Bill and is beaten by him."

"This sounds familiar." Soren smiled.

"Let's put aside the value-based interpretations we're used to and look at this happening, just as is. I believe what we'll realise then is that Jack is smaller than Bill, or Bill is somehow swifter or stronger than him. Another reality is Jack's pain after being hit. If we saw the issue within these limits of objectivity, that would be the only reality we'd observe.

"But the problem is that we add a psychological and internal burden to that physical pain, as if we're witnessing something shameful. We say to Jack, 'You weakling!' or 'Shame on you!' By saying these things, we're conveying two messages simultaneously to a child's mind. First, 'You're a weakling.' Second, 'Your weakness is a cause of shame and disgrace.'"

"Can I say something?" Soren said.

"Yes?"

"Perhaps someone does that to push their child to work harder?"

"Maybe, but if that person thought a bit more, they might change their minds."

"How?"

"We remain negligent of some significant points. First, children are fundamentally different in terms of physical and mental capacities. There's always someone weaker or stronger, smarter or less intelligent, in every field. No human can always outdo others or win in all encounters. Obviously, the responsibility is on every parent to provide suitable intellectual and physical grounds for their children's potential to flourish. But it's unfair and unrealistic to expect any person to invariably beat others or to always be number one."

"Sounds right," said Soren.

"As I'll discuss later, comparing people is an essentially wrong and unjust practice due to their innate and natural diversities."

Soren said, "I've always thought that although Hans is bigger than me or stronger, I have other capabilities that he may not. For instance, I can write easily. In the future, Hans could be a good sports trainer, and I could be a good teacher or author."

"Completely right. That's where another point is. If all people were the same at doing all things, society's activities would freeze! Such things as the economy, art, science and politics would simply stop."

"People wouldn't need each other's help or cooperation anymore."

"Exactly!"

Soren remembered the fight, and for the first time, he wondered if Shabe had had similar experiences.

Shabe continued. "Like we said, children are particularly receptive and farmable. Babies are born with virtually no idea of the world around them. They have little knowledge of themselves and who they are. They receive almost all their understanding about things from their father, mother, and those around them. In a nutshell, a child's worldview takes root and takes shape within the family.

"Due to their natural trust in adults, children make conclusions about the meaning, worth and importance of things based on the attitudes and reactions they can see from adults. That's how our worldview takes shape from childhood. If parents frequently discuss monetary issues as essential at home, the child concludes that money must be a fundamental and sensitive matter. If parents or elder siblings love reading and books, the child concludes that books are valuable and enjoyable things that are important in their lives. Likewise, if grown-ups show respect for others' rights and exercise care, both in words and actions, the child learns that it is necessary to regard others' rights and needs.

"However, the most significant point is that children develop their sense of worth, even their identity, from adults. The way adults treat a child tells the child clearly who they are, how dear they are, what their worth and place is among others. It's not exaggerating to say that adults' behaviour towards a child defines that child's identity. Due to their naïve and sensitive mind, the child accepts the definition and absorbs it deeply.

"When a mother says to Jack, 'You're quite hopeless,' she tells him who he is and what his identity is. The mother is defining Jack for Jack. Afterwards, Jack, who depends on his parents for his knowledge of everything, including himself, readily accepts that he's a weak and hopeless person.

"Grammatically speaking, you can say that affirmative sentences are imperative sentences, concerning children. It means we should be wary of saying 'You're quite hopeless' because, in effect, we're telling the child, '*Be* quite hopeless.' In such a case, for the rest of their life, an image of incompetence and hopelessness can become a constant reminder of who they are in their own mind."

Soren interjected. "But what about the things we learn on our own, without adults? I mean, sometimes, we see or experience things that don't match what we're taught. Doesn't that change how we think about ourselves and the world?"

Shabe nodded. "You're absolutely right, Soren. Our own experiences can either reinforce or challenge what we've learned. As we grow, we start to compare what we were taught with what we see in the world. Sometimes, these personal experiences can even lead us to question or redefine our values and beliefs."

"I get it. So it's about finding our own understanding of things, right?"

"Exactly."

After thinking for a while, Soren said, "So it's pretty important how you treat a child, isn't it? Looks like the family shapes the child's whole personality and their fate too. With my little sister, Melody, I've always tried to be careful how I treat her. I'd hate to make a bad impression on her."

"That's very thoughtful of you, Soren. But don't underestimate how other factors outside the family can also play a role in a person's life. Factors like education, genes, inheritance and life events also play a large part. Sometimes, a person ends up possessing characteristics quite different to those of their family or the environment they've grown up in."

"You're right, but surely, that's more of an exception?" Soren said.

"Correct. Apart from exceptional cases, environment and family generally play an essential role."

Soren nodded.

"Okay, let's carry on," Shabe said.

Soren interrupted. "I guess it's best to encourage children by admiring them, right? To do our best to give them a good image of themselves and improve their self-confidence?"

"Not exactly."

"Oh, how come?"

"Well, if encouragement means paving the way for children to develop their talents, I do agree. Every parent should do that. Even so, excessive admiration or unnecessary praise can be as destructive as reproach and blame. Value-judgement and labelling can disrupt the natural growth of a person."

Shabe paused to take a sip of his tea and stroked Tara's head. "We should be aware that any praise or admiration tends to be a kind of evaluation, which is necessarily extrinsic and external, while our real needs and states are intrinsic and spontaneous. Excessive praise and commendation, in particular, can transform our inner motivations into external incentives, making us dependent on others."

Shabe set his cup down on the table, a thoughtful expression on his face. "Soren, have you noticed that traits like shyness or timidity are hardly ever objected to in society, while aggressiveness or being sharp-tongued often face confrontation?"

Soren thought about his classmates. "Yeah, I have. It's like when Jake pushed Clive out of the way to cut in line for the school play tickets. Clive just stayed quiet, and no-one said anything. But when Andy spoke up about our art teacher being unfair with the roles, he got in trouble. It's like people are okay with Clive being quiet, but they don't like it when Andy speaks his mind."

"Why do you think that's so, particularly since the problems that timidity or shyness can cause to the person are often bigger than those caused by aggressiveness or boldness?"

"Timid or bashful people are more likely to be persecuted and have their rights taken away?"

"Yes, especially in societies where the law isn't strong enough and where winning your rights is primarily dependent on your personal strength. Timid people tend to lose far more."

"Okay. Well, why is that?"

"I believe that in judging people and their behaviour, what mainly concerns society is its *own* benefits, rather than an individual's, so in this case, the dangers from an aggressive or fearless person—especially to someone who wants to claim their own rights—far outweigh any dangers from a shy or fearful one," said Shabe.

"Interesting!"

"As I mentioned before, saying: 'You're quite hopeless' conveys two messages simultaneously to Jack's mind: that he's no good and that this is shameful."

"I suppose it also tells the child that *we* are the one who defines who he is," said Soren.

"A very smart point, Soren. Thank you. That's actually the false language, as we said. Conveying a lie as a truth. This is when a destructive conflict takes root in a child because, having an innocent and receptive mind, they accept the painful reality that they're no good. This is where the child finds themselves facing an unsolvable riddle. First, that they're a hopeless case; second, that they shouldn't be because hopelessness is a disgraceful weakness.

"Once a child believes they're hopeless or incompetent, the only solution left is to do whatever it takes so no one notices this shameful trait. They try to keep this flaw hidden. From here on, a human's stressful endeavour to conceal their embarrassing secret begins."

"How are you supposed to deal with a child, then?" asked Soren.

"Well, it's not just a matter of a couple of encounters. Critical reactions prevail in society, even among adults. Adults, too, rebuke each other and blame themselves because of their failure or problems. The child can see how painful these reproaches are and how everyone tries to escape them. They witness how some people try to take revenge or torment each other through false language and how these behaviours bring about hatred and hostility among people."

"Do you mean that this happens all over the world?"

Shabe nodded. "More or less. The more people in a society understand human psychology and the importance of a sense of agency, the more informed and constructive ways in which they treat each other. But it appears we still have quite a way to go to reach a good level of awareness."

"Sounds right."

"Once these feelings of dependence and humiliation sprout, they can grow bigger and bigger, creating a vast network of problems. One of the first outcomes is the shaking of one's self-confidence."

Shabe noticed Soren appeared perplexed as he processed the statements. "It's a lot to take in." He smiled. "Later on, I'll discuss what the true meaning of self-confidence is and its nature. Remember how we said that, in our explorative journey, we should try to discover all the places and learn about them?"

Soren nodded.

"A person whose mind and thoughts are polluted with an embarrassing image of themselves can hardly like themselves or enjoy inner peace. They have to hide the unpleasant thing in themselves so that nobody discovers it. And that thing is their self. What agony could be greater?"

"But what if you change yourself? What then?" asked Soren.

"Well, you cannot believe something evil by nature and at the same time try to reform it."

"Can you clarify that a bit?"

"You see, you can encourage your child, or anyone, to discard a wrong habit or behaviour only if you believe they are inherently good, but what is not good is the behaviour. However, if you tell your child and make them believe they are inherently bad, and, for example, ignorance, clumsiness or weakness is part of their nature, you cannot expect them to change."

"I see. Just like a mirror. You can wipe the dust off the mirror if dust is dust and mirror is mirror," said Soren thoughtfully.

"Excellent. But if a mirror is made of dust or if dust is part of the mirror's texture, you cannot talk about cleaning or wiping it off."

"Makes sense now. Thank you."

"Of course. And that is what blame and reproach do to us. They attack your character or identity, not the problems or points to be improved. So the only thing is to conceal the so-called truth, rather than improve or change for better."

"I don't want to be morbid, Shabe, but isn't that why, when shame or self-blame reach an unbearable point, some resort to suicide?"

"Yes, that does happen sometimes. You can also see how some people try to conceal the painful feeling of worthlessness by buying a more expensive house and a more luxurious car or struggling for a higher social status."

Soren shook his head. "I guess there's no solution, is there?"

"Of course there is! Otherwise, why would we even bother writing this book? What I mean is that continuous suggestions of pseudo-values can force our minds into an awkward conflict, hindering our sensible thinking."

Soren sighed with relief.

Shabe went on. "The other point is that due to the value-stricken view, a value-seeking person tends to pursue most of their goals, not just because of their merit or real use but mostly for the supposed value attached to them. People often may not really like something or care how much it actually suits them; rather, they go after it to gain positive labels, whether it's education, occupation, a future spouse or even clothing and furniture."

"Yeah! One of my dad's workmates bought some really expensive furniture. It probably cost as much as a big car, but they've covered it all with a thick cloth so it's not stained," Soren said. "When I saw this, I thought that was too funny! They'd spent so much to have beautiful furniture, but they covered up all its beauty."

"That's a great example, Soren. Even then, people can't always get peace of mind, as they have to divide their attention between what they're doing and how the neighbours are going. Their main concern is whether they can win the 'well done' and 'good job' medals in this endless marathon."

A pause. "I'm not exempt from this, to be honest," Soren admitted. "There was a skateboard craze at school a couple of years ago. All the popular guys were doing it. I begged Mum for a board too, even though I didn't really like skateboarding. Eventually, she got me one, but I didn't ride it more than a couple of times. It was just because I wanted to look cool."

"We've all done something like this. At least you're aware, so I commend you for sharing that."

"But I still can't understand what harm there is in admiring or praising."

"First, I should reiterate that encouragement, such as loving and paying attention to children and their needs, is absolutely necessary. However, what's not very helpful is trying to motivate our kids by using over-the-top verbal admiration."

"How does that harm?"

"Suppose you enjoy studying a foreign language," said Shabe. "Naturally, you do this out of pleasure or interest, so your study is a self-motivated activity, and you enjoy it because it's smooth and dynamic. Then someone arrives and learns that you've got considerable knowledge on the subject, and they praise it. They say, 'Oh, you're so talented' or 'What a knowledgeable person.' By doing this, they are *interpreting* you as knowledgeable or intelligent. Though there might be some truth in such a remark, because you're human, you naturally like being admired. You enjoy this. But when it's repeated, you can become dependent on it, just like a drug. Increasingly, your focus will be split between studying and social praise."

"Right."

"Gradually, it can get to a point where you don't study the language for its own sake anymore; you learn because you want to gain recognition. On top of that, you begin to fear losing approval, and this places another burden on your mind. Thus, learning becomes simply a means to an end: to get praise and renown."

"Oh, I see."

"But the problem doesn't stop there. The other nuisance is that you tend to be mentally and emotionally controlled by external factors. It will be others who decide what you ought to do before you know how you feel about it yourself," said Shabe. "The reason is that society has put you on the drug and can withhold it at will. This is how society takes control of how you think and feel and manipulates you, like a slave."

"Wow. I'd never thought of it like this before."

"Another emerging problem is comparison and competition. Obviously, society does not give praise and admiration only to you. It gives it to others as well. So you are all more or less on the same drug, and you're struggling to get more. Rivalry is inevitable! Such a competitive climate not only disrupts your peace of mind but also distorts your equanimity. And such rivalry has several aspects. First, each of you tries to gain more value and rewards, and the obstacle to this is other people, which means resentment and hostility is likely."

"Makes sense," Soren murmured musingly.

"Second, the ones granting the approval you're striving for are other people. And they won't give that approval, at least not overtly, because they're your rivals. Admitting your success is equivalent to betraying themselves. Ironically, because of your dependence on the drug, the third drawback is that your control is seized by your rivals, and by taking it away whenever they wish, they can hurt or subdue you." Shabe closed the book. "Did I answer your question?"

"Yes, very well. Thanks. But what's interesting to me is the agreement we made in the beginning."

"What do you mean?"

"I can see it's actually a very exciting condition! I mean, if we just looked at things with a fresh perspective, we cannot imagine what we'd see!" said Soren.

Shabe chuckled. "Yes. I call it the miracle of the fresh look!"

"Interesting. Hey! That wouldn't be a bad title for the book. What do you think?"

"Um, perhaps. But it does sound a little propagandist." Shabe chuckled.

Soren also grinned.

"Well, when do you say we meet next?" Shabe asked.

"Up to you, Shabe."

"How about I call you later?"

"That's fine. I'll be waiting." Soren said goodbye and headed home.

CHAPTER THREE

THE CROSS-EYED SERVANT

Shabe lay on the couch, reviewing his notes, crossing some sentences out as he went and jotting down new points raised during his discussions with Soren.

The doorbell rang. Tara hopped up from her slumber and ran ahead to the door, wagging her tail as she waited for Shabe to open it. Soren was on the porch, holding a paper bag as Tara cavorted around his feet.

"Come on, Tara, you'll scare Soren." Shabe laughed.

"Good day, Shabe." Soren smiled.

"Good day. Come on in. We've got a lot to do today!"

Soren gave in to Tara and patted her, then followed Shabe into the house. "You mean reading the book?" he asked.

"Yes, of course. Many lands are waiting for us to explore them."

Soren removed a large cake from the paper bag and handed it to Shabe.

"Wow! Chocolate cake! Thanks! Lovely. Bet it's homemade."

"My mum baked it. She loves to cook."

"Oh, tell her I said thank you. I think some of this would be great with a cool drink. What do you think?"

"Couldn't agree more."

Shabe set the cake on the table, then headed into the kitchen. Soren sat down on the sofa. He could hear the rummaging of cutlery as he waited, scratching Tara's ears as she nestled beside him.

"My mother was an excellent cook too," Shabe announced from the kitchen.

"*Was*? Oh, I'm sorry to hear that."

Shabe returned, carrying a tray with cutlery and glasses of fruit juice. He set them on the coffee table.

"Why are you sorry? Death and life aren't two separable things; death is just as necessary as life. You know, without death, people likely wouldn't have much enthusiasm or excitement for life."

Soren struggled to accept Shabe's claim. A life without death would be beautiful. A life without death would omit a lot of suffering from life. "I'm not sure," Soren said. "I wouldn't ..." He stopped himself, remembering their initial agreement. "Why do you say that?"

As if he knew what the boy was thinking, Shabe smiled and paused a moment. Then he sat down in the armchair opposite Soren and handed him some cake on a plate. "Well, what's the place you'd most like to visit?"

"Um, I guess that'd be Egypt. I'd love to explore the pyramids and see all the wonderful things you've shared about Egypt for myself."

"That's a great wish. And I'm sure you will. Now, close your eyes for a moment."

Soren eyed Shabe.

Shabe insisted, "Close them!"

Soren shut one eye with a cheeky grin.

"Stop clowning around and shut both eyes!"

"Okay. Okay."

"Imagine you've just won a three-day ticket to Cairo, including business-class airfare and accommodation in a luxury hotel with great food and facilities."

Soren opened his eyes involuntarily. "Wow. That would be amazing!"

"Close them!"

"Sorry."

"How excited are you going to get?"

"Very. I'd want to set off as soon as possible."

"And I bet you'd have a lot of plans?"

"Oh, of course."

"Now, imagine you've just arrived."

Soren smiled at the thought.

"What are you doing?"

"I'm walking around," Soren answered, eyes still closed. "Taking it all in."

"Must be exciting! You'd hate to miss even a minute of the experience. You would want to make the most of every moment, wouldn't you?"

"Yes, obviously."

"Well, now, what would you say if you had to remain in Cairo for the rest of your life?"

"What? For good?"

"Yes. Forever."

Soren's smile began to fade.

"Tell me, are you still so excited that you want to wake up early every morning to rush to the pyramids and take photos of the Great Sphinx? Give it some thought."

Soren opened his eyes and stared at the floor. "No, I guess not. I think things would be different then. Egypt would lose much of its interest. I may want to leave altogether."

"Precisely. Most of the excitement you felt was because the journey was so short. You understand why?"

"Not really …"

"Because whatever we can have without limits, we tend not to appreciate. It can become tedious, even tormenting."

"Yes, I can imagine that."

"And that's exactly like life, Soren. All our joy and excitement for living is because it's short and unpredictable. If we truly think about it, death makes life worth living. You could say that life's limited length gives it a particular value. Otherwise, you can imagine what a mundane thing life would be. Mind you, death has other functions as well."

"May I add something?"

"Yes?"

"If any creature born in the world never died, after a while, there wouldn't be any space for new things," said Soren.

"Right. Or suppose there was an animal whose body had already stopped working, but it never died."

"Ugh. That'd be horrible." Soren took a sip of his juice after a moment of thought, as if it could wash the image away. His thoughts returned to death. *Like Shabe said, perhaps it is necessary.* "When did your mother pass away?"

"Around four years ago. You know, my mother was originally from Iran."

"So that's why you know Iranian literature?"

Shabe nodded. "I also know Persian well. It's the language of Persia, which is now known as Iran."

"Oh, you can speak Persian?"

"Yes, because my grandmother talked to me in Persian until I was ten. She'd read Persian books to me and would tell me Persian tales. The Eastern world has an amazingly rich culture and literature."

"Oh yes, I've heard that. And is your name also a Persian name? I hadn't heard it before."

Shabe said, "Yes, actually. My full name is Shahab."

"Shahab," Soren repeated, trying to feel how it was pronounced. "What does it mean?"

"It means a 'shooting star.'"

"A shooting star? That's beautiful."

"Thank you. My mum picked the name for me. She said it reminded her of something fast and bright that disappears before anyone can hold onto it. I guess she thought I'd be that kind of person."

"Did she turn out to be right?"

"Maybe. Still figuring that part out," Shabe said, smiling faintly. "She loved stories and poetry. She knew lots of poems by heart and would frequently quote from them."

"That's a coincidence. My mum is also very much into reading and writing. A literato, she calls herself."

Shabe smiled. He picked up his cake and took a bite. "A literato and a great baker. Well, we can start now, if you're ready?"

Soren nodded with a mouth full of cake.

Shabe picked up the book and flicked to where they'd last left off. "Right. Before we set about exploring the core parts of the discussion, it'd be helpful to examine the general properties of arbitrary interpretations and the resulting *false values*.

"Obviously, to know a problem and its consequences, we should understand the underlying causes and backgrounds. But, Soren, before we begin, I should mention a point about some of the terms we often use in these discussions."

"Key terms?"

"Yes. In these discussions, I've used several words when referring to an afflicted person. These include the *value-stricken* human, the *self-lost* individual, the humiliated person and the *outwardly* person. Remember, we use various terms because the problem afflicting the individual in question is a diverse one. It's not easy to cram its multiple aspects into a nutshell. In fact, each one of these words can reflect different aspects of a person's difficulties, hence the variety in terminology."

"Right." Soren nodded, attempting to make a mental note of the terms. "I see."

"As we'll see, there's a relationship between *pseudo-values* and the mind's habit of interpretation. *False values* are outcomes of interpretation; interpretation, in turn, encourages these mental notions. So values and interpretation are not separate things; they're two sides of the same coin.

"For example, if my mind interprets wealth as glory, then I'd try to obtain this value, which is merely a product of my own interpretation. That's why I've used the word *interpretation*, or the labels, together with the words *pseudo-value* or *value*, for short.

"But what's meant is invariably the same process, attaching values to things and attempting to get these values, in your own imagination. Briefly, the variety in the terminology shouldn't leave us puzzled. It shouldn't make us feel that the discussions lack coherence or unity.

Remember, we're talking about the same human who's been afflicted by different problems."

"That makes sense."

"For instance, when we say the *value-stricken human,* we mean the human obsessed with empty values. When we say *self-lost person,* we refer to someone who's given up the home of their being to the wants and beliefs of others, rather than living a life built upon their own beliefs and values. As a result, this individual smothers their own identity with a fake persona.

"Likewise, by using the term *masked person*, we're trying to show how such a person covers their face with a pretty, popular mask, or one who can see things only through the masks. They can hardly see beyond the masks they put on the world's face.

"And talking about the *humiliated person* reveals the fact that all these plagues can be seen as various manifestations of one deep and vast affliction called humiliation. I'll share more about humiliation down the track. To sum up, we're discussing different aspects of a single but multifaceted difficulty."

"I think I've got it," Soren said. "Isn't it strange how we end up creating these interpretations and values ourselves, and then they trap us? It's like we're building our own prisons."

"Yeah, that is strange. It's almost like we're both the builders and the prisoners at the same time, as you said."

"Shabe, what if you added these explanations to the book too?"

Two But Nothing!

"Oh, absolutely. Good point! Cheers!" Shabe made a note in the book. "Well, the first characteristic of the pseudo-values is that they're comparative. We want to start with interpretive values that are based on comparisons. Basically, without comparisons, pseudo-values wouldn't exist.

"For example, if I looked at Jack's attributes without comparing them with other children, or those of an imagined child, Jack wouldn't be seen as a weak or timid kid. I wouldn't judge Jack as fearful or brave, clever or clumsy. I would merely see Jack as he is, with a detached perspective."

"Pardon me, but isn't it sometimes necessary to compare things?"

"It is, of course. Like many other things, in its right place, comparison is a helpful tool for understanding and selection. It's even inevitable. Think about when you go shopping for a shirt. You need to compare what's available in terms of size, material and colour to decide which one fits and suits you or which one you can afford. It's the same when you're deciding on a job. You compare available positions to see which occupation best suits your abilities and your interests. In such cases, comparing is a practical, valuable method."

"Agreed." Soren shut his eyes for a second.

"Even so, we need to remember there's no need to compare or judge people based on our personal likes or standards. No human has been born to fit with your tastes or mine or to live the way we think they should. People are free to choose their own way of being and living!

"Throughout history, judgemental attitudes have only caused hatred and horror and led to fighting, oppression and backwardness. We need to see people and accept them just the way they are."

"But what if I see someone making a mistake or doing the wrong thing?"

"Well, we have a right and a responsibility to talk to each other about what we believe is right or wrong. But what I'm opposed to is when we insist we are right without good reason."

"Okay. But what about the law? Doesn't the law force people to behave in a particular way? We even punish them if they don't, don't we?" Soren said.

"All right, good point. Law is a contract among residents in any community to obey a set of pre-agreed rules. All those who live in that society must be bound by that agreement … unless it's illegitimate, deceitful or oppressive."

"Makes sense."

"So comparison, in relation to people, is a blind and unjustified approach, and holding a comparative mindset is selfish and destructive."

"Excuse me again, but I often compare people. Like when I was trying to see who could be a friend on the cycling team. Or I remember when my dad was looking for a secretary. He looked at the candidates' characters and resumes to choose a suitable person."

"In both those cases, you're judging people based on your own needs or standards, and that's fair enough. But you shouldn't think of your comparisons as absolute or final. Because your judgements are personal and subjective."

Personal and subjective. Soren thought about his own friendships. Rob was a kind and caring friend who Soren had recently met, but at times, he felt disappointed with him for not spending as much time with him on the weekends as he would've liked. But Rob hadn't actually promised to spend time with him, especially before they became friends. *Maybe my expectation was based on my imaginings or, as Shabe put it, I compared Rob to the ideal friendship I already had in mind. Perhaps it was wrong to expect someone to give more than they'd ever offered.*

He felt glad Shabe had helped him recognise his unrealistic expectations. He knew this fresh insight would help him frame future relationships more fairly and logically.

Shabe continued. "I also want to say, comparison can be basically pointless. Why should you compare your job with mine and then feel embarrassed or inferior? The comparative nature of false values means they're imaginative and subjective, rather than absolute or real. In other words, they only exist in our imagination."

"What do you mean?" Soren said.

"It means, if you don't compare your height, which is, say, 140 cm, with my 180 cm, you'd simply say 'I am 140 cm tall.' You'd see this fact for what it is. So there wouldn't be any feelings of sorrow or regret. It's only when you compare your height with mine, and with *value-laden* standards, that you might say, 'I'm too short,' and then feel you're missing out."

"Yes, I see."

"The pride attached to having a tall, well-built figure comes from comparing it to the shame attached to having a stout, chubby figure—and vice versa. Neither is imaginable without the other. That means if either is removed, the other will disappear too."

"That's an interesting point." Soren nodded his head as he remembered. "I can definitely say it felt horrible, being called that."

"Yes, and we'll talk about humiliation soon. For now, let me share something." Shabe cleared his throat. "Rumi tells a good story in his *Masnavi.*

"Once there was a master with a cross-eyed servant. One day, the master ordered the servant to fetch a jar of vinegar from the cupboard. The servant obeyed, but to his surprise, he found two jars of vinegar side by side, not one. Unsure which one to grab, the servant returned to his master and explained the situation. The master was sure there was only one jar and told the servant to try again and be more careful this time.

"The servant went off, only to return and insist there were indeed two jars. The master became aggravated and was about to shout at the servant for his carelessness when he remembered the poor man was cross-eyed. So he decided to show the man that seeing two items was *his* misperception and not a reality.

"He called the servant over and told him to go and smash either one of the jars. The servant went back to the closet and soon returned to his master, astounded. 'I smashed one, but now there's neither!'

"'That's right! It was only your own poor eyesight that made you see things doubled.'"

"Amazing!"

Shabe put the notebook down. "See how easily we can make a basic mistake of believing in two conflicting ideas, while neither actually exists!"

"Yes, I can."

"It's very easy for my mind *not* to see you simply as you are. Instead, it tends to compare you with someone else or with an imagined person, so it attaches such labels as stupid, lazy, antisocial or knowledgeable to your character."

"That's a clever story, Shabe. But here's a twist. What if smashing the jar wasn't enough? I mean, what if the servant still saw things doubled? Sometimes, even when we smash our false beliefs, the habit of seeing things in a distorted way can stick around. How do we deal with that?"

"Good point, Soren. In fact, smashing the jar means you have woken up from illusion, and you're no longer cross-eyed. As soon as you question your unexamined thoughts, you are no longer cross-eyed."

"I couldn't agree more. So if you stop needlessly comparing yourself with others, you can be yourself! You can be comfortable! At school, some boys try to copy an athlete or actor's style or the way they speak. It's as if they're trying to clone themselves into their heroes. It's stupid, I think."

"Yes. When you blindly follow something, you lose your freedom. When you are a captive, it's difficult to be happy. You see now how comparativeness is the primary property of conventional values?"

"Yes! That's clear to me now."

"Well, okay. Let's go on to the second difficulty of interpretive values. I think you're going to like it."

"How come?"

"You'll see."

Blurry Lenses

Shabe flicked the page over and read. "*Interpretive values* are not clearly defined or understood. There's almost no consensus on them. Every person or group has their own definitions for each value, which may differ.

"Say, Jack's involved in a fight. Some call him timid because he came off second-best, while others tell him he's civilised for not being as violent as his attackers. Some consider Jack's behaviour as weakness, while others regard him as decent.

"At a personal level, the way such judgements are so subjective and ambiguous can leave you confused and frustrated. At a social level, they often cause misunderstanding, even hatred."

Soren blushed. "This seems to be based on a true story, doesn't it?"

Shabe smiled and went on. "Suppose I saved my wages for several months and bought an expensive car so you and everyone would think I was important. I'd be very frustrated if I found out you called me a show-off behind my back. That would really stir up bad feelings between us, wouldn't it?"

"Sure would!"

"Well, a great source of human ignorance is the habit of groundless interpretations or …"

Soren finished, "… judgements."

"Yes."

"That's why the Bible says to avoid judgements."

"Right. But, Soren, do you think it's possible to eliminate judgement altogether?"

"Um …"

"In a general sense, we need to judge—or you could say, *decide* or *discriminate*—in nearly every moment of life, don't we? I need to be able to decide which friend is reliable to share a secret with or ask for advice in a crisis. You have to weigh up which bicycle to buy or what major to study at uni."

"Even having this conversation now means we've concluded that reading and thinking are right, and wasting time is wrong," Soren commented.

Shabe smiled. "Exactly. Judging is inevitable in life, if you think about it."

"So judgement means deciding something is right or wrong, or good or bad, doesn't it?"

"It does."

"Then why do they say, 'Don't judge'?"

"Well, in such statements, judging means accusing or condemning. In our vague way of thinking, we've extended that to mean any kind of judgement. However, discarding *all* judgements is just plain wrong. And, in fact, impossible.

"What *is* wrong is pre-judgement because it can lead to wrong or unfair conclusions. For example, if I tell you not to judge your classmate as lazy merely because he arrives late to class, I mean that you shouldn't blame him for that. There might be many reasons why he's late that you're not aware of. 'Do not judge' means 'Don't blame others based on insufficient information.'"

"Sounds right."

"As Rumi advises, we should penetrate words, mottos and ideas and dig up the true meaning. Otherwise, we might be misled."

"Interesting."

"Yes, there's far more to words than we usually imagine. Words form our thoughts, and our thoughts tell us how to decide or act and how to feel." They were both quiet for a while, then Shabe said, "Shall we go on?"

"Can you suggest a few more examples?"

"Of course! But before I do, do you remember what we said in class recently about examples?"

Soren thought back. "Yes, I do." He smiled. "You said examples are good because they help us understand ideas, but we should be cautious because, sometimes, an example can be wrong or irrelevant."

"Yes."

"And you said some people use examples to mislead us."

"Glad you remember! I mentioned this to warn against accepting any ideas without adequate reasoning, as sometimes, you can be misled by examples—and that applies to whatever *I* say too. Please tell me about any faults or criticisms you notice about my remarks."

"Okay, will do."

"Now, suppose you don't invite me to your party simply because you don't have enough space. However, I interpret that as insulting or disrespectful and get offended. Or something crops up, and I can't come to your party, and you think I'm dismissing you and get upset. Therefore, we get sad or offended at each other because of our own interpretations."

"So our own imagination, rather than reality, tends to make us happy or sad," Soren said.

"Yes. Our imagination or understanding may be right and realistic or wrong and unrealistic, but in any case, we are invariably affected and moved by *our* understanding, rather than directly by the outside facts. You could say, we live in a world that our understanding filters and shows us, rather than living first-hand in the outer world."

"That's amazing, isn't it? The idea of living here." Soren pointed to his mind. "Not there?" He pointed to the environment.

"Well put, Soren, and that's how our knowledge and understanding works. The more wise, knowledgeable and skilled we are, the more power we have to deal with life's constant questions, challenges and problems. We can't change the entire world, but we can improve and increase our own knowledge."

"And knowledge is power."

"Exactly." Shabe picked up his glass and drank. His gaze ran over the pictures on the wall, and he was quiet for a moment. Then he went on. "My father was a porter, Soren," he said. "When I was a child, I used to feel embarrassed because of his job. Any mention of it would offend me, and I suffered a lot as a result. Whenever my classmates spoke about their parents' jobs, I'd get upset because I felt as if they were boasting."

"Really?" Soren found it difficult to imagine Shabe as a naïve child.

"Obviously, my suffering was rooted in my lack of insight and awareness."

"But perhaps they did that really to hurt you."

"That's right! That's what I want to say. If you're aware of the baseless values many people use to show off, you'd see them as weak and pathetic, not strong. You'd feel sorry for their pain, rather than resenting their behaviour."

"Very liberating." Soren smiled, staring into the distance.

"Mind you, it works the other way too. You've heard some people boast about their parents' jobs or wealth and expect admiration for that. They tend to interpret anything, even irrelevant remarks, as an insult to their prestige and get upset. There's an interesting point here."

"What's that?"

"Depending on social approval brings misery equally to the poor and the rich."

"Oh! I'd never considered that before. And this comes from value-based interpretations?"

"Yes, it does. I'm glad we're going through the book together. I'm positive good results are waiting for all three of us."

Soren narrowed his eyes. "Huh? Three?"

"Yes: you, me and the book!"

Soren laughed. "Oh, right!"

"I'd like to finish up the parts on the nature of values. What do you think?"

"Yeah, okay."

"Great. One moment. I've got something to show you."

Shabe disappeared into another room. Soren was wondering how these aspects of people's lives and relationships could be put into a story when Shabe returned with his brown leather bag. He rummaged through it, pulled out a photo album. He turned to a page and showed Soren.

A cartoon picture showed a bald, fat man in a tight suit riding a skinny, exhausted donkey along the middle of a long road. The rider held a stick with a rope, like a fishing rod. Attached to the end of the rope was a carrot, dangling near the animal's salivating mouth. Obviously, the donkey was determined to reach the carrot, despite his fatigue.

"They say a picture speaks a thousand words," Shabe said. "In this album I've collected images I've found impressive. Some of them are quite eye-opening."

Soren watched with a smile. Shabe turned to another page. Soren saw an extremely emaciated three- or four-year-old African child in the middle of a desert. The poor child was crouching, head resting on his bony chest, nearly dead. In the background, a vulture sat eyeing the child. Clearly, the predator was waiting for its prey to take his last breath.

Shabe saw profound distress in Soren's eyes. The boy sighed deeply, turning his head so that the image left his line of sight.

"I'm sorry. I didn't mean to disturb you, Soren. But we're on a journey to the world, and sadly, these are all part of the world's truth. We can't close our eyes to reality, can we?"

"I suppose not. But what can be done, really?"

"Actually, that's part of the question we're trying to answer. But we can't be satisfied with superficial answers, remember? We're after a helpful answer for effective action."

"Mm. I wish I had enough money to feed all the poor kids in the world."

"That's a kind thought. But shouldn't we be looking for a more useful remedy? Feeding the poor is a humane thing to do. Still, I believe anyone who wants to do something about poverty and misery should focus their efforts on the *system* of poverty."

"What do you mean?"

"Think of poverty as a system, and a vicious one at that, but however much you try to feed the poor, the evil system still produces more poverty. So instead of being carried away by the idea of endlessly providing for poor people, you could think about reforming the behaviour, relationship and culture responsible for perpetuating this poverty."

"There doesn't seem to be a simple answer for anything."

Shabe nodded. "As long as poverty is a system at work, it's not really effective to satisfy a number of individual hungers because the root cause is still in place. Well, shall we go on after we stretch our legs?"

"Please."

Superman

Shabe put the album away and picked up where he left off in the book. "Another problem is that society's expectations and values often contradict each other."

"I'm not sure I follow," Soren said.

"Well, one of the primary social values is wealth and the status it brings. Rich people are looked up to, and high status is often seen as glorious and respectable. At the same time, society expects the individual to be kind and compassionate. So far so good?"

Shabe paused for effect, then continued. "Wrong! If you wish to go after wealth and high social status, you need to be as smart as possible.

You have to compete with others and beat your rivals to gain greater wealth and a higher place. In such circumstances, you often can't remain a sincere friend to others or cooperate with them because they're your rivals, and helping them hurts yourself."

"So the conflict is between being kind and being clever."

Shabe closed the book. "Precisely. But here's another conflict that's fascinating—or a little ridiculous—whichever way you see it. It can be called the *prohibition of values* or the *tantalising nature of values*."

"Tantalising?"

"Yes, a blatant paradox. The point is, despite the importance society attaches to values, once you reach them, you're not supposed to enjoy them or feel proud of them."

"That *is* ridiculous! Why?"

"When you like or need something, you work towards gaining it. You spend time and energy on it. Right?"

"Right."

"And when you get it, naturally, you care for it and perhaps even treasure it."

"Yes …"

"Can you give me an example, Soren?"

"Um, if I read a book review and like it, I buy the book and read it. I'm also careful my little sister, Melody, doesn't think it's a colouring book. And my mum loves music; she plays the piano. She looks after her instrument, has it tuned regularly and takes care so it's not damaged."

"Great examples. So it's natural. We look after things that are important to us."

"Yes."

"Well, that's not the case with pseudo-values. When you obtain a value, you aren't allowed to like it, at least not openly. You'll remember, wealth and power are two of the most socially important and admired values, so many people go after them quite passionately."

"True."

"Now, suppose you're a porter, and you're distressed by the way many look down on you for your occupation. You reach the stage where you've had enough. You decide to work hard and dedicate years of your life to trying to improve yourself and become a rich and important person. You can see that it's not money or social status that you'd be trying to achieve. Instead, it's the honour associated with these things."

"Ahh."

"If you feel proud of your wealth or fame and others sense that, you can be accused of being arrogant and snobbish," Shabe said. "And if you expect praise and admiration, they say you have some sort of complex or that you doubt yourself."

"Uh-huh. And is this what you mean by tantalising or forbidden values?" Soren asked.

"Correct. Because if you have wealth, power and prestige, you are encouraged to ignore it and behave like someone who doesn't have these things. Even if someone admires you or pays you sincere respect, you're still not supposed to enjoy it. If you do, it's best to keep that hidden."

"Right. You can't openly declare yourself to be an important person with a high position," Soren began before pausing. "It's ridiculous that society admires those who have wealth and prestige but only when they don't show them off or act as if they care about them!"

"The paradox is that you must work hard for many years to attain something, but once you get it, you aren't allowed to enjoy it."

"Yes. Tantalising. I see." Soren smiled, remembering the picture of the donkey and the carrot. "But what's the reason for these inconsistencies?"

"The reason is that society is well aware that pride, honour and seeking fame are all different forms of what I like to call *begging for admiration*. Behaviours like this reflect an inner poverty and lack of self-worth."

"Begging for admiration. Interesting term!"

"There is a second lesson too, about how futile it is to try to gain social approval," Shabe said. "Hang on a moment." He collected the bag and stood up, disappearing into the other room.

Soren contemplated his words. *So mocking is a form of deceiving? Or is it? If so, you shouldn't be tricked. Perhaps by ignoring the mockers, you can indirectly tell them you've discovered their hidden intention. They can't fool or hurt you with their words and gestures.* Soren felt relieved. *I just wish those two fools, Hans and Daniel, knew these things too!*

Shabe took a piece of red fabric from his bag and unfolded it. A cape, Soren saw. Entangled in the material was a large, cut-out 'S' in a triangle badge that fell onto Shabe's lap. He stuck it to his shirt on his chest. Soren couldn't help but chuckle.

Shabe stood up and waved his hands in the air like a magician. In a deep and mysterious tone, as if he was advertising a thriller, he said, "Superman! The legendary hero! The man for whom nothing is impossible! Superman flies over skyscrapers; he crosses seas, deserts and forests and hurries to help the weak! Superman breaks through the boundaries of time and place. He can fly through thick walls and travel to the past. Superman!" Shabe froze, fist still raised.

Soren clapped his performance, unsure how it was relevant but knowing by now not to question Shabe's teaching methods. He'd soon find out.

Shabe bowed. "Thank you, Soren. Did you like it?"

"Very amusing."

Shabe removed the cape and returned to his armchair, putting the costume pieces away in the bag. He picked up the book and asked, "Soren, do you know the reason why people often get unduly offended by each other?"

"Um …"

"Believing in Superman."

"Well, *I* don't believe in him any—"

"Not *that* Superman." Shabe chuckled. "People often have exaggerated expectations of one another. They aren't faultless, which is natural; however, they expect others to be infallible, which causes offence and disappointment when they find out they aren't. The root cause of these excessive expectations is wrong and thoughtless values."

"What are they?"

"Social interpretations often won't tolerate any fault or imperfection. They expect you to be absolutely perfect, to be Superman. You can tell because, often, plenty of labels are attached to any shortcoming, with all sorts of blame and reproach.

"This is where intolerance and frustrating expectations arise. If you slip up, you can be labelled irresponsible, inconsiderate, timid, stupid and the like. And, as all these labels are contaminated with disgrace and hatred, they bring about guilt and anger.

"Yet we all know that no one's perfect, and Superman is a mythical figure. If people were the ideal versions of themselves, no action would ever be necessary, nor would any growth take place."

"And if this was the case, life would be an extremely boring and static thing," Soren chipped in.

"Right! Actually, there wouldn't be any life at all because life means motion and action, while perfection involves stillness and stagnation. Nevertheless, these irrational social interpretations fail to acknowledge a simple truth.

"For example, if a teacher can't answer a question, sometimes, they'll avoid admitting it because they fear they'll be accused of lacking knowledge. So they tell a lie or make up an excuse so they don't have to answer to save themselves from any stigma."

Soren remembered Shabe saying, "I don't know" or "I have to think about that" on several occasions in class.

Shabe continued. "Or, if you lack the courage to do something, it's difficult to admit you're scared. Odds are, you'll be accused of cowardice, which bears a social stigma."

Soren said, "Sometimes, when you show you're scared, it can make things worse. When you're being bullied, for instance."

"That's right. Excessive fear is even paralysing. My point is that giving annoying labels to people doesn't help. Labelling turns these unpleasant self-images into part of a person's identity. When that happens, shaking it off becomes far more difficult."

Blind Traditions

Shabe refilled their glasses with orange juice and took a sip. "Soren, do you think getting angry, shouting and screaming is good or bad?"

Soren swallowed some juice with a loud gulp. "I think it's bad."

"Well, you could be right, but think about the mental pressure that fake values put on us. The first and most straightforward type of conflict is when baseless interpretations disagree with human needs and feelings. We know anger is a natural reaction of the body, propelled by hormones released in the blood.

"Within natural limits, getting angry is not harmful; it's actually natural and necessary. But suppose, for some reason, you get angry and start shouting. You're likely to be accused of bad manners or even savagery. So you feel you must repress your anger to avoid being labelled rude or uncivilised.

"You know, in some cultures, when a male cries, it's a sign of weakness and hopelessness. Yet weeping is a normal reaction. It's a fascinating mechanism of the body to regain its calm and relieve emotional pressure. Why does it have to be interpreted as weakness?" Shabe noticed a smile on Soren's face. "Does that remind you of something?"

Soren nodded. "I was just thinking about how I usually blame myself whenever I get angry and feel some sort of guilt. But now I can see that the guilt was suggested by society. I know society has always frowned upon anger, but I never thought to question it and find out the truth. I see that getting angry is a natural state, and there's no sense in blaming it."

"Very well put, Soren! I completely agree. Even if it's excessive, blame and labelling rarely heal it. Blame and hate cannot help us improve; we need empathy and education."

"I agree."

"Soren, forceful environmental suggestions rob us of the chance to think and choose our ideas. Our minds get crammed with suggested beliefs that make decisions for us. Even respectful etiquette can deny some of your natural needs!"

"How come?"

"Suppose you don't like me for some reason. But you have to force yourself to smile and give a reluctant 'good morning' when you see me. Otherwise, you'll be seen as impolite."

"Yes!" Soren said. "Sometimes, my parents feel tired and don't want to go to a party. But they go because they're afraid the host will think they dislike them."

"Why shouldn't we acknowledge each other's feelings and ideas?" Shabe asked.

"Sometimes I don't show I'm feeling sad because I don't want to hurt someone else."

Shabe took another sip of juice. "Care to tell me an example?"

"Okay. My friend Jessica needed a study buddy for our English exam. She'd asked me to help, as I do quite well in the subject, and we agreed to meet the day before. Henry, my cat, was badly sick, and I wasn't feeling good at all, but I didn't let Jessica know because she was relying on me to help her for the exam."

"You had good intentions. It means you care for others' feelings. But that's quite different from pretending for fear of judgement or blindly following social norms. By the way, did your cat survive?"

"Oh, yes, and he's fine now. My mother took him to the vet, and they gave him some medicine. He must have caught something, they said."

"Glad to hear that." Shabe peered down at his dog, Tara, with a grateful smile. "Anyway, one time, I was at a friend's place when his wife came back from work. As she was taking her shoes off, she sighed in relief and said they'd been hurting her feet all day. We asked her, 'Why do you wear them? Why not wear more comfortable shoes?'

"She said her old shoes were far more comfortable, but she'd received many compliments for her new shoes. So that's a clear example of torturing yourself for the sake of external approval."

"That just reminded me of a movie." Soren stared off into the distance. "Actually, I think it was a TV show. Anyway, the story was about a tribe a few hundred years ago. They tied young girls' toes with ropes so that, after a while, the tips of the feet bent down and gradually changed shape. It was painful and even dangerous, but they said it was a tradition to make females' feet look smaller and prettier. Horrible!"

"Yes. It can be surprising for us to hear about things that are considered normal for many cultures. Like slavery. Difficult to believe *humans* used to be traded like common goods! Nevertheless, even today, we're hardly aware that fads and fashions and imitative values are doing more or less the same to our own lives!"

"Can you give me an example?"

"I might enjoy farming and being in nature, but I decide to become a politician. I deny my natural calling, and so I ruin invaluable days of my life, all so you'll regard me as a person of power and importance. In other words, I spend my life striving to gain *outward values*."

"What does an outward value mean?"

"In this case, the act of farming brings me joy and pleasure, while being a politician doesn't. However, being in politics does win me respect and praise from the outside, from other people. Inside, it's more pressure and grief than joy or satisfaction."

Shabe placed the book down on the coffee table and leant back on the armchair, falling quiet for a minute. He patted Tara, who was resting against his calf, wagging her tail.

Meanwhile, Soren's mind had begun to drift. He knew many people with comfortable lives and decent situations who still compared their lives to others' or to what they'd read or seen in the media about some actress or millionaire. He himself had done that too, which both surprised and disappointed him.

Shabe picked up the book and sat up straight. He cleared his throat. "Following values often means wearing a mask. A mask consists of deceit, pressure and frustration and, of course, guilt in denying your own common sense and alienating yourself from your nature."

Soren wondered whether Shabe had learnt this lesson at the circus.

Advertisement

Shabe picked up the remote control, switched the TV on and flicked through a few channels until he reached a program comprised of advertisements only. First, a commercial for a beverage showed a couple relaxing on a tropical sandy beach, popping open a can and eagerly drinking from it. The next advert featured a family joyfully driving on a winding forest road along a cliff, smiling and joking together as they successfully manoeuvred to avoid hazards and obstacles. The next commercial was for some sort of tonic, followed by a chic cosmetic set, apparently turning a fifty-year-old woman into a thirty-year-old. Then they saw an advert for an insecticide, then for a painkiller and so on.

Shabe turned the TV down and said, "Soren, these different commercials have one message in common. What is it?"

"They're all telling you to buy their products."

"Exactly. They're telling you to give the outcome of your work to them. 'Get our product, and give us your *days* in return.' Soren, what else do you think all ads have in common?"

"For one thing, they're all designed to be as attractive and fascinating as possible."

"Right. They try to tempt you in different ways to buy from them. And the other thing is that ads are always repeated. Why?"

"So that they become fixed in your mind? Kind of like lessons!"

"Yes. But I believe the more attractive a lesson is, the less you'll have to resort to repetition and memorisation to take it in. The most effective learning takes place involuntarily, when you're fully absorbed in what you experience, without your mind being divided between what you're seeing or reading and the idea of an upcoming exam."

"I fully agree. Just like your lessons."

Shabe shared a warm smile and went on. "You've seen before that the mind can be trained in nearly any way, positive or negative, so that it can act for a person's benefit or even loss. Fake values prevail in society as inherited custom and traditions. And tradition is often something stale and imitative, devoid of question, analysis and creativity. Soren, in the self-lost person's life, advertising has a tremendous implication, far beyond its usual sense. You could say that in one sense, we're profoundly *advert-stricken people*."

"Can you clarify a bit?"

"Sure. When we talk about advertising, what comes to mind are radio or TV ads that promote particular types of food, clothes or cars or advertisements during elections or similar things."

"Right."

"But if, as Rumi advises, we pull aside the veils of appearances and dig deeper through, we'll see that whatever is said or done—in order to suggest a particular idea to our minds, through repetition, exaggeration or embellishment, rather than facts or reasoning—is a form of advertisement.

"As such, humiliation, insult, ridicule and even praise and compliments can all be various forms of advertising, suggesting particular images and ideas to our mind through intimidation or emotional stimulation, rather than allowing us to liberally think, analyse and decide."

Soren seemed to be following carefully.

Shabe added, "Suggestions influence the mind and make it surrender and follow, especially when accompanied by the triggering of sensations. Take the feelings of awe, pleasure and greatness. Or the opposites, such as worthlessness, grief, pain and humiliation."

Soren grinned. "What a horrendous situation. We're hypnotised beyond recognition!"

Shabe laughed and answered, "You can't be hypnotised as long as you're alert."

Soren nodded with a smile.

Shabe went on. "The reason kids and young adults often seem stubborn and rebellious is because of these pressures to adapt and conform, at least partly. The individual initially feels these values are alien and awkward. Still, society keeps pressuring them to comply, through the tools we talked about before. As a result, their psyche finally surrenders. But to soothe the feeling of reluctance, they close their eyes to all these contradictions.

"Right now, you and I feel frustrated about many persuasive so-called etiquettes and courtesies that we have to obey. None of us can really make sense of them. Yet we don't usually feel the pain vividly, as we've grown accustomed to denying our emotions."

"And our reasoning," Soren added.

"Absolutely."

"But if we ignore others, could they take offence?"

"Yes, but I didn't say we should ignore or disrespect others. What I'm saying is that when we pay respect or give attention because of pressure or imitation, we're just paying lip service with nonsense words and gestures."

"Okay. Well, I suppose I have an objection to what you said about custom and tradition."

"Objection?" Shabe smiled eagerly as he leant back into the sofa, lacing his fingers together. "Good! Go ahead."

"Is it good to receive objections?"

"Of course. Imagine, if no one ever objected or criticised but simply agreed to everything. Would any error be corrected? Would any progress be made?"

"I'm not sure."

"All improvements have happened because people have objected to the old ideas or methods. Praise and admiration do less to improve things."

"Mum always says one way to judge if your actions are right is to imagine what would happen if everyone did the same thing you're doing."

"That's very interesting, indeed. But you haven't told me your objection yet."

"Well, I think traditions aren't always a bad thing," Soren admitted.

"Can you explain?"

"We have good traditions as well. Like celebrating the new year, visiting sick people or giving congratulations or condolences."

Shabe pursed his lips. "Mm. I guess you're right. They're good traditions. Your criticism is sensible. So, let's say tradition is not necessarily bad, but what is wrong is being *tradition-stricken*."

"Which means …?"

"That we shouldn't accept habits and traditions blindly but must judge them consciously and select them independently. We should drop the wrong ones and keep the good ones."

"Great. I agree."

"You see?"

"See what?"

"Your criticism helped me to correct a mistake and clarify a good point. Thank you!" Shabe smiled at Soren.

"You're most welcome," Soren said with a proud smile.

"Now we're going to learn the most important weakness of the interpretive values, which is their nothingness and nonsense. We'll see why fake values are nothing but a bunch of empty words. Understanding this point is the key to the problem, so it's crucial to have this fully clarified."

"I'm all ears."

"No, Soren. Please have a head and mouth!" Shabe chuckled.

Soren burst into laughter. "Great advice!"

Shabe also kept laughing.

The Sunglasses

After a moment, balancing his glasses on the tip of his nose, Shabe said, "Interpretive values are merely a bunch of imaginary concepts, because these so-called values aren't made up of anything real. They're made of words that only represent things."

"You've mentioned this before, but I didn't really get it."

"I'll give you an example." Shabe stroked his chin. "Imagine I have a highly respected job as the manager of a company. Realistically, the job has given me considerable privileges—a decent income, easier duties and wealth. However, it has also earned me the title of 'sir' and the associated status and respect. As a prideful person, which of my privileges do you think I'd boast about most?"

"What do you mean?"

"Which benefit of the job I just described am I likely most proud of?"

"Your wealth and power?"

"Right, but think about it at the deeper level."

"I guess being called *sir* and the respect you receive?"

"Exactly. So what really matters to me is not merely the reality of my job; it's also the value-laden words, such as people saying, 'Yes, sir.' These are often even more sensitive."

"I see."

"And it also works the other way. If, for any reason, someone happens to say they didn't think I was much of a person because I was a garbage man, how would I feel?"

"Probably angry. You'd hate them."

"That's correct. Now the question is, what really troubled me or made me resentful? They haven't changed anything about my situation. What made me angry was the notion that I wasn't much of a person because I was a garbage man."

"Okay. So you've been offended by insults that aren't true."

"Exactly. Another example. Suppose I'm struggling financially and don't have such a comfortable life. Of course, realistically, poverty is a problem. As a poor person, I'd be deprived of decent clothing or accommodation and might have to do unpleasant jobs."

"Yep."

"Now, if someone saw me and called me a junkie, I'd get pretty upset. But the question is, what's really offending me? Is it my financial problems? Does being called a junkie affect my nutrition or financial state?"

"No. I think what really upsets you isn't your old house or clothes; it's the word 'junkie,'" Soren said.

"Right. I'm not offended or disturbed by realities but by the words related to them and their *value-laden* meanings."

"But, Shabe, we see these words as insults."

"Well, what makes me sad or glad aren't the words 'sir' or 'junkie.' It's the interpretations my mind makes of these."

"But people also have the same understanding."

"That's correct, and that's probably why we easily believe it, but that doesn't mean there's any truth behind it."

"It means everyone imagines these words can harm them, so we also believe this?"

"Words are not swords or bullets. They're nothing but sounds and vibrations."

Soren chuckled. "Yes, Shabe, but even a loud enough clap can cause an avalanche."

Shabe laughed. "I like your sense of humour! The book could use some of that. But using your interesting metaphor, you know why the avalanche, despite being so huge, can be triggered just by a clap?"

"Umm."

"It's big and heavy, but it doesn't have roots. It's merely a pile of snow with no anchors to the ground. Soren, I know it can hurt when someone insults or ignores you. And I agree that is wrong and impolite behaviour. But as far as mental and emotional matters are concerned, others can hardly hurt you without your own collaboration. You're not hurt by the word or gesture the other person says or makes; you're hurt by the importance you give to that action. You're hurt because you subconsciously identify yourself with their words or actions. The stronger you are, the harder it is for others to impact you with their judgements or valuations. Being strong means believing in your own values, beliefs and reasoning, rather than being vulnerably dependent on the likes and dislikes of others."

"That's profound! So that's why even a small tree is more stable than a huge avalanche—because it's got roots. If you want to add that to the book?" Soren said with a grin.

Shabe said, "Oh, that's awesome. Of course!"

Shabe wrote down a few lines and said, "Going back to our discussion, suppose I have a luxury car. My car is a vehicle for transport, but I use it as a tool to show off my income. Addiction is a hazard to my health, but I look upon it as a stigma. My old clothes are in good condition, but I feel ashamed about having to wear them. The more we become dependent on words, the more distant we get from reality. The more attached we are to our interpretations, the less sensitive we become on realities. That's how we gradually get submerged in fantasies and illusions every day."

Soren grinned. "Then we should probably bring a life vest."

Shabe raised an eyebrow. "What?"

"You know," Soren chuckled. "Or a blow-up tube. Whatever keeps us afloat."

Shabe laughed. "In a bit of a clowning mode today, aren't you? I suppose we don't have to read much today if you're not in the mood."

"No, no. I'm just kidding around."

Shabe smiled. "I was joking too," he said and pulled a pair of sunglasses out of the brown leather bag. Offering them to Soren, he asked, "Can you put them on, please?"

"Sure." Soren did so, then peered around the room curiously.

"Well, what colour is my shirt?" Shabe asked.

"Grey."

"And this table?"

"Dark grey," Soren answered.

"And the building outside the window?"

"Grey again."

"And the sky?"

"Grey!"

"Now take the sunglasses off. What happened?"

Soren placed the sunglasses on the coffee table. "Well, everything changed. The colours changed."

"And then what happened?"

"Things were real again."

"Why?"

Soren shrugged. "Because I took the glasses off."

"As long as you had the sunglasses on, what you saw was not the world. It was the colour of your own sunglasses. Only when you removed your glasses could you see the world, the world itself, direct and first-hand."

"Yes. I know how glasses work. But how is—"

"Are you certain you know how sunglasses work?"

"What do you mean?"

"Can you be sure right now that we aren't wearing sunglasses on our brains?"

"Sunglasses on our brains?" Soren echoed.

"I'd say we are, most of the time. A pair of sunglasses with lenses made of labels, prejudgements, indoctrinated feelings and borrowed ideas."

Soren nodded thoughtfully. *That wouldn't make a bad cover design, a brain wearing dark sunglasses.*

"And as long as we're wearing these glasses, we can hardly see the world and its truths. Rumi said all this, eight centuries ago.

*'You are wearing dark glasses.
That's why you see the whole world dark.'*

"If you listen closely to the way we talk every day," Shabe suggested, "you'd be surprised by how often we use the false language and make cliché statements. Worse, how often we *think* in this language and how much we feel through it. I reckon if we were somehow reprogrammed to be free of this language, we wouldn't be able to think at all."

"What words, for example?"

"Well, stingy, for instance. Great man. Patriot, coward, disloyal, conservative ..."

Captain Heap. Dwarf. Clumsy, Soren went on in his mind.

"These words are the rails on which our train of thought runs," Shabe continued. "Without them, our mind would become paralysed. When you stop and think, you'll realise how difficult it feels to look into things without those terms.

"We're often concerned about the nature of things so we tend to think through the lenses of words and symbols. Our feeling happy, sad, angry, proud, hopeful or disappointed all come from words, rather than realities. During a relationship, the values we associate with others are constantly in our minds. In fact, the way we feel about our family, friends and others is largely dictated by words.

"Let's say a person cut me off on the freeway. I'd be thinking to myself, 'That guy is an absolute idiot.' If I thought about it, I'd discover what's really annoying me is the term 'idiot.' I can't see the actual person or what they've done as they truly are. I simply see him and his character adorned with the mask of an idiot.

"Without realising it, my anger is also directed at those words and the feelings they carry, not at that person or their action. If I looked at the person and what they did as they actually are, with no mask, I might see only a mistake or an illness. But that sounds too difficult. Being obsessed with the words injected into my mind and the feelings that follow, it seems too hard to take off the thick mask and see the world first-hand."

Soren's eyes drifted to the window, where he caught a glimpse of a white seagull floating past in the blue sky. He began to imagine invisible sunglasses on the faces of everyone around him. How many were dark and made of some impenetrable material? *Likely too many.*

He returned his gaze to Shabe's glasses. *Shabe's lenses are clear. They don't distort his view of the world. They help him see things more closely.*

Shabe stroked his chin. "Everything has already been defined in our *value-laden language* and given a label. The value-stricken person is not a free human. They are virtually chained from the inside. They think and feel through borrowed words and labels! They love them and organise their life according to them. The masked person is an imitator of most things. They copy and follow society, which itself is blind and has little insight on matters.

"If I weren't blind or confused, I'd ask myself, if someone called me a fool or insignificant, would that really shrink my being? So why should I be troubled by a few empty words?"

Shabe removed his glasses, giving them a quick wipe on the hem of his shirt. "When you think about it, Soren, what's so terrible about not being an important person? What problems have been caused through not being famous or sought-after? What's the danger of not being distinguished?" Shabe asked, putting his glasses back on.

Soren tugged his ear. "I guess you're right, but I reckon it'd be quite enjoyable to be famous. Everybody would recognise you when you walked down the street."

"But think a bit more. Wouldn't it actually be the other way around?"

Soren lifted an eyebrow. "How could it?"

"People don't usually have much to do with unknown persons, but famous people are frequently targeted by jealousy, scandal, robbery, blackmail and even murder. Just look at newspapers and TV. You'll see loads of examples. The French philosopher Michele de Montaigne said, 'Peace and fame will never live together.' Rumi has a few words to say, too.

'People have made ladders of pride and brag.
The ladder will eventually collapse.
The higher you climb, the more foolish
You'll break your bones harder.'

"Being famous or important means you have a special place in society and you're always being observed closely. Think of British royalty! And most celebrity lives. It means you're not free to do or talk about anything you wish to. You'd frequently have to censor yourself. You couldn't suddenly decide to go shopping or take a trip or enjoy your life the way you'd really like. If you defied social values, even in a minor way, you'd suffer a lot of scandal and misery. You really wouldn't be free to be yourself. So fame means limitations. No freedom and pressure put on your life and a psyche by the public."

Soren said, "So the lesson here is, whatever thing or situation you come across, first you must take off your sunglasses and *then* look at it."

"Soren, you can't imagine how enjoyable it must be to be rid of this grey world and see things in their real colour. The peace and joy that comes from liberation is indescribable."

"Sounds fascinating," Soren agreed, imagining himself removing the mask and burying it in Shabe's garden.

"Well, that brings us to the end of today's discussion."

"Um, excuse me …" Soren said.

"Yes?"

"I just have a question, but I'm not sure if I can ask it."

"Oh, don't worry. Go ahead."

"You've told me about your father's job and about your previous work in the circus. Can you tell me a bit more about your life and how you grew up?" Soren asked hesitantly. He felt Shabe would be kind enough to answer the question he'd wondered about for so long. "I'm keen to know, if you don't mind?"

"Oh, of course." Shabe began quietly, his voice heavy with the weight of memory. "You already know, Soren, I came from a poor family. I had several siblings, and life was tough. I had just turned twelve when my father took me out of school and sent me to work in the circus, where a friend of his was employed.

"From dawn to dusk, I laboured, both physically and mentally. The pay was low, and things were harsh. Still, I was glad to help my family and support my younger siblings."

"Oh, it must have been very difficult," Soren said. "I'm very sorry to hear that."

Shabe spoke musingly, as if watching the scenes of those still-vivid memories. "Yes, Soren, it was bitter and harsh, but in hindsight, I'm not sorry today. I owe much to the lessons I learned from that uneasy life and even from those not-so-nice people. Without those pains and challenges, I doubt I would have ever learned any great lessons in life."

"When did you study, then?" Soren asked after a moment's pause.

Shabe smiled faintly. "Whenever I could. I never missed a chance to read, think and write. No matter how exhausted I was."

"Oh, you wrote as well?"

"Yes, I kept a diary, writing down everything: my memories, what I learned, the strange characters I encountered and their lives and the things that made me think. Over time, I learned a great deal, not just about circus life but also about people, about suffering, joy and meaning."

"Were there any good friends around?"

"Yes, thankfully. I had a few like-minded friends—quiet souls like me. We usually talked at night when our work was done and the noises had faded away, allowing us to be ourselves at last. We shared our thoughts and experiences, trying to make sense of it all."

"And did you travel?"

"Of course. We travelled a lot. It was both tiring and interesting. I saw lots of different places and met many different people. Those events expanded my outlook and taught me many precious things. By the age of sixteen or seventeen, I was much more travelled and experienced than children my age and learned lessons not just from books and classes but from life, first-hand, with all its challenges and realities."

"Fascinating!" Soren's mind was immersed in everything being shared.

Shabe paused and looked Soren in the eyes. "You know, from the outside, the circus seemed like a world of joy, laughter, colour and music. To the audience, it was magic. But inside, it was something else. Behind the scenes, it was exhausting and stressful; it was like a glittering cage. We made others laugh, but we rarely laughed ourselves. I never felt like I belonged there. I was always an outsider, somehow observing. And I felt that contradiction every single day."

Shabe sighed, then went on. "As the years passed, my life improved. I rose through the ranks and eventually became a manager. I was no longer financially struggling. My family was better off too. But even then, something felt off. I had grown accustomed to that life; it had become familiar, almost safe, in a peculiar way. So leaving wasn't easy. I could clearly see it was a life I had outgrown yet still felt attached to. For a long time, I struggled internally. Part of me resisted change. Another part longed for it. Eventually, I made my decision. I said goodbye to the circus for good."

Soren nodded slowly, sensing the weight of that inner war. "That's such an amazing story," he said, unable to hide his wonder. "And your family, Shabe? What happened to them? Where are they now?"

"My sisters and brothers are all right. They live in other cities. I moved here because I found it a beautiful and quiet place. I had been here once, Soren. Probably before you were born."

"Oh, wow! Sounds like a dream to me!" Soren exclaimed. "So you had seen this town before …"

"Yes."

"And what about your father?"

"My dad was a tough man. He rarely gave us a smile or a hug. But that's okay. I believe we shouldn't blame our parents for what they didn't share with us because they probably didn't enjoy it themselves either."

Soren was staring at Shabe, saying nothing but just trying to digest each sentence.

"He strongly opposed my decision to leave the circus, especially now that I was a manager and made good money. He ridiculed the idea of becoming a teacher with a much lower income. And he passed away, years ago."

"Oh, I'm sorry." No sooner had he spoken than Soren remembered the talk about death and the journey to Egypt. "Though death is another side of life, as you said."

"That's right, Soren. Thank you for your empathy, though."

Another pause. Soren seemed lost in thought, his eyes unfocused for a moment, as if the story had stirred something painful inside him. He saw Shabe in a different light now, all of his teachings and their discussions making much more sense in the light of what he had just learned. All of the pieces fit together—Shabe's experiences, his insight, why he was who he was. It was as if a picture had moved out of the shadow, into a brighter space.

"So did I answer your question?" Shabe asked.

"Absolutely. Thank you for sharing all that. I think I'll carry this with me for a lifetime. I really enjoyed today. Thank you."

Shabe's face softened. "And I enjoyed talking to you. It's rare to meet someone who really listens." He placed a gentle hand on Soren's shoulder. "You're coming tomorrow, aren't you?"

"Yep!"

"Good. See you then."

"Goodbye…um…one more thing."

"Yes?"

"Is it ok if I share your story with mum? She'll be astounded to hear about it."

"Yes, no problem at all."

"Thank you!"

Soren walked home slowly, pondering the day's lessons. Soon, he reached town, where various billboards, large and small, now replaced the trees.

A bit further ahead was a grocery shop. Sprayed across the windows in large neon letters was a big slogan: 'SAVE EACH TIME YOU SPEND WITH US.' A bus with a loud engine roared past, its stinking exhaust filling the air. Along the side, a huge advertisement of an attractive woman caressing her face and holding a bottle of lotion peered back at him. 'Beauty is Eternal,' the ad read.

Across the street, an A-frame stand in front of a pizzeria presented appetising photos of its menu. The backrest of a wooden bench displayed the portrait of a political candidate dressed in neat clothes. The caption read: 'Vote for a better future with Eric!'

Soren thought to himself that adverts were really just ways of setting traps and catching prey. But if you never advertised, how could you sell?

Henry, the cat, was stretched lazily in front of the door when Soren arrived home. He got up and silently met Soren as he climbed the porch steps, purring and rubbing against his calf.

"Hungry, are you?" Soren asked him. He let himself and Henry into the living room. The house was filled with the delectable aroma of frying cutlets. Soren could hear the satisfying sizzles of hot oil. He felt his stomach rumble.

Soren found his mother in the kitchen, hovering over the chopping board as she prepared a salad.

"Hi, Mum," Soren said.

"Hi, darling." Sally smiled. "How are you?"

"Great, thanks. Where's Melody?" Soren picked up a slice of cucumber.

"Asleep," Sally answered, chuckling. "She went on a play-date today and got completely tuckered. She was asleep in the car before she even had her seatbelt on."

Soren smiled as he picked up a piece of carrot.

"And how was your meeting?"

"Great," Soren said through a mouthful of food. He went to pick a yellow leaf of lettuce when his mother shook her head at him.

"Instead of picking at the food, how about you go and wash your hands, and we'll talk about it over dinner."

Ten minutes later, Soren was sitting at the dinner table with his mother while Henry ate from his bowl beside them on the floor. Soren and Sally were soon deep in conversation about his day. He told his mother about the way people wore masks, the harm in believing in Superman, the troubles of being a celebrity and the way advertisements could be a sort of entrapment.

And, of course, he shared Shabe's life story with Mum, his voice full of excitement. Sally listened intently, deeply drawn into the tale of Shabe's hardships, endeavours, contemplations, and the long path he had travelled to become who he was now.

"How interesting." She said. "I did think there must be an unusual life behind all of this."

"So did I," Soren replied, musingly.

There was a moment of silence.

"But where do the labels and values of particular words come from?" Soren wondered. "Can you avoid them if you start young? And how exactly do we remove our masks?"

"Certainly interesting things to think about, Soren. It seems like you have a lot of questions. To be honest, I think I have questions of my own as well."

Soren chuckled. "The more you learn, the more questions you have. But Shabe says as soon as you stop following the meanings people put on things and start to think about the true meanings for yourself, you begin to live in a world you have discovered by yourself, not one that is made by others."

Sally smiled at Soren fondly. "Quite big words. But really thought-provoking, I will admit. I'll wait for Shabe's book to be published. I'm sure many more answers are in there."

"What questions do you have?" Soren asked.

"I'm just a bit unsure about some of the things he said. If we get rid of all values, what standard would there be for our behaviour? Honesty and empathy are core values in friendships. And of course, there's lying, betrayal and theft. Aren't they truly bad things?"

"Hmm," Soren responded. "That's a good point. Well, Shabe says the values he's opposed to are fake ones. But I'll ask him about it tomorrow."

Soren's internal monologue rarely seemed to cease these days. New ideas and questions persistently arose from the depths of his mind.

After dinner, Melody awoke, and Soren played with her for some time. Melody seemed to enjoy every moment of the game and laughed heartily. The innocence of her joy and laughter reminded him Soren the first chapter of Shabe's book about how society treated children.

I can't imagine Melody lying or making fun of others. Right now, she's happy and carefree. But that doesn't mean she'll always be that way. What really happens that causes these problems in later life? Hans and Daniel were once sweet, innocent children too, just like Melody, weren't they? What happened to turn them into such mean bullies? God forbid Melody turns out like that.

Watching the dark shadows from the tree outside his bedroom window dance along the wall, Soren knew he'd try never to let that happen. He lay in the darkness, mulling over what he'd discussed with Shabe.

An idea erupted in his mind, like a sparkler. He quickly sat up, flicked his lamp on and took a seat at his desk. He opened to the first blank page in his notebook and began to write...

He wasn't sure how much time had passed. Many pages were covered in black ink. Many sentences were crossed out and replaced. Then his train of thought was interrupted by a faint knock at the door.

"Yes?" Soren said, looking up from his notebook.

The door opened, and Soren's dad appeared in his pyjamas. He squinted into the room at Soren, adjusting to the brightness of the lamp. "Son, why aren't you sleeping?"

"I'm writing something," Soren answered. "I'm sorry. Did I wake you?"

"No, I was just getting a glass of water. You must be writing about something pretty important to keep you up so late."

"Mmm! Sort of."

His dad nodded. "Maybe you can tell me about it when the sun's awake."

Soren smiled. "Yeah, I will."

"Just don't stay awake too long. It's not good for you. Goodnight, love."

"Goodnight."

Soren looked at the clock. Just past midnight! Realising this made him yawn. He put down the pen and closed the notebook. The cover read: 'Upon a Time: Stories by Soren Dustin.'

CHAPTER FOUR

BEHIND THE MASK

Shabe answered the phone. "Hello?"
"Hi, Shabe. It's Soren."
"Hey! How are you?"
"I'm okay, thanks, just a bit confused."
Shabe laughed. "Oh, I wouldn't worry too much. A bit of confusion or bewilderment is necessary. As Rumi advises,

> '*Sell smartness and buy bewilderment.*
> *Smartness is doubt; bewilderment is vision.*'"

Soren laughed. "Well, that's a relief."
"Are you okay for five o'clock in Forest Park? Next to the coffee kiosk?"
"That'd be great."
"See you then."

Dense shade from the colourful trees enveloped the park, protecting passers-by from the scorching June sunshine. A road slithered around the park like a long, grey snake. Road signs reminded drivers to be cautious and slow down.

Cyclists passed through—male, female, young and old. Some were dressed in Lycra and could pass for professional competitors. Others idled around, enjoying their afternoon.

Some bikes amused Soren, like the ones so low to the ground that the cyclist had to pedal lying down. Another sort had two different-sized wheels. Some bikes required two people to pedal, their legs in perfect sync as they maintained balance.

The pleasant breeze cooled Soren's cheeks, flushed from his own cycling, as a flock of colourful parrots squawked loudly overhead. When he arrived, he got off and walked his bike to the small lake in the centre of the park, where he noticed the ducks drifting in pairs, occasionally diving beneath the water to feed. He found Shabe already seated beside the kiosk, reading a newspaper.

Soren rested his bike against a tree trunk. "Good afternoon!" he called out as he approached the bench.

Shabe's gaze lifted, and he returned Soren's big grin. "Good afternoon, Soren. Looks like you're a bit hot. A cold drink would be great, don't you think?"

"Mmm! Can't think of anything better."

Shabe went to the nearby kiosk, returning with two juices. Soren took one gratefully and took several large gulps.

"So, Soren, your mind's a bit cloudy, huh?"

"You could say that," Soren said. "I've got a few questions."

"And I'm sure the answers aren't far away." Shabe took a sip of his juice as he eyed Soren watching more ducks waddling past them on the footpath, seeking stray crumbs.

"How do you know?" Soren asked, turning to Shabe.

"I was like you once. I had just the same concerns and doubts. Well, perhaps a bit different. But if you need an answer to a particular question now, go ahead."

"Mum asked me something I couldn't answer."

"Glad to hear your mother's joined in. What was her question?"

"She said that if we disposed of all values, wouldn't that lead society into chaos? She wondered what standard we'd be left with to judge good and bad if we rejected values."

"I see." Shabe rubbed his chin. "Like I said, in this context, we're not discussing moral values or ethical good and evil. We're criticising pseudo-values, which are unfounded ethics. Society is full of nonsense values. And the popularity of fake values has blurred the face of true values. Let me make that clear."

Shabe delved into his bag for a book: *History for Children*.

This is for kids, Soren thought.

As if he could hear, Shabe said, "Although this book is written for school kids, it still has valuable things to tell us."

"Yes. I'm beginning to see that you can find lessons in everything."

"Even in the simplest of things," Shabe agreed, pushing his glasses back up his nose. "In the olden days, people in many primitive tribes, even some civil societies, considered objects such as wood, stone and trees to be holy or sacred."

Soren settled into his seat, awaiting a fascinating story.

Shabe went on. "They imagined that particular trees held mysterious healing powers, and specific pieces of metal could cast magical spells. They even hand-carved some sculptures from rock or wood, then worshipped them as idols! They believed these idols to be gods or goddesses and credited them with tremendous supernatural powers. Disrespecting these objects was believed to have grave consequences. They referred to these lifeless, non-intelligent objects with awe and reverence and safeguarded them devotedly. Animals, even humans, were sacrificed to these idols, and bloody battles broke out in response to these idols being disrespected.

"At the same time, other phenomena, regarded as sinister or devilish, were avoided. Often a certain rock or a sign was thought to hold Satanic powers and was used against an enemy." Shabe closed the book and put it on the bench.

Soren picked it up, flicked through the pages and muttered, "Superstitions."

"Today, when we hear such stories, we're surprised by their ignorance. We see their traditions as stupid and superstitious. Know why?"

"Because we know better?"

"Yes. Thanks to the advancement of knowledge and science, we've unveiled a lot about nature's powers and have found the causes behind many happenings. We know now the supernatural powers those tribes attributed to those objects never existed. So the magical properties of those objects were all in their own minds, not in those objects."

"Interesting. Many things are just here," Soren said, pointing at his head with a chuckle. "And not out there. Is that it?"

"Exactly! In the real world, objects were simply what they were: a piece of metal or wood, a stone or a tree. Nothing beyond that. Their conflicts were over nothing! If they'd understood then that what they fought over, mourned or feared only existed in their own minds, all that suffering would've disappeared immediately, and their hatred would have been replaced by peace and friendship."

"I bet Rumi had something to say," Soren said.

"Absolutely!" Shabe said.

> *'People's fights are like children's,*
> *All nonsense, empty and futile.*
> *Each imagines their toy horse to be a real vehicle.*
> *Each is boasting about their playthings.'*

He explains our problems so charmingly and precisely, don't you think?"

"He's a genius," Soren agreed. "You said that, often, when it comes to mental issues, understanding and remedy are the same. I'm getting that more and more."

"Glad to hear that. We should understand that false values are the same as imaginary powers surrounding the realities of things, like an invisible cover. The humiliation that makes us feel sad and the greatness we're proud of are *nothing!* Just interpretations of our own minds, like the sacred halo those people saw around those things.

"If I look into myself deeply enough, I might realise those I hate aren't necessarily horrible; very often, it's my mind that is full of hate, Hate lives in *me*, nowhere else. And I carry this hate in me wherever I go. Have I provided some clarity to answer your mother's question?"

"Yes, thank you." A leaf landed on the back of Soren's hand. He examined its veiny texture and began to fiddle with it. "I have a question, though."

"Mm?" Shabe took a sip of juice.

"Even though I realise these values are false impressions, a lot of people still believe in them. Wouldn't that create some disagreements?"

"Well, first, remember, no matter how many people share an illusion, the truth doesn't change. *Value-worshipping* is a massive intellectual and emotional fantasy. But even if an illusion is widely accepted, that doesn't make it real. Second, interpretive values are neither necessary nor helpful. Denying them is denying a bunch of lies. And, as most hatred results from these *illusive values*, once they're gone, humans return to a state of peace and tranquillity.

"Even if others don't realise the nothingness of such values, *your* realisation of this frees you from a futile struggle, and that's a big advantage. Do you remember when we read Omar Khayyam in class?

> *'Hell is but a flame of our futile struggling.*
> *Paradise is but a moment of our peaceful unburdening.'*

What he means is that the time you waste stressing about things is a hell made by your own futile struggles, and the moments you spend enjoying life create a paradise from your own wisdom."

Shabe leant back on the bench and gazed around the park. It was still sunny, but the afternoon breeze rustled the overhead leaves and cooled the air. "We finished our discussion of the nature of the values yesterday. We learned that fake values create an ideal personality in our minds. What I call the outward I."

"Which is who we are not and is controlled from outside of us. Is that right?" Soren asked.

"Exactly. And today, I'd like to discuss the problems that arise when you make the effort to reach this imposed personality. We'll see if it's even possible to achieve such a personality."

Shabe put the *History for Children* book back into his bag, then grabbed his notebook. He shifted on his bench a little and cleared his throat. "I call this chapter *Behind the Mask*." Shabe flicked through the pages of the notebook. "I think by now you understand that fake values involve limitless expectations from the individual. Yes?"

"Mm. Think so."

"The demands they fail to satisfy just reproach and blame us. Then society forces a human to have a personality that aligns with its expectations, the outward I.

"The first problem about this *I* is that you have little power over it; instead, society determines what sort of personality you must have. And it's society that decides whether your personality is or isn't approved. If it's not, various types of pressure and hostility await you.

"So it's no wonder the outward person remains in a state of worry and suspension. Naturally, constant concern about approval and validation creates a life of worry. From this point on, your being becomes a home for an imposing guest, replacing your true thoughts and feelings. If you stop to ponder a bit, you'll clearly feel the presence of this imposing guest."

A Destination Not to Reach!

Soren watched Shabe expectantly. "Go on."

"The apprehension about what people think about you stops you from having a happy life, and we're going to see why. To avoid getting bogged down in theories, let's look at what actually takes place in the course of a typical life and its concerns in society. I call it *typical* because we all are acquainted with the processes involved in it."

"Okay."

"As you know, unrealistic expectations can create a fragile self-belief in an individual, who tends to look down on themself as a result. They'll carry the picture of a faultless, *ideal personality* in their mind of who they want to become—a character with no faults or weaknesses, admirable in every respect. And loveable."

Soren nodded, the image of Superman coming to mind.

"Soren, have you noticed how we become anxious and offended even by the mildest criticism? Or how we get annoyed when some aspect of our appearance is criticised?"

"I've definitely noticed that. Actually, I've always been self-conscious about my height," Soren admitted. With a grin, he added, "But you could say it's growing on me."

Shabe chuckled. "Very good! Well, isn't that because we are insecure about our merits and values?"

Soren nodded, thinking of the ideal version of himself he'd imagined: intelligent, compassionate, creative, strong, fair and, of course, a great author. However, while he worked towards becoming that person, criticisms made against any of those aspects hurt, especially when they were his own.

"You know," Shabe began, "the point we tend to miss is interesting. Our wish for an *ideal personality* is the result of something we dislike about ourselves. If we just accepted ourselves as we are, there'd be no point in hiding our reality and replacing it with a fake, embellished thing. So the base of the ideal personality is evading oneself.

"Because of brainwashing, we come to believe that our actual character is shameful and unlikable. So we wear the mask of an acceptable person, hating our true self and projecting a *fake self*. In other words, our ideal personality is based on self-hate and lies."

Soren's mind drifted to the circus. He imagined Shabe, in costume, sending the audience into peals of laughter. Then, unintentionally, he imagined *himself* as the clown in the middle of the scene and the large, enthusiastic crowd. He saw the balloons twisting in his hands, water spraying from his props and his large orange shoes squeaking with each exaggerated step. A smile crept across his face as he pictured the crowd laughing and clapping for him.

But the moment quickly soured. He became uneasily conscious of the strong overhead lights that would blind him, the unpleasant greasiness of the heavy makeup, how itchy he would feel under the oversized red nose, how annoyingly his large orange shoes squeaked with each step and how difficult it would be to move easily wearing the ill-fitting blue overalls. His stomach tightened with the fear of making a mistake and embarrassing himself in front of so many people, turning the imagined laughter into something far more intimidating.

A loud quack from a passing duck brought him back to reality.

"Showing off a flamboyant personality not only does little to alleviate my problems," Shabe continued, "but even makes things worse. I'm aware I'm hiding beneath a mask and blaming myself for having to continue with this hypocrisy and pretence. What's more, the bigger and more admirable the outward I is, the larger the chasm becomes about who I really am. The more unbridgeable the gap is, the deeper are the feelings of sorrow."

"Why don't people just try to improve instead of reproaching themselves, then?" Soren asked.

Shabe's gaze drifted to the sky. He took a deep breath. "Good question. That's because feelings of imperfection become an integral part of our mentality. As long as we hold that assumption, no matter how much we move forward, we're still really at the same spot."

Soren sat quietly for a moment, absorbing Shabe's words. "So, it's like no matter how much you achieve, it's never enough because you're not fixing what's inside, which is the real problem," he said slowly, his voice laced with both curiosity and understanding. "Is that why people feel trapped, even when they have everything?"

"That's completely right. I might work hard for years to save money or build a reputation and become very popular. After some time, however, I realise I still feel inadequate and unhappy. In fact, I'm even less happy, and less energetic. It's because denying myself has turned into a truth for me."

"So denying yourself has become your mind's default?"

"Exactly! Just like this motorcycle."

"Huh?" Soren raised an eyebrow.

Shabe pointed to a bulky, black motorcycle whizzing past on the street.

"What do you mean?" Soren asked.

"The feeling of not being good enough can act like the engine of that motorcycle."

"I don't follow." Soren frowned.

"How far can that motorcycle travel without its engine?"

"Not far. Not at all, actually," Soren said.

"Right. In fact, the very source of the movement for the motorcycle is its engine. Similarly, the feeling of not being good enough is the *outward person's* motivation."

"I see." Soren nodded.

"When Rumi warned, 'These outward things are all but your plagues,' that's what he meant. Trying to release yourself by doing more of the same thing won't work. The more you struggle, the deeper you fall into ignorance and suffering.

"Now, imagine your current car has no issues, but there's a new model just out, so you borrow money to buy it. You're actually pre-selling years of your life merely to keep up with the trend so people won't call you cheap or sneer at your old car. This means victimising yourself to please others!"

"Even when you think you're ahead, there's always something new to chase, right? So you can't ever win," Soren said. "The image of the donkey and the carrot springs to mind."

Shabe nodded. "As the social labels will always be above you, even when you work harder to upgrade your life, you can't ever have peace of mind because, at any moment, somebody can mock your car or house or disappoint you just by uttering a few words. I'm sure you've seen people who trade years of work to pay for changing their body or face when there's nothing wrong with them, merely because it's the fashion?"

"Yes! A boy at school had his ears pinned back because other kids called him 'wing-nut' and 'big ears,'" Soren said. "Bet that hurt."

"Yes, but I'm sure you know, we aren't referring to any particular person or group in our discussions," Shabe said. "We're examining the typical pains of a masked person's life."

Shabe picked up the newspaper he'd been reading and flipped open a page folded on the corner. The left-hand page was covered in small ads for cars, fashion and beauty products. Models posed beside text that read, 'Because youthful skin never goes out of fashion' and 'The most trusted car dealership.'

On the page facing it was an image of the remains of a bird's nest on the ground. with recently deforested land in the background. Beside the broken nest, lifeless baby birds were lying in the dirt as the mother eyed them mournfully. In bold letters, the headline read, 'DEFORESTATION: THE ECOLOGICAL TRAGEDY.'

Soren felt a twinge in his chest. He peered up at Shabe, who gave him a thin-lipped smile.

"Soren," Shabe began, pushing his glasses up again, "Many of us are worried by pollution, deforestation, extinction, tsunamis, global warming and things like that. But what's behind all these catastrophes? Isn't it the constant operation of factories that demand land-clearing? And don't they also require an insatiable supply of natural resources?"

"Of course," Soren said.

"So what's driving this cycle of production and consumption? Isn't it the popular belief that you should keep up to date with fashion and upgrade your bags, shoes and cars routinely so you appear cool and aren't accused of being low-class or outdated?"

Soren scratched his head. "Yes, I think it is."

"So can you see how far these mind-sets can push us?"

"Mm. Yeah. Mum says tragedies happen when we don't think about what we're really doing."

"Beautifully profound! I've read some of your mother's columns. They're always thoughtful," said Shabe. "But getting back to social labels, apart from destroying nature, the other problem is the mental and emotional complications of a pretend life. As well as constantly feeling regret and blame, the outward person often struggles with other torments. Knowing their pretend personality is nothing but a decorative mask, they're always anxious, afraid they'll be unmasked as a fraud. This leads to even greater efforts to suppress themself. And violence against yourself creates anger towards others."

"Yes. I can guess why."

"I hate you because the pressure I'm suffering is because I'm afraid of your judgements. This build-up of anger and our readiness to explode puts pressure on our psyche. It's only natural that grudges and violence towards others will flow from our inner anger and suppression. All these are the effects of an alien self, an imposed identity. If you fail to understand the problem, its roots will go deeper into your being. However much you struggle, you'll only become more entangled."

Soren recalled the survival film Shabe had run. "Just like that butterfly caught in the spider web," he said.

"Exactly." Shabe smiled. "Suppose you and I work for the same company, but your rank is higher than mine, so you enjoy a higher level of prestige. As a result, I'd feel inferior and jealous of you because I'd wish *I* enjoyed that value and status, not you.

"If you noticed this, it would be like removing my mask and revealing my weakness, and I'd probably feel hostile and resentful if I had to do that. So I'd have no choice but to swallow my feelings and pretend to be your friend.

"This puts further pressure and frustration on my psyche, but I can't reveal that either. Nor can I admit that I feel this puts me beneath you because the very society that put me in this predicament also warns that these are shameful feelings. So I try to deny all this and blank out this complicated puzzle of hate and inferiority. That's how my mind would get deeper and deeper into ignorance and self-deception."

"Does everyone suffer like this from these things?" Soren asked.

"No. People are affected to varying degrees. If you're less affected, you're lucky, but we should never be unaware of ourselves. We need to be alert to understand just how far this problem can go."

The Mind and the Burden of Identity

Shabe folded up the newspaper and tucked it into his bag. "Great confusion arises when our mind becomes a place to hold our identity, as the mind is meant for thinking, not for preserving identity."

"What do you mean?" Soren asked.

"Well, you are always who you are, whether you think about it or not. Thinking 'I am this' or 'I'm not that' doesn't change you, does it?"

Soren scratched his head. "I don't think so."

"When an identity is imposed on your mind through indoctrination, you gradually develop a mental self, an imposed one. That's when your thoughts become obsessed with constantly catering to that identity. That's when identity can turn into a serious obsession. You start attaching some labels to it and detaching other ones. In doing so, you imagine your identity is changing, but it's really just thoughts playing in your mind."

"Okay." Soren nodded. "I think I'm getting it. It's interesting! Could you explain it a bit more, though?"

"I will, sure, but I have a feeling you're going to tell me something. Something good, or maybe something exciting?"

Soren gaped. "How did you know?"

Shabe chuckled. "Well?"

"I'm writing a new story!" he burst out.

"Really? That's wonderful."

"I think our talks have pulled an idea out from deep in my mind."

"Have they, now? Well, please go on."

Soren rubbed his hands together. "I have been thinking about it for a while, but finally, a few nights ago, I was up late, and I got up, picked up a pen and started to write! It's not complete yet, though."

"What's the theme of your book? Do you have a title yet?"

"I don't want to tell you yet. I want it to be a surprise. I haven't told anyone. The first draft might be ready next time we meet. If it is, I'll bring it over and read it to you."

"Excellent. I look forward to reading it."

Soren smiled diffidently.

Shabe was quiet for a moment. "Well, let's move on, then."

"Yes, please."

"Perhaps the most fundamental problem with the outward I is that this phenomenon is made of thought."

"You've lost me," Soren admitted.

"See, the problem here is when a person builds an identity for themself out of thoughts and then they spend time caring for this *mental identity* and fixing its problems. So what's the function of the mind? Obviously, thinking and reasoning, using words and images."

"Sounds true."

"The mind itself cannot touch or change the essence and nature of objects. Nevertheless, the identity and features a person assumes for themselves only live in their mind and memory. This identity is entirely mental and imaginary, but they consider it a real one. That's the main problem, and that's the reason for the constant worry and obsession."

Soren found he could only process Shabe's words with difficulty. "I'm sorry. I still don't quite understand."

Shabe pointed to a small bed of orange flowers beside the lake. "When I see those flowers, my mind records an image of them in my memory, along with the word 'flower.' And because of the good feeling I experience by seeing them, I add the words 'pretty' and 'lovely.' So, I say, 'the lovely flower.' Right?"

"Right …"

"Now, my mind's image of the flower is one thing, but the flower out there is another. Okay?"

"Yes."

"Also, the word 'lovely' doesn't have the same quality of loveliness as the flower. The mind can never actually touch the flower itself. It doesn't have access to the loveliness of the flower itself either. All it can do is simply hold the image. The flower and its qualities are live and flowing entities, while the word 'flower' and the adjective 'lovely' are nothing but words and a picture, and pictures are permanently fixed, static things."

"Then where are my true aspects?"

"Well, they're not in your mind; they inhabit your being. They're the modes, feelings, inclinations, abilities—all the specifications and properties that exist in your being, whether you think of them or not, or whether others recognise them or not. An attribute that may be taken away by words is not an attribute; it's a thought."

"Very profound. But there's a question."

"Sure."

"If my identity is not something imposed or dictated, as you said, I can still think about it, can't I? I mean, I'd still have an image of my features and character in mind," Soren said.

"You would. However, when your self-image is real and authentic, you don't have to be worried about it. It becomes a source of worry and anxiety when it's something borrowed and dependent."

"I see. But what if I want to improve my abilities or my character or attributes?"

"That's a great goal, but you would need to work and train and attain genuine merits and real capacities. Still, the mere act of thinking and obsessing would not change you."

"Sounds very sensible." Soren stared at the orange flowers, dancing gracefully in the breeze. He rubbed the back of his neck as he silently repeated, *An attribute that may be taken away by words is not an attribute; it's a thought.* He felt as if something had shattered in his mind—an illusion, perhaps?

"Here's another example," Shabe suggested. "We say the lion is a brave animal. Obviously, we don't have access to the lion's quality of braveness, nor its modes and feelings. The bravery in the lion's being is an inner mode and forms a part of its existence. What we carry in our mind is just a word or an image of the way it is. *Brave*, as we know the lion will fight other animals when necessary and is hardly afraid of enemies, as far as we know."

"Yep. That's true."

"So I think it's clear that our natures and qualities are one thing and our mental understanding of them is another."

"And our subjective interpretations of them is still another thing!" Soren added.

"Well said!"

"But what happens when we mix up mental images with qualities?" Soren asked. "Mum's told me a few times I'm clumsy, and so I've recorded the image of a clumsy Soren in my mind. My aunt said I was generous when I shared my ice cream with Melody after she dropped hers, and I've created the image of myself as generous alongside the image of clumsiness."

Shabe seemed to be following closely.

Soren went on. "Also, teachers have said I'm intelligent, and so I've recorded the image of an intelligent Soren in my mind. I still think of these images of myself as pieces of my identity, although they were imposed upon me by others. And now I wonder how to maintain these qualities of who I am."

Shabe was rubbing his chin, so Soren continued musing aloud. "But the mind doesn't have access to my qualities or abilities to preserve or change them."

"That's right." Shabe nodded.

"Strange how our mind plays with us like that. Why does it?"

"Suppose I'm not doing very well in a subject, and my brother calls me stupid," Shabe said. "Once 'stupid' is recorded in my mind as a word, along with an image, I imagine that's my attribute. I tend to miss the point that my intelligence or talents are simply what they are, and cannot and will not be changed by what anyone calls me or says about me.

"As a result, I start collecting evidence that I'm intelligent, like winning a competition or coming first in a test, to wipe away the claim of 'stupid.' If I succeed, I feel I've captured the quality of intelligence, and then I'll be in a state of fearful enjoyment."

Soren wrinkled his nose. "Why would you be fearful?"

"I'd be afraid someone might take this attribute away by humiliating me again. I don't yet understand that characteristics and qualities can't be taken away, or granted, by words or judgements. And the quality I think I've acquired wouldn't be real; it'd be merely a word or a label. How can a label or a certificate take away quality from me or add to it?

Ask yourself, what real quality comes with a medal? Would a genuine quality really be like that?"

"No, I don't think so."

"What we often miss is that attributes are not in your mind; they're what you are—even if you're not aware of it. The self I hold in mind is a collection of thoughts and images, but I'm not those thoughts or images. I'm made up of many modes and qualities to which the mind and its thoughts have little connection …"

"… let alone others' minds."

"Absolutely. Despite this obvious fact, I'm constantly obsessed with my identity or character being ruined or damaged."

Soren leant back in his seat. After a long pause, he asked, "But what if someone is not after words, images or awards. What if they just want to obtain useful qualities, but those things represent those abilities?"

"What's an example?"

"Someone wanting to have a stronger body, for instance, or to become more knowledgeable on a subject. Medals, titles and certificates could be the by-products of these qualities or tools I might need to be able to achieve something real—for example, a certificate to practise as a psychologist."

"I see." Shabe moved in his chair a bit. "Then ask yourself, now you've got an A or a medal, what truly matters to you: the education or the physical strength? Or do you want the titles of 'smart' and 'strong'? Suppose you gained that strength or that knowledge, and your father says, 'But you're still the same hopeless son.' How would you feel then? Wouldn't that ruin your joy and pride? Wouldn't you feel depressed or frustrated?"

"Yes, I suppose I would."

"Why? Your dad wouldn't have taken anything away from you. Just a few words. So why the dismay and sadness?"

Soren sat silent, unable to respond.

Shabe let him be for a moment, removing his glasses to clean them with the hem of his shirt.

Soren sighed. "You're right!" Then, excitedly, he said, "I have a question!"

"Go ahead."

"You say bravery is a genuine attribute of the lion, but timidity is a mental label."

"Yes."

"Say there's a lion that understands human language, and I tell him he's timid. The lion might then become timid from my suggestions. Right?"

"Right."

"So the lion would have developed an attribute by receiving a label or an image, wouldn't he?"

"No." Shabe shook his head and put his glasses back on. "The lion didn't develop an attribute. His bravery is still there, but he'd behave under the influence of an image you imposed on him of a timid lion."

"So why, then, does this timidity persist? I mean, if timidity isn't really part of his being, why does it continue to be there?"

"Excellent question. The reason for the lion's persistent fearfulness is that he's cross-eyed!"

"A cross-eyed lion?" Soren crossed his eyes, making Shabe chuckle.

"Yes." Shabe nodded. "Look. The lion imagines two things: that he is timid and that there's an accompanying picture of his timidity, while they are in fact one and the same."

"I kind of get it. Could you explain it a bit further?"

"Well, suppose you're clever, which is true." Shabe smiled. "Whether or not you hold the image of being clever in mind, your intelligence still remains there. True?"

"Sure."

"Or suppose you possess great physical power. Whether you see yourself as a strong person or not, or even if you're totally unaware of your strength, it still exists. True?"

"True."

"That's not the case with mental attributes. If the image of a timid person leaves your mind, you'll stop behaving like one."

"Okay. I get it," Soren said.

"And that's the difference."

"Between?"

"Between genuine attributes and mental ones. You are timid because you believe you are; if you stop believing you're timid, you won't be timid anymore. That's what Rumi calls cross-eyedness, which means seeing an illusion. Our problem is that we assume our timidity is one thing and our image of it is another. We take our timidity as reality and our image as a reflection of this reality. We don't see the fact that it is the very image that causes the timidity. You know what I mean?"

"I think so. That reminds me of The Hall of Mirrors."

"In the circus?"

"Yes. I saw it once when we visited the circus. It was both interesting and a bit scary."

"Excellent example. In the hall, when you look into one of the mirrors, you'll see a distorted version of yourself, and if you come to believe it, you'll act upon it."

"Just like little kids do. They touch their nose to make sure it's the right size or stretch their body to stretch it to their normal height. That's amusing, isn't it?"

"It is. This illusion causes the problem to persist."

"So that's the reason we call these *mental attributes* and not real ones?"

"Exactly! And that's why Rumi says if either of the jars is shattered, neither will remain. If you take the image of being timid off your mind, your fear will fade at the same time. When one goes, neither remains. Does that make sense?"

Soren grinned then took a large gulp of juice. "I see. But when you're cross-eyed, you'd see everything in an illusion, even your own cross-eyedness, wouldn't you?"

"You would. And that's the problem."

"So, doesn't that mean you can never get out of illusion?"

"You'd remain within this vicious circle until you learnt a different outlook, when you get out of the box and start to see things from outside the box."

"How can you learn that? I mean, who can show you that different outlook?"

"A person who has broken out of the circle."

"Just like the cross-eyed man's master."

"Yes. Who do you reckon he could be, Soren?"

"The master?"

"Yes."

"Um, a wise teacher or an insightful parent, I guess."

"That's right, but it can be yourself too, when you step out of the rut of your habitual thought. It can be a fresh outlook that sees not only the world but also *you* and your beliefs and assumptions and evaluates them all. A reason that looks from above, not only at things but also at you and your thoughts!"

"You mean, the eyes to see the eyes?"

"Exactly."

The Outward I and the Inner Mechanisms

Shabe paused long enough to allow Soren to digest what they'd just discussed. Then he said, "Before we go any further with the *false I*, it's necessary to clarify something. When we're talking of the *I* in these discussions, we're not referring to a human being with a body, mind, thoughts, feelings and with individual and social rights and duties.

"No! Every human being needs to have a name and an identity and to possess a separate individuality to set boundaries for their rights and responsibilities; that's not the issue. What's concerning is the false picture that's been built up by baseless remarks and biased opinions. What we're referring to as the *mental I* is an identity that's value-based and generated by society; this comes about from blame and pressure and the unfair and often paralysing expectations of society."

"So we're kind of referring to the ego?"

"Correct, and that's the message mysticism has for humanity. Mystics teach that if you expel this outward I from your being, what remains is your own reality and your natural feelings. Inner conflicts will fade away"

"I have always thought that conflict cannot be a natural mode or way to behave," Soren said, waiting for Shabe's perspective.

"Conflict always takes place between at least two extremes," Shabe answered. "If you feel there's conflict in you, it means two opposing forces are at war in your being. Particularly at the level of identity, conflict means that two identities are living in you at the same time. One is you, while the other is an alien within you."

"Could there be more. I mean three, ten or even a thousand?" Soren asked jokingly.

"There could," Shabe said, chuckling. "Joking aside, it is very possible to have more than two things conflicting in you, including selves or identities," he said. "But we're simplifying the matter here for easier understanding."

"That makes sense, and it's so scary!" Soren remarked.

"Well, your true identity is freed only when the false *I* vanishes. Doesn't feeling conflicted show that something's going wrong in there? Doesn't this inner struggle reveal that your actual being is suffering and is trying to throw something alien out of itself? Rumi calls,

> *'Oh, mankind, you're in agony because of this ego.*
> *The bird of your soul is paired with an alien bird.'*

"As I said, I've called this nuisance-being *the imposed self*, or *the outward I*, because it's dictated by others telling you how things should be."

"There must be an inward I and a genuine self then, too?"

"Correct. The inward I refers to my true attributes, just as they really are, without being dependent on others' judgements."

Soren fluffed his shirt around to get some fresh air on his skin. "So it's the outward I that is responsible for all these troubles?"

"Yes, it is. So we should put all our efforts into getting rid of this imposing alien and its pressures."

Soren spotted a monarch butterfly floating over the lake. Its wings resembled the flowers in the nearby garden bed. Soren imagined how safe the butterfly must have felt in its cocoon. All the same, had it not left the comfort of its home, its safety, it wouldn't be living freely in this park. It would be a worm living out its life in the prison of the cocoon, never to feel the breeze beneath its wings, and probably suffocating to death.

Shabe cleared his throat. "Well, having said that, we'll turn to the discussion of the psychological mechanisms. Karen Horney was a German psychoanalyst who did great work in that field. She believed that conflict is the root cause of nervousness and inner distress.

"In her book, *The Neurotic Personality of Our Time*, she posed a very significant question. She asked what kind of anomalies lie in social values that can create conflict in the individual, causing various mental and emotional difficulties."

"That's a good question."

"As we've seen, the main reason for our conflicts are the inconsistent values imposed by society. What's more, it's not only the imposed ideas that cause the problem. The fact we have hardly been given the chance to think and decide for ourselves has undermined our right to think and choose. It has taught us that others are the authorities, and we are the followers."

Soren clenched his fist and waved it mock-menacingly. "So society's to blame!"

Shabe chuckled and said, "Soren, having said all that, we shouldn't ignore an important point: the fact that many of the problems are caused by society and social factors doesn't mean as individuals we are free from any responsibilities or that everything has to be corrected by others."

"So we all have a duty?"

"Definitely. Society is composed of single individuals like me and you. We are perpetuating this system. If everyone blamed others for the problems and denied their own roles and impacts, who'd solve them? No. People must try to build their own health and well-being.

"Suppose there's a plague of tuberculosis or diphtheria in your town. If you get the disease, you cannot simply blame other people for your illness and say they didn't look after themselves and so made you ill. Nor can you say that just because everyone is ill, you won't remain healthy. You need to be vigilant and practise hygiene to stay well."

"And you need to get vaccinated," Soren added.

"Exactly."

"So mental distress is caused by surrendering to society's contradictions?" Soren asked.

"Very well said," Shabe said. "That's a more precise way of putting it and is more enlightening. Thank you. And this surrender brings many types of distress. I've called this as the *outward I* and the *inner mechanisms*."

Shabe found the page in his notebook and pointed to the title. "What complicates our problems even more is when mental and emotional reactions get stirred up, like fear, anger, jealousy and pride. These reactions are the tactics that your mind resorts to in order to ease the burden of these inner pressures. However, these solutions require some sort of self-deceit and unawareness."

"Are they deliberate behaviours?"

"More or less. Some of these mechanisms, such as hate and jealousy, are less intentional, while lies and pretence are more deliberate."

"This's a fascinating topic to me. Can our bad behaviour be unintentional or sort of automatic?"

"If you don't attend to this issue smartly and quickly, it can reach a point where you turn into a virtual robot. We've all seen people who look confused and disoriented, as though they're cut off from the world around them. This can happen when your mind is overloaded with too many confusing ideas and conflicting obligations."

"Like mental indigestion." Soren laughed.

"A great description," Shabe said.

"When my Auntie Rosie comes over to visit, she just starts going on about when she was young and how beautiful she used to be. After a while, she'll change the topic to how rude and badly behaved young people are today and how good children and everything used to be in her day. Then she turns to the topic of how many noble gentlemen wanted her to marry them and the ones she rejected. She goes on and on, and she doesn't seem to care if you're interested or not." Soren laughed and looked back at Shabe.

Shabe laughed too and said, "That's a good example of getting sunk in your own mental world, where you're unaware of yourself and what you're actually doing. I was going to say, in different situations these mechanisms can dominate the person and influence their thoughts and behaviour. We all have experienced such situations. Sometimes, these reactions even shape important decisions in a person's life, and it can end badly."

"Oh, really?"

"I knew a man who married a woman even younger than his daughter after his divorce. However, they had very little in common, which was obvious. After this second marriage also failed, we were having a friendly conversation. I asked him why he'd married this young woman in the first place. You know what he said? It was for revenge against his ex."

"Goodness …"

"It's quite sad. Sometimes, you can summarise a person's entire life in just a few defensive reactions."

"Like attention-seeking or revenge," Soren said.

"Correct. So you can see why a good knowledge of inner mechanisms can help us better understand our problems. Let's now take a closer look at what triggers these mechanisms. But before we dive in, there are a few important points to consider."

"Sure."

"We're not talking about basic survival mechanisms like fear and escape. Instead, we're focusing on how these and other mechanisms function in relation to pseudo-values."

"Wait. I think you've lost me again!"

"Shabe smiled. "Let's hold hands tightly so we don't lose each other as we navigate this busy and convoluted—but fascinating—land!" he joked. "We are talking about when these reactions are activated to defend our value-based identity, rather than to protect our well-being as a human."

"Got it. Thanks."

"The other thing is that these mechanisms generally consist of two aspects: intellect and emotions. And there's a constant mutual relationship between the two."

"What about our actions and behaviours? They would be the third aspect, I suppose," said Soren.

"A great point, but as I said, we're dealing with the inner roots or bases here, hence the inner mechanisms. We're going to tackle the acts and behaviours down the track."

"Fair enough. And they affect each other?"

"Yes, the emotional side activates the intellectual side, and that triggers the emotional aspect, and so on."

"Like a cycle."

Shabe nodded. "Exactly like a cycle, and the self-lost person gets increasingly tangled in this complex network. A third point to beware of is that many seekers of peace and liberation—even therapists—use the wrong approach to control or suppress psychological mechanisms."

"You mean we shouldn't try to control our fear or anger?" Soren asked.

"I mean we should be aware that, as long as we're trapped in the cobweb of inflicted beliefs, inevitably, moods like anger, anxiety and depression will surface. In other words, all these feelings are the natural offshoots of one main root: self-loss. As long as the main cause exists, little will come out of dealing with the effects."

"Okay."

"The last point is that we don't all use the actions and reactions of psychological mechanisms equally. The form and type of these mechanisms depend on the person and their psychological structures, including their needs, learnt patterns of thought and behaviour and sensitivities. Also, one or more of these tactics might be activated by the individual, depending on the situation."

"I was actually wondering about that," Soren said, sipping his juice.

"The first mechanism is fear, the main root of the problem."

Fear

"Like I said, fear, in its various forms, shapes the entire foundation of self-loss. In other words, you could say that the whole structure we call self-loss stands on fear and anxiety, and society uses it for various hunting tricks," said Shabe.

"Is that like the story of the lion and the fox?" Soren wondered. "Perhaps society is the fox, and the person is the lion? It's interesting to dig into my story, isn't it?"

"Great allegory. Society is a conservative structure. It devises various false values because of fear of an individual's defiance or disturbance of the status quo. Society is afraid of an individual being free and independent, so it tries to control their ideas and feelings, even at the price of jeopardising that person's happiness.

"If you look a bit closer, you'll see there's a network of fear dominating society, ruling many people's relations. Nevertheless, as the individual gradually sinks into this network, not only do they give in to its demands, but they also become part of it, serving it and reproducing it.

"And that's why it's common for people who've been abused to abuse others. Same with those who've been humiliated or intimidated. Sadly, in our relationships, fear has superseded love as the propelling power, and this replacement is the gravest tragedy to humanity."

"The network of fear," Soren murmured, staring off into the distance. "Just like the internet, but instead of computers, it's people who are connected to one another, and instead of exchanging information, they exchange fear."

"The network of fear," Shabe repeated, stroking his chin. "I like that. Great example, Soren!" Shabe wrote a quick note in his book, then added another idea before he put his pen away. "Imagine computers with interpretation software installed, with servers across towns and countries connecting them to one another. Most of the information exchanged across the globe is polluted with the virus of fear. Soren, what do you think the servers are?"

Soren thought for a long moment but ultimately shook his head. "Not sure."

"I'll let you think about it. But let me share an experience, a familiar one."

"Sure."

"Many years ago," Shabe said, "when I was looking for work, I took a job-seeker course. We were given several principles to follow when we were at an interview: to always smile, maintain eye contact and stand or sit in particular positions and not others. This helped to impress the employer by seeming like a friendly, confident and respectful employee and could increase your chance of getting the job.

"Personally, I had a problem with that sort of masquerading and pretence. Why should I pretend to be a person I'm not or behave in ways alien to me, just to deceive someone into letting me work and make money? How could such a job, where I wear a mask and maintain a fake persona, ever make me happy? This is an example of the humiliation of a human and taking advantage of our natural needs. If I genuinely liked a job, I'd be full of happiness and energy for it, and this would reflect naturally in the ways I acted, spoke and behaved. And if I didn't, why should I have to suppress my true feelings just to hold a job I'm not really made for?"

Soren shrugged. "Because they set rules to make sure their staff behave in friendly and polite ways?"

"I know that," Shabe replied. "But that's not the question. I don't mean we should behave in rude or unfriendly ways! The question is, why should I show interest in something that's not interesting to me? Or pretend I'm happy and comfortable when it is not true? Why should suppressing who you really are and how you feel be a precondition for a chance to survive? This, to me, is soft slavery!"

"Yes, I agree."

"Indeed! We talk passionately about freedom of expression and freedom of opinion. So why do we use various civilised tools to suffocate each other's feelings? If we accepted each other's feelings the way they are and didn't force each other to show off and censor ourselves, wouldn't it benefit both of us?" Shabe leant back on the bench and added, "That's not respect; that's putting on a show."

"Then why *do* people force each other to pretend in the first place?"

"Fear and doubt!"

"Doubt about what?"

"Disapproval. If you're in doubt regarding your worth, you're afraid of not being approved of. That's actually what the outward I points to. We're depending on others for our sense of self-worth. So we use etiquette and courtesy to force others to approve of us and tell us we do have worth and value. The incoming party joining the game plays along so they won't be accused of rudeness."

"I see. A two-sided game."

"Well put. That's a social aspect of fear prevailing in our relationships. The other aspect is more inner and individual.

"One significant point about psychological tactics is that they're all just different forms of one mechanism called fear, or apprehension, if you like. Reactions like anxiety, anger, stinginess and pride are all manifestations of fear.

"In the structure of the outward I, all of them, one way or another, preserve a positive value and prevent a negative one. Due to self-loss, the driving force in humans' lives has turned from love and pleasure to fear and urgency. And there's an immense difference between the two and how they feel.

"Imagine a beautiful day. Two people have gone to a scenic forest to take a pleasant hike. One of them is at peace with their surroundings, but the other person fears they'll meet an angry bear. How would each one experience the trip, do you think?"

"Completely differently, I'd say."

"I agree. The first man strolls leisurely, occasionally stopping to take in the view. He's taking his time in the forest, enjoying the tranquillity, listening to the melodious singing of the birds, watching the picturesque waterfall and the trees and the flowers. He's immersed in the wonders and mysteries of the forest, enjoying every moment.

"However, the other person, worried about bears at any moment, doesn't get the chance to see the trees or listen to the birds. They can't enjoy the scenery because they're relentlessly in fight-or-flight mode.

For them, each moment is spent in terror. Now add to the story that no bear actually exists, and all that constant worry comes merely from the man's anxious mind."

"I can imagine."

"That's the difference between living by love and living by fear. As Rumi says,

> *'The world is refreshing itself every moment,*
> *But we are standing still,*
> *Heedless of the constant refreshment.'*

"Living by love is to live in the present, and in peace. Love for yourself, for others, and for the universe; love for little sparrows, for white, multi-shaped snowflakes, for sweet little kids and love for watching nature and breathing in the petrichor of the rainy air.

"Living by love is a life of harmony with yourself and with the ever-refreshing moments of life. When you live like this, you feel profoundly content and blissful. But living by fear is a life of endless escape and stress, of running and haste. Haste hardly allows that person to see anything. It's difficult for them to feel anything beyond their fear. So they seldom get moments to watch the beauty of life. Fear makes you blind to yourself, to others and to life."

Soren thought of one of his teachers at school who taught English. She was young, in her thirties. He'd noticed her lack of enthusiasm. She was intelligent, but he and his classmates knew she had little desire to be there. She quickly got frustrated with her students, refused to take part in excursions like the other teachers and avoided most people at school. She never even noticed that the maths teacher was always smiling at her.

Shabe checked his watch. "Well, Soren, I hope you're not too tired. Today, I'd like us to finish exploring the mechanisms."

"Oh, okay. How many mechanisms are there?"

"A lot, but I've dealt with the more important ones, such as jealousy, pride and anger, which takes us to our next topic."

Anger

"So, Soren, how would you define anger?"

"I think anger is a feeling you use to defend yourself against an enemy. Kind of like Mr. Hardy in an episode in the *Laurel and Hardy* series."

"Interesting! Go on."

"Hardy was sensitive to the sound of horns, and he got very angry when he heard one. Once, on a voyage, Hardy was beaten up by a fugitive murderer who was illegally on their ship. At the fight, Hardy kept begging Laurel to blow the horn so he could gather enough strength to beat the bully. Laurel did so, and Hardy was able to beat the bully and save them both from being killed by him," Soren said, laughing through the story.

"That's a memorable example," Shabe agreed, laughing. "Anger is a reaction to help you fight against danger, just like in Hardy's predicament, when the danger was something real and serious. But in the value-struck person, anger's function is often to protect false values. Like I said before, the humiliated person holds a blind and multi-layered anger, which is nevertheless natural."

"Natural?"

"Yes. Rather than letting people follow their true needs, interests and callings, society creates false needs and wishes, and forces or tricks them into a pointless, exhausting competition. This feeling of obligation gives you a curious sense of indignation and frustration."

"But you said we're often angry with ourselves?"

"That's right." Shabe nodded. "Anger is a double-edged sword with one side facing the value-struck person. The mindset of this self-lost individual is that they aren't entitled to be at peace with themself.

"Social suggestions have convinced them they're unimportant and always guilty of something, and so they tend to hate and disown who they are. What's more, they also feel guilty and angry because of having to suppress themself."

"So that could be why some people are cruel?"

"Very likely." Shabe nodded. "Society has values that condemn expressing your anger or resentment, and so you often have to suppress them. As a result, anger and resentment turn into a blind complex in many people. That's why you often see people who hurt themselves or torment other people or even animals that have done nothing wrong to them! And, it goes without saying that this development of resentment gives way to new complications. These problems cause issues both in the individual and social life in general."

Soren gazed into the distance, his eyes unfocused.

Shabe went on. "At the individual level, issues such as frustration, self-harm, stress, nervous diseases, and at the social level, problems like violence, aggressiveness and committing crimes ... They all result from hate and anger."

Once again, Soren was reminded of Hans and Daniel and their aggressive, bullying behaviour. He looked down, his voice quieter. "So they're trapped too, in a way. All that anger ... It's like they're hurting inside, but they don't know how to deal with it, so they lash out."

He could now see why he often felt sorry for them. He had been thinking about them a lot lately, trying to understand them with the help of the new discoveries he'd been making. He'd noticed the sorrow and anxiety in their faces. Even after nearly a decade of schooling together, the signs had always been there, but Soren hadn't taken much notice of them before.

Soren *had* noticed Hans often came to school with bruises, but he'd thought little of it. Bruises were common in teenagers playing sports or rough games with friends. But recently, Soren had walked past when Hans and his younger brother were being picked up from school by their father, who had been yelling all sorts of unnerving comments. Empty bottles had rattled loudly as the boys clambered into the car. Soren had only seen Hans's dad a few times, but each time it was the same, or worse.

Daniel's story was different, but Soren wasn't sure it was any better. Everyone at school knew both his parents were doctors. Daniel often bragged about that. They had a massive house on the river, drove expensive cars, and went on a lavish holiday together every year. But Soren had never seen Daniel's parents.

While Soren's mum, Sally, was in the audience for every school play or award ceremony, clapping proudly for her son, Daniel stood sheepishly on the stage as he inspected the rows of parents. His were never there. Soren often avoided him for the rest of the day, knowing he'd feel deeply sad and embarrassed.

Soren's father and Daniel's had crossed paths briefly throughout their careers and, for a short while, had been friends. Soren's father had visited Daniel's one evening after work and later told Sally and Soren about their gorgeous house, filled with art, shelves of medical books and framed awards hanging on the walls. It seemed like the only place Daniel had in the home, besides his bedroom, was in a small baby photo in the hallway.

No wonder Hans and Daniel had become such close friends, despite the differences in their families. They both suffered the same pain: neglect and helplessness. Soren knew now that was why he didn't want his mother complaining about their bullying. He felt sorry for their pitiful situation.

"I used to wonder why some people mock others or hurt them for no apparent reason," Soren said before falling quiet for a long moment. "I think the answer is obvious now: blind anger and resentment."

"I'm guessing you're referring to your classmates, Hans and Daniel?"

"Yeah," Soren answered. "Although I often get angry with them and their behaviour, I do sort of sympathise with them."

"Yes, I get it. One who's harmed does harm. But the problem is, others often take revenge on such people and retaliate in different ways."

"That's what I've thought about too. But I think it's natural to want to get back at those who've wronged you."

"I understand, but one thing for sure is problems are hardly ever solved by revenge. The reason for hurting is being hurt; the problem is increased by revenge. As this continues, it results in a sinister cycle of harm and revenge, which damages everybody. And it will continue unless ..."

"Unless what?" Soren asked.

"Unless someone decides to break the chain, which is only possible through love and care. Understanding is the first essential for caring. Rumi says,

> 'Love is the fruit of knowledge.
> Who can access this throne falsely?'"

"He likens being caring to being on a throne, does he?"

"Yes, what he's saying is that a deep and genuine love requires a high level of insight and understanding. And only those with true greatness and nobility can rise to such a level."

"Sounds very wise."

"Soren, if you throw a small rock into a cup of tea, what happens?"

"It splashes around."

"Correct. Maybe even half of the tea spills out, right?"

"Yeah, it does."

"Now, what if you toss it into a small pool?"

"Probably just some small waves."

"Right. Now imagine throwing that same rock into a large, deep lake or even the sea. What do you think happens?"

"Almost nothing. Maybe a few tiny ripples."

"Exactly."

"What's your point?"

"The bigger and deeper your being is, the less you're shaken by what others say or do."

"I get it. That's really true," Soren answered.

Shabe continued after a pause. "Let's turn back to Hans and Daniel."

"Sure."

"Remember when we talked about the way we see ourselves?"

"Yes. The self-image?"

"Yes. If you tend to harm others, chances are high that deep in your mind, you hold a self-image of a negative person. This drives you to take it out on others who you think have given you that annoying picture of yourself. The more we try to stop that person by hurting them back, the more we reinforce that image, causing them to behave accordingly. The more that person is faced with violence or is excluded, the less they believe they can really change or improve or love others and be loved."

Soren felt a sense of remorse, as well as embarrassment. *He* had wanted revenge against Hans and Daniel, instead of thinking about breaking the chain.

"As you know, Soren, the school staff are trying to help kids with problems, such as Hans and Daniel. I'm sure your help would be very relevant."

"Why?" Soren asked with surprise.

"They haven't treated you well, obviously, and so they naturally don't expect a good reaction."

"They didn't receive one either," Soren said.

"No, but right now, if they received care and friendship from you, that could break the chain of hate and enmity and stop this vicious cycle. You know what I mean, don't you?"

Soren imagined offering friendship to Hans and Daniel and could already imagine their response. *Can't beat us, so you want to join us?* Soren could almost hear Daniel's voice but realised it was actually his own fear speaking. "You think that'd work?"

"It's worth a shot."

"Well, what do you think I could do?"

"I'd like us all to arrange some get-togethers so they can rely on our support."

"And then we can try to get them to let go of the negative images they have of themselves," Soren added.

"That's right."

"Do you have any ideas?" Soren asked.

"Not yet, but I will. Soon."

"I'd just be glad to help."

"I'm happy you say that. If we succeed, imagine how we'd feel, the profound pleasure of easing someone's pain."

A few moments passed in silence.

Jealousy

"Soren, what's the reason people feel jealous of each other?"

"Um, because you have something they don't. Just like James in our class."

"James Bennett?"

"Yes. He's the tallest in my grade, as you know. Everyone listens to him when he talks. I've felt jealous of him, sometimes, I should confess."

"Right. That's why I say jealousy is, in fact, reverse admiration, a compliment standing on its head."

"Interesting. How come?"

"The true concept behind jealousy is that you're secretly admitting the person you're jealous of is more successful than you are. In fact, what we call jealousy takes place when we see some sort of value in someone else and feel frustrated that they possess something we crave but don't believe we ourselves can acquire. And we call this frustration jealousy."

"Amazing!"

"Ironically, because they feel inferior, value-stricken people usually feel unsure of their real worth and abilities, so they're very susceptible to jealousy. One point to remember: although on the surface it seems like jealousy is over things like money, wealth and social status, it's actually over the values associated with these things. In other words, what triggers jealousy is other people's apparent importance, achievements or popularity."

"Makes sense."

Pride

"Soren, how often have you considered pride?"

"Quite often."

"Great. When we say pride, we mean arrogance and snobbishness, don't we?"

"We do, but ..."

"I should note that what we mean here is false or wrong pride, or the outward pride."

"You mean being proud of your social values?"

"Precisely. You can be aware of your genuine worth and capacities and hold onto them. This is what we often call dignity or self-worth, which is great. But being outwardly proud means you take pride in your public image and status, and you try to defend it, often at the cost of your true worth and growth. We usually call that pridefulness."

"Great difference, isn't it?"

"It is. So, you could say the prideful person holds a high-profile, social image of themselves and thus constantly tries to bring the way they communicate and behave in line with this image. It means they must always be careful not to do anything to damage this image," said Shabe.

"I think that's why many people look down on others. They believe everyone else is beneath them," Soren replied.

"Yes, that's often the case but only on the surface!"

"How come?"

"Some people refer to that as *self-worth* or *self-esteem*, but really, their pent-up fear and pain prompt this mocking behaviour. Superiority is a reflection of inferiority. Openly or furtively, a prideful person feels that their real personality is something shameful and so they keep their behaviour under control, so others don't discover their true face. Why would you keep your reality hidden unless you believe it is ugly or embarrassing?"

Soren rested his chin in his hands as he drifted deep into thought. "Pride is another kind of mask you wear to seem superior."

"Yet it's a kind of dependence, dependence on the approval of others. Most of our sorrows and insecurities arise from dependence of this kind. Two main points to remember about these mannerisms: first, the true motive behind tendencies like pride and snobbery is a fear of worthlessness."

People want to matter, Soren thought.

"But when you genuinely feel independent, you don't see any reason to put on a shaky mask. As an *inward person*, you never doubt your values, and so you don't fear others' valuations. This means you don't have to be anxious about what others think or say about you. In fact, any value borrowed from others is imported, and precarious. External validation is rootless and undependable. It's like throwing buckets of water into a dried-up spring."

"And the mask becomes so familiar that you forget who you are, underneath it," said Soren. "You trap yourself in an image, and after a while, that image controls you."

"Precisely. Wearing a mask of pride is a kind of *self-violence*. The conflict between the inner and outer sides can only mean that the prideful person sacrifices their peace and comfort for a false, outward image. Nevertheless, the more they wear the mask of prestige, the more they're excluded and resented."

Soren raised his finger.

"Do you have a question?"

"I was just going to say that my uncle is quite proud of himself. When you were describing the prideful person, he came straight to mind. He's reluctant to greet others and yet expects respect from everyone," Soren said. "Oh, and he hates proud people and can't stand snobbery, which is odd."

"Well, that's natural," Shabe said. "There's little authenticity in prideful behaviour. The person pretends to be someone they're not. Society notices these fakes. By nature, humans—including proud ones—love authenticity, power and truth. And they naturally hate weakness, lies and deception. The unfortunate outcome is that when the self-important person competes in a lose-lose game like this, they only gain loneliness and exclusion in the end."

"Like Uncle Will," Soren added. "Go on, please."

"Because deep down, he doubts his worth and place, the self-lost person tends to over-react to everything that triggers the apprehension. They tend to be pessimistic towards what others say, take everything personally and hold grudges. Such a person imagines their sensitivities are natural and plausible, but what actually torments them frequently are their own interpretations of what others do and say."

"Sounds very familiar."

"It should."

"You mean …"

"We are supposed to deal with real and tangible problems and questions we all face and feel every day. Otherwise, what would be the benefit of it all?"

"Right. I agree."

"Understanding these aspects plays a significant role in providing relief from the pain of self-loss because, looking closely, the interpretative person lives in a world of these sensitivities, more than in the world of realities. Sometimes, it's to such an extent that you could say interpretive-minded people live in a world of their own."

"Just like astronauts."

"Yes?"

"They travel in the open, limitless space, while they actually exist in the tiny space of their capsule machine!"

"I like that! That's very similar to the allegory Rumi uses. Rumi likens that situation to walking in an open field wearing tight shoes. What matters is your own shoes that cause pain and hurt your feet, no matter how wide and massive the field is."

"Exactly."

"A person who believes they should be looked up to because of their social status constantly worries about being neglected or insulted," said Shabe. "As their entire worth relies on their status, they're in constant fear of losing it. As this over-sensitivity is an integral part of this person's mentality, their psyche is like an injured body that screams at the slightest touch. We can't have a truly happy life unless we drop these burdens."

"But sometimes, someone really wants to hurt and upset you. Don't you think it's natural to get angry or offended then?"

Shabe sighed. "First, even if anger is something natural, hate is definitely not. Hate is a destructive force in our being. It's meant to destroy, not create. It's neither necessary nor helpful, not for you, nor the subject of your hate."

"What about hating things like bullying and abuse?"

"That's right. We can hate abuse, ignorance or dishonesty, but we don't hate people. We want people to be free from these plagues."

"Just like our plants. Dad used plant medicine last season when some of them got a disease. We hated the diseases but loved the plants and flowers."

"Excellent, Soren. We want to keep our plants and get rid of the illness. That's what we should do for each other as humans if we see anything wrong or flawed. The only results from hatred and resentment are enmity, stress-related disorders, heart attacks and premature ageing. Imagine what a hell of a world it'd be if we all hated each other because of our faults and mistakes! Where's the place for caring and helping each other to improve, then? Which one is more useful: you helping me get rid of my faults or hating and fighting me because of them?"

"But sometimes, it's just too difficult!"

"I understand, but look at it like this. You'd feel pity for those who have no bread to eat or no home to sleep in, right? So why do we hate those who don't know how to live better and behave better?" asked Shabe. "We sympathise with those who suffer from financial poverty. So why don't we feel sorry for those who suffer from emotional or intellectual poverty? Why don't we try to help them out of their ignorance? Don't they also need our help?"

Soren's eyes widened. "That's a very good point."

"What's more, as we said before, even if that person does mean to hurt you with their insults or sarcasm, it's still naïve of you to get upset."

"Why?"

"Because it's you who believes they're taking your value away. Otherwise, you'd laugh at their nonsense instead of hating them."

Soren slid his hands down either side of his face, in a way that made his eyes appear wild, almost scary. "I wish I could reach into myself, pull this filthy ego out and strangle it!" he burst out.

Shabe watched him patiently.

Soren leant forwards on his knees, gazing into the distance, exasperated. Then he took a deep breath and let out a sigh. "Sometimes, I hate myself because of my fears and misery, and I just can't find any solution to it. It's so frustrating!"

Shabe gave him a sympathetic smile. "I appreciate the way you feel. Like I said, I've also been there, and I've seen it in others too. But remember, you need to be very smart in the course of self-discovery. The ego is a cunning being, with so many tricks. It can easily play games with you. You could escape its traps in one spot, only to fall prey to it in another.

"One thing to look out for is our emotions, like anger and resentment. They're all natural reactions to an entity inflicted on us by the environment when we were innocent children, without any intentions on our part. So we shouldn't reproach ourselves for having these feelings, nor should we try to suppress them. And we shouldn't fool ourselves and try to ignore our problems either. Denial and self-deceit do little to solve our issues, just as overlooking things and blaming others don't help us out of them."

"So what should we do?"

"Learn to be aware of what's going on in us, without any shame or hate. Admit the existence of our sufferings, and relieve ourselves of them by increasing our awareness. We should also beware of afflicting others, particularly innocent kids, with the same way of thinking."

"But if we don't suppress our anger, does that mean it's okay to act on it?"

"Of course not!" Shabe shook his head.

"No?"

"Accepting your anger or fear doesn't mean you should unleash them and allow them to govern your life. That's in blatant conflict with the goal of self-flourishing: to grow into a peaceful and confident person. Reproaching ourselves or deceiving others doesn't help. It only complicates matters. In other words, we may respond, but we shouldn't react."

"As you said, we shouldn't let our minds fool us."

Shabe smiled, then sighed. "Remember we said that incomplete answers are often useless, or even harmful? Self-loss and its repercussions prevail in society like an epidemic, easily transmitted from one person to another. Unpleasant feelings emerging is a natural consequence of this disorder.

"Once they get this, a wise person will stop abusing themself, whether they're self-reproaching, self-censoring or self-tormenting. As this burden of self-violence lifts, not only does their pain fade away, but also the shadows of ignorance and self-deception.

"When this takes place, they'll have taken a big step towards liberating their true self and getting closer to a state of peace with their whole existence. Being at peace with yourself is a prerequisite for being at peace with others, with life and with the world. After all, how could you care for something to heal and flourish if you don't like it?"

"That's beautiful," Soren said, "but one question?"

"Go ahead."

"From what you say, it sounds like there's no such thing as free will, and we're destined to behave in certain ways. I mean, they say it's predetermined, right?" Soren asked.

"Neither free-willed nor predetermined," Shabe responded.

"No? How come?"

"I think, instead of the terms *free will* or *predetermination*, we could say *share*," suggested Shabe.

"Not sure I follow."

"Every human is part of the universe; a piece of humanity and its history of thoughts, deeds and development. Any one of us is an integral part of this integrated being. Meanwhile, every one of us has a share of this system and what takes place in it, whether it's an active or passive share," said Shabe.

"But take the psychological issues; who's to say these aren't transmitted between people, just like viral epidemics? If I'm abused by, say, my parents, I'd also tend to abuse others to sort of exhaust my anger or take revenge, or as a learned pattern to protect myself. I tend to ignore that this is useless, that such measures don't usually help me out, but they aggravate my pain further and just complicate my problems. In these circumstances, it's hardly possible to judge who's guilty and who's innocent.

"The truth is, each of us has a share in this process and plays a role in the circus! My violent or ignorant parents' share has been hitting, reproaching or neglecting me. However, my choice—to resort to tricks, pretence or revenge—has its own share in my problems. It was me who consciously or instinctively decided to resort to lies, self-deception, abuse and various tools to soothe or escape my difficulties."

"So what you mean by *share* is the role everyone takes in this play?" asked Soren.

"A very good portrayal. Others put me into this trouble in the first place, and they made me resort to a painful mask. However, what I need to realise is that at the moment, *I am* the main actor of this play, and *I am* the one operating this vicious machine, no one else. That's what it means to talk about our share in our own happiness or sadness."

"Makes sense, really."

"Soren, holding onto the image of yourself as an innocent, oppressed person— abused and unfairly treated by powerful yet ruthless others— can feel reassuring and comforting. It justifies our mistakes, explains our faults and weaknesses and alleviates feelings of guilt and self-hate. It also shifts responsibility from our own shoulders onto other people, circumstances and external forces.

"However, this comfort comes at a cost. A victim mentality strips you of your power, undermining your ability to choose, act and bring about change. It turns you into a powerless, dependent being, with little hope for improvement, freedom or a better future. The more I grow aware of the pains involved in this mask, which I'm fervently attached to, the more my problems would be solved and my agonies would fade away."

Soren scratched his head. "And that would solve everything?"

"My main source of worry is the mask. I live behind the disguise because it provides me with comfort and pleasure, and over time, I become attached or even addicted to it. But preserving this mask also brings considerable worry and anxiety. If I realised how much agony was involved, I wouldn't care how I looked to others because the stress it brings actually outweighs any comfort and pleasure.

"Being someone I'm *not* is stressful, and I live in this constant worry. If I stop viewing the mask as something dear and important, the fear will cease, and I'll feel light and free. Does that make sense, Soren?"

"Yes. But should we call it *fault*, instead of *share*? Like everyone is at fault in some way?"

"I don't think so," Shabe said. "Fault is associated with a sense of guilt. The precise meaning of *fault* is inadequacy and error. However, we can't judge people's abilities on different occasions and on different matters. We're not in their shoes, so we can hardly measure how far various factors, like emotional pressures and intellectual abilities, have been at work to shape their decisions and behaviours."

Shabe paused. "You know, Soren, when I was a kid, I noticed my classmates' nice clothes and pricey toys, and I wanted the same. I stole a pair of shoes once, and a couple of toys a few times. I was severely punished and never did that again. I'm not saying whether that was right or wrong, but who could really judge a child's capacity to handle the pressures of that longing and deprivation properly?"

Soren was stunned. He stared at Shabe, eyes wide, as if seeing him for the first time. "You?" he said quietly. "I can't believe it. I mean …" His voice faltered. "I always thought you were born different. Like you never slipped, never got lost."

"That's a wrong assumption, Soren. We all have our vulnerabilities."

Soren pondered that for a moment. He looked down, then back. "I didn't know longing could do that to a child."

Shabe gave a soft smile, looking Soren in the eyes, compassionately. "Longing can be louder than conscience when you're small and hungry—for food, for warmth, for dignity. I was just a boy trying to feel equal."

Soren nodded slowly, the weight of it settling in his chest. "It makes me wonder how many people carry stories we never see."

Shabe placed a hand gently on his shoulder. "That's the beginning of compassion, Soren." After a pause, Shabe continued, "Soren, how could we judge such complicated factors as someone's level of intelligence, their knowledge and psychological capacity, and, on the other hand, the pressures of these unfavourable circumstances?"

"So we shouldn't be hard on ourselves?"

"Feeling bad because something has gone wrong, including something you may have done, is natural to some extent. But there's no point in blaming yourself for every mistake you make. If you make a mistake and then decide to put things right again to make up for it, what's the point in torturing yourself? Being unkind to yourself never helps you become better."

"Then *blame* is something like *doubt*?" Soren said.

"Why?"

"I remember in class you said doubt is a good bridge but a bad home. You said we should doubt things but not leave ourselves in the hands of hesitation. We should think and discover the truth and move on, as far as we can."

Shabe's mouth widened into a grin. "Way to go, Soren!" he said. "And I'd add, to free yourself from pain, you need to step out of the cycle of deception and self-torment. When you look closely, it can often be a relief to find you had a primary role in your own problems."

"How would that relieve anything?"

"Because you'd realise that *you're* in control of your own happiness, not others. So rather than seeing yourself as a captive, you'll discover your own power, and that will reinforce your sense of liberation. You'll find that peace is just an arm's length away."

"That is liberating to know, actually. We just need to be more self-aware."

"Liberation is the fruit of awakening."

Self-Deceit

The lights throughout the park came on, including the one beside Shabe and Soren's bench, illuminating everything with a soft warm glow. Soren couldn't see the ducks anymore and assumed they'd gone to bed for the night.

The evening air was still, but pleasantly cooler now, to Soren's relief. A sliver of bright orange hovered over the horizon as the last of the sun's rays disappeared. People still continued to amble through the park with their dogs. Soren looked up to see the faint glimmer of stars through the branches. He felt he could sit here all night.

"Are you up for the next topic?" Shabe asked.

Soren checked his watch. As they had rung his mother, Soren knew she wouldn't be concerned about his absence for another few hours yet. "Of course. I've never had such meaningful lessons!"

"Are you saying our lessons at school aren't great?"

Soren's mouth opened as if to speak. Instead, he remained quiet, feeling his cheeks reddening. "I didn't mean that—"

"I'm just kidding," Shabe said, chuckling to himself.

Soren relaxed.

"I don't claim everything taught at schools is useful or necessary, after all," Shabe added. "Well, how about a cup of tea?"

"Actually, I'm a bit thirsty. I'd prefer water."

"Sure."

Shabe returned from the kiosk with the tray of the drinks. Soren took the water and drank fast, as if trying to quench something deeper than thirst.

Shabe held his tea for a moment, watching the steam curl upward, then blew gently and took a small sip, thoughtful. He smiled. "We're going very well, I think. We'll cover the whole book before we return to school."

"How many more chapters have we got left?"

"Three more. Some consist of our conversations."

"I'm so glad I'm helping with this!"

"Well, the next topic is self-deceit."

"I'm ready."

"To recap, feelings of fear and inferiority are unpleasant for the person experiencing them but also shameful and censored by society."

"That's right," Soren said.

"So this means certain sentiments must be kept hidden, even from yourself. In fact, due to the conflicting features in the imposed self, it's inevitable that conflict will arise in us. Nevertheless, our mind has been trained to cherish this identity, so we ignore the contradictions. Preserving the outward I means we must deny our reasoning and deceive our consciousness."

As Shabe spoke, Soren thought about his own feelings and discovered a new insight, almost as if looking in a mirror that reflected his and others' thoughts and feelings. Or perhaps a camera with a unique lens that could see through the masks people felt compelled to wear—the deceits and the displays they put on—capturing people for who they really were.

Identification

"Soren," Shabe said, "I'm sure you've witnessed scenes of fighting between fans at football matches?"

"Yes, I have. It's terrible! I don't understand it."

"Why do you think people fight over teams, even though the teams probably don't know who they are?"

"Because it's their favourite team, and they want to defend them."

"Yes, that's what it looks like," Shabe said. "But remember when we started our journey? You said you'd prefer precise answers."

"Yes. Well, what's the real reason, then?"

"I believe these people identify with a certain team, so they now regard that team as part of their character. What they love is not that team; it's their own identity."

"Oh. Yes! A few weeks ago, some guys at school were fighting over soccer results. Something about an unfair penalty. But still. I thought they were fighting over something personal."

"Well, in fact, this *is* personal, as it's their character they're fighting over."

"Ah, I see."

"This is called *identification*, a fundamental issue with immense emotional and practical ramifications."

"Identification," Soren repeated. "It sounds like how you define your identity."

"Sort of. One way to make up for the emptiness of the outward I is resorting to the technique of identification. That means linking yourself to what you regard as significant or honourable to cover your feelings of emptiness or inferiority."

"How do you mean?"

"For example, my mind might link itself to my luxurious house, my fancy car or even my late grandad's important position. Or it might identify itself with big names like a political party, a fashion designer or a religious sect. Feelings of worthlessness form the structure of the outward I, and this identification provides some relief from this agony. You've heard people boast about their positions or aggressively claim to come from the best country in the world?"

"Yeah! Or when people brag about beating *you*, even though we were only watching the game from home!"

Shabe laughed. "Exactly. Ridiculous, isn't it? Identification is a vivid example of blind-mindedness, living in a world of fantasy and imagination. We don't bother to ask ourselves what my car or my favourite team's win or loss has to do with my personal identity. What value does it add to *me* if my car is the latest model or my mum has an important job? Virtue? Wisdom? Kindness? Beauty?"

"But what if someone really wants to watch the sport or buy a specific car just because they really like it?" Soren asked.

"Well, that's absolutely fine. You should do what you want to do and buy what you want to buy. But it's ridiculous doing these things and expecting them to enhance your identity. And isn't it pathetic if you need to borrow your worth from your bank account or from some celebrity, all while you have an ocean of marvels in your own being?"

"Why are so many people unable to see that?"

"Under the pressure of social blame and demands, the mind is affected by haste and foolishness. It desperately seeks ways to cover its agonies. As a result, the mind resorts to tactics of attack, deceit and denial. But not only do they *not* solve the problem, they give birth to further complications!," said Shabe. "Identification might soothe my discomfort or warm me with a sort of makeshift pride. However, if I'm blinded by fake values, I don't realise I'm continuously creating inner suffering and outer tragedies."

"Mmm. Not entirely sure I follow," Soren said.

"When external things, like my team, become part of my identity, it's only natural that if the team wins or loses, my character is also endorsed or weakened. The opposite happens too. If my favourite celebrity is involved in a scandal, I can feel ashamed and inferior. One moment, I feel proud. The next, humiliated. I'd hardly have a moment to enjoy peace and certainty."

Soren finished off his water while Shabe took a large sip of the masala tea.

"Have you noticed how much it upsets us when someone tells us that our car is scrap or our shoes are outdated?" Shabe asked.

"Yeah." Soren nodded. "So we have something like negative identification as well?"

"You mean ..."

"I mean we identify ourselves with negative or shameful things also, like our faults and mistakes."

"Well said! Exactly. And even when the negative or unpleasant things are not related to us or to our identity at all."

"But why do we do that if it's hurtful?"

"It's become a mental habit. Remember, we said blame and reproach turn every fault into part of your self-image?"

"I do. Everything seems to be so related."

Shabe nodded. "It's like a prism. From each angle, you see a different aspect of the image, while they are all the same thing."

"I like that simile. It makes a lot of sense."

"You know, Soren, when I was a child, I felt embarrassed about the poor suburb I came from, as well as my father being a railway porter. It was as though I had committed a crime. I was always careful not to let anyone know. I was cautious of all the other pains that arise from identifying myself with my suburb, my parent's job, shoes, car, and a myriad of things totally unrelated to my identity. And I thought if anyone found out, I'd crumble with humiliation."

"I get that. I've done that myself," Soren said, recalling comments he'd heard about his father's car that had struck him more intensely than they should have.

"Yes, and it's not only that. Identification has vast and profound implications. It's a way of seeking approval, and it intensifies dependence. When I say I'm proud to come from a particular race or ethnicity, what I'm really doing is pleading for people to approve of me and say that I'm not insignificant. And if I don't get this approval for any reason, I'm overcome with frustration."

Soren asked, "So the real meaning behind these things is to get approval and attention, right?"

"Yes, and to soothe the pains of emptiness and inferiority. If you feel worthwhile, deep inside, you don't see any point in seeking valuation from others."

"But I think it's natural to like your town or country, isn't it?"

"Of course. You naturally grow to care for and love the place where you grew up and formed memories. It's appropriate to care for that place and try to protect it and keep it flourishing, whether it's your country, your hometown, your home or even your street.

"But being proud of something or someone has nothing to do with loving them. Love is a sincere inner feeling towards a thing, but being proud means showing it off to others. When someone really likes something, they don't use it as a tool to prove themself to others."

"Ahh." Soren nodded. "I can see the difference!"

"The other problem is division, war and human tragedy."

"I can imagine."

"When I separate myself from others as a member of a certain group, faith, nation or sect and proudly boast, it's natural for others to say the same about their own nationality, religion or culture. The natural outcome of this is separation, hatred, enmity and tragedy. In fact, when people separate themselves from others and start thinking in terms of 'us' and 'them,' they can more easily abuse, torture or kill other people. And this is precisely what identification does."

"Like what happened in the Second World War."

"Yes. So much tragedy for a mental illusion and the ocean of other miseries humanity is still grappling with. We say we're after peace and friendship, that we despise war and slaughter. We cry for the innocent children suffering at the hands of violence and show sympathy for babies left hungry each day. Yet the way we talk and behave really paves the way for hatred, disunity and war between white and black, Christians and Muslims, the villagers and city dwellers, Westerners and Easterners," said Shabe. "They're all tragedies created by identification. The soothing effect of the outward I and its thirst for approval blinds us to these abhorrent facts."

"I think I'm getting this!"

"But, Soren, I'd like to add something more. There's a form of identification we all fall into, and unless we recognise it, we remain trapped in illusion. I'm referring to identification with the mind, or more precisely, with our own thoughts."

"That sounds serious," Soren said. "Go on."

"This kind of identification means viewing your thoughts as your true self. Many of us find ourselves deeply absorbed in our thinking. When you think about it, it's easy to see we often spend more time inside our heads than being present in the real world. We're constantly lost in images, inner conversations and imagined scenarios. And before we know it, we start to blend with these thoughts."

"You mean …"

"We sometimes lose sight of the fact that our thoughts do not define us, they're simply what our minds are projecting. We have to remind ourselves that we're the audience, not the film itself. And we can and must master and manage our own minds!"

"Yes, I can really vouch for that!" Soren said.

"Have you noticed how a painful thought can feel like it takes over our lives? Instead of saying, 'A thought of failure crossed my mind,' we may say, 'I am a failure.' In this way, the thought starts to mix with our very identity. We tend to treat our thoughts and mental images as if they were part of us, almost like extra limbs."

"So whenever a memory, worry or inner image pops up, our feelings can rise or crash with it. We can feel like a boat tossed around on a restless sea, and in those moments, our emotions, judgements and imagined stories become our self-image. When this happens, instead of our mind working for *us*, we find ourselves working for *it*. The mind takes the lead, and we end up virtually as its hesitant servant."

"Mmm. That's intense," Soren murmured.

"It is. And this is what we call *identification with the mind*. That's why becoming aware of this and moving beyond it are vital steps towards clarity, calm and inner wisdom."

Soren frowned. "But why would we keep doing something that brings so much suffering?"

"Because we take it for granted. We have hardly experienced another mode. It feels normal. Remember when we said that blame turns every mistake into part of your identity? It's the same with thought. Most people don't even realise it's happening. What's more, the mind creates the illusion of control, assuring us of safety. If I think more, worry more, judge more, I'll be protected. However, we end up ensnared in greater confusion."

Soren nodded slowly. "So what's the way out?"

"The first step is to realise that you are not your mind. The mind is a tool, like a device or a machine. It is something you own, not something you are. You are the one who observes the thoughts, not the thoughts themselves."

"Wow. That's an excellent idea."

"Try this. The moment you catch a fearful thought, say, 'There's a fearful thought' instead of 'I'm afraid.' It's like a crack opens in the illusion. That's where freedom begins. Separate yourself from your thoughts, feelings, memories and imagination. Stop building your home in your mind. Stop surrendering to the voice in your head. Instead, own and manage your thoughts and feelings like a master. We'll discuss this identification more later. It's absolutely crucial. It's both awareness and technique at the same time."

"It's great you're telling me about this. Thank you," Soren said.

Self-Blame

Shabe finished off his tea, took a breath and said, "I hope these points make sense."

"I can understand new things if I can take it slowly. Right now, I feel there's so much ground to cover. It'll take a lot of reflection."

"It definitely will. As I said, when the book is ready, I'll hand you a copy so you can review the topics for yourself. I'll also be available for any further discussions, if you like."

"Thank you so much." Soren smiled. "Mum is also very eager to read the book when it's published."

"We'll certainly share it with her. A few more points, and we'll leave the rest for our next catch-up. Okay?" said Shabe.

"What's the next topic?"

"I thought you'd want to know what our current topic is." Shabe chuckled.

"Oh, right. Getting ahead of myself." Soren scratched his head. "What's this topic's theme?"

"Blame and reproach. The final discussion about the pain of living behind the mask."

"Stupid mask," Soren mumbled under his breath.

"As I said, blame and reproach form the start of our suffering. Blame is a sick mentality that plays a major role in preserving the outward I. In short, you could say that self-blame is built on three main pillars. The first one is shame, when the outwardly person is told they're inferior, second-rate or incapacitated. The second is guilt, as the person denies their reality to procure their ideal, socially approved image, silently kicking themselves for their inadequacy. The third pillar is doubt. As this person's values and beliefs are often empty and borrowed, they often feel doubtful and hesitant."

"These are the ABCs of the blameful life," Soren joked.

"Or the SGDs."

"SGDs?" Soren asked. "Oh! Got it," he laughed after a pause.

Shabe also chuckled and went on.

"Because such a person has to suppress their reality to reach the socially approved image, they're often grappling with guilt and self-reproach. And because most of their beliefs and feelings are alien and outward, they often experience doubt and hesitation. This means, whatever the self-lost person does or doesn't do, they remain ashamed of it, as there are always other values to demand the opposite. Blame is a major cause of deception."

"Why is that?" Soren asked.

"Well, it's for fear of blame that people deny their problems, which hinders their personal growth and improvement. If we stopped blaming ourselves for our mistakes and weaknesses, we'd see them as they are, and would try to improve them. But when you form the habit of constantly reproaching yourself, this pushes you to resort to other deceptions or justifications to ignore your problems and save yourself from further blame. In fact, you preserve your external face, at the cost of your real growth and improvement."

"But you said in class that mistakes are part of learning," Soren said. "They're essential!"

"Yes." Shabe put the book down. "You can hardly imagine any learning or growth without errors, mistakes or pitfalls," he answered. "Well, let's finish it here for today. Thank you for your interest and support."

"Any time."

"Shall we meet tomorrow morning at my home?"

"Sure. What time?"

"As early as you can wake up."

"Of course. See you then. Thanks."

"See you."

Pedalling his bike home, Soren thought about Shabe's statement: *bewilderment is an introduction to wakefulness*. He now believed it wholeheartedly and knew he was a walking example.

After the fight with Hans and Daniel, he'd felt confused about who he was, what was good and what wasn't. If it weren't for Shabe's mentoring, so much knowledge and understanding would have passed him by. Shabe had shared not only the answers to many of his important questions but also what questions to ask first, and even what a real answer looked like.

Soren was so immersed in his thoughts, he was surprised to see he'd reached the short driveway to his home. He saw his father's car in the yard, with its wind-up windows, chipped paint and rusty steel bumper. But it had character. Memories. And it had his father's musky, sweet smell.

Soren glanced into the yard next door. Their car was just over a year old. He recalled how perfectly the paint reflected the world around it, right after his neighbour polished it every week.

Looking back at his dad's car, an idea came to him. He stopped and asked himself what the reality of this car was. It was about eighteen years old—a bit older than himself. It had some desirable features. For instance, its brand, Toyota, had built-in safety features, and it had versatile capacities. Its strong engine could do 180 kilometres per hour. The car worked efficiently and had served the family very well over the years, and had never to let them down, just like a caring, loyal friend. So how could it be considered *scrap?*

Soren recalled Shabe saying that judgement was impaired by baseless comparisons. He compared his father's car to the neighbour's. It took only a couple of seconds for the reasoning behind the *scrap* to make sense. Embarrassing, though mostly disappointing. When he reached the porch, he got off the bike and rested it against the wall. He walked towards the stairs and went to put his foot on the first step but stopped midway.

The conversation about identification came back to him, and he almost laughed at himself for being so oblivious. He had identified with the scrap car, attaching it to his character, and thus condemned himself. From there, he got into a conflict between a new, fancy car and an old, outdated car, which meant he was torn between being respected and admired or being pitied and pathetic.

"Hi, son."

Soren's head shot up, seeing his father standing near the front door.

Melody appeared from behind her father's legs, waving at Soren, as he clambered up the porch steps.

"Hello, Dad! Hi, Melody!"

"How did the ethics lessons go?" David asked.

"Ethics lessons?"

He scratched his head. "That's what your mum called it, I think."

Soren hugged Melody, giving her a kiss on the cheek, and said, "I suppose it is sort of ethics."

"So how's it going, then?"

"Good. Fantastic, actually. We're writing a book together. Mum is going to read it. She will be the first one besides us. I'm sure you'll like it too. It's all about life."

"I'm sure it is." His father smiled. "Let's go in. Dinner's ready." He led the way to the dining room.

Soren asked, "Will you read it, Dad?"

"I'm not sure if I'll have time, Soren," he said, sitting down at the table. "I'm sure your mum will tell me all about it, though."

Disappointment washed over Soren. He helped Melody into her seat at the table before taking his own. Hesitantly, he said, "But, Dad, don't you think these matters are important? That they do deserve some time? Why is reading less important than work and other things?"

"You're right, son, but I'm at work from dawn to dusk. No time left, really."

"Shabe said what we call time is actually *priority*. When you say, 'I don't have time,' it means you do the things you regard as important, and if there's any time left over, that's when you read. Because the truth is, we *do* have time. It's the one thing we will always have."

His father was taken aback. Then a smile crept over his face. "That's excellent reasoning. Well done! You're right!" he said, putting his hands up.

Soren stared at his dad, pleased.

"And I must say, I'm enjoying this," David added.

"The book?" Soren asked, confused.

"No. That Shabe is spoiling your morale, like Socrates did to the youth of Athens!"

He glanced at his dad in surprise. He knew his father had been an adventurous young man, as he'd often heard anecdotes about this time.

He also knew his dad would sometimes read philosophy books as well as get involved with political activities. And, of course, that he loved Socrates.

But Soren wondered why young people read, discussed and fought for their ideas but seemed indifferent about reform and change as they got older. Why did they put those important concerns aside and just focus on money, work and business? Such a pity.

"Just kidding! I'll make time to read it. I promise."

Sally and Dave had talked about the changes they'd noticed in their son since he started his regular meetings and discussions with his teacher, and they were both very glad about it ...

That night, during dinner, a new movie played on the TV. It was set in the Second World War, showing Germany's invasion of European countries and the destruction and massacres that followed. The sad, pensive narrative highlighted the racism and destruction, as well as the love, devotion and resistance that emerged during this massive historic incident.

Soren remembered what Shabe had said about people slaughtering each other when they set themselves apart by identification because of their differences in skin tone and heritage, by some races viewing themselves as superior and others as inferior.

He asked himself, *Can humans really be better because of their race? The way Hollander cows are better than Mexican ones? Or the way the Arab horse is superior to the German one?*

CHAPTER FIVE

THE OFFICE

The cool dawn breeze brought over the petrichor of the dense forest. Multicoloured birds emerged from the trees where they'd nested, chirping melodiously. The sun beamed through the fluffy clouds, tinting the sky yellow, orange and purple. Soren was grateful for the morning's coolness before the inevitable heat arrived.

The azure sea appeared boundless. Soren felt as if the constant dancing of the waves in that hazy morning atmosphere was calling him. Boat engines fired up, one after another, heading out to sea, reminding him of the presence of civilisation in the heart of nature.

Shabe had suggested meeting for an early breakfast today, to enjoy the beauty of dawn and because the mind experiences greater alertness in the morning. It seemed he was right.

They sat on the veranda of Shabe's home, overlooking the sea. Soren cleared the table of the remnants of their breakfast, and then they went inside. Shabe quickly wrote a thought in the book.

Through the window, Soren could see the beach was filling up with swimmers and pedestrians. As he watched a dog chase after a ball, his mind drifted to Shabe and his time in the circus. *Was the circus responsible for most of what Shabe knows?* Then he noticed the crowded bookshelves and answered his own question with a no.

He admired Shabe's understanding of the world. How much reading and travelling had it taken to learn so much? And of course, how much thinking and analysing? How had Shabe's earlier life enhanced and shaped all that? Why did so few people discuss these essential topics? Weren't these the things people faced every day?

Soren was surprised by how little attention was paid to such vital matters; instead, people usually wanted to chat about the weather, television shows, recent purchases or some upsetting incidents on the news.

"The magnitude of our being is reflected in the magnitude of the concerns of our lives," Soren remembered hearing in class.

Shabe stopped writing. "Okay, Soren. Today's discussion is about the tools used by society to subdue and enslave the individual."

Soren was pulled from his thoughts. "Subdue and enslave?"

"Yes! We're going to look at the tools society uses to inject its preferred outlook onto our minds and the ways this creates problems for us."

Soren imagined a gigantic hand injecting a potion into someone's brain with a syringe. The thought made him cringe. "Last night, I watched a war movie about the invasion of Europe during the Second World War," he said. "I remembered you talking about identity and racism."

"Funny, I was watching the same movie! You're totally right. I have another topic related to the same theme I'd like us to start with today."

"What topic is that?"

"It's what I like to call *the office*."

"The office?"

"That's right. It's chapter five of the book. You'll remember we talked about how society makes up values to control and take advantage of an individual, attempting to implant a *collaborator I* into their mind. Society wants to make sure we remain meek members who never defy its rules."

"Yes, very curious. But sad, though."

"Indeed. What I'd like to add here is that to keep you obedient, it's not always necessary to have somebody present to force you to obey. Instead, society installs a virtual *office* or *agency* into your mind, and you invariably follow the orders, even in private. This office is the outward I that you assume as your identity. The construction of this office starts when society bombards your mind as a child with comments about who you are and who you should be. These suggestions create the office in your mind."

"That's similar to last night's movie," Soren said. "Invading countries and abusing them."

"Yes," Shabe said. "However, instead of a direct invasion, the colonising countries dispatch their representatives—like armies, soldiers, puppet politicians, missionaries, and the like—to the lands they colonise. These representatives use various tools, such as deception, violence and propaganda, to keep the country under control. This is how the wealth and resources of the colonised country are so easily looted and taken to the dominating nation."

"A bit like leeches that cling to your body, sucking your blood to feed themselves."

Shabe nodded. "A telling simile. Society does similar things to you through suggestion and repetition."

"And the leeches are the thoughts you hold onto in your mind."

"Precisely, and the resulting feelings and actions. You need to get rid of them to get relief."

"I remember you said in class that governments treat people the same way people treat each other."

"Yes, generally. You could look at it from that angle. And remember how I also said that the outer world is the reflection of the inner one?"

"I do."

Shabe smiled. "Society keeps you in a state of fear and hope—fear of shame and hope for approval. Following this colonisation, you become a submissive slave. This captivity can happen so smoothly that you are totally unaware of it. You may even enjoy it."

Soren thought of the intoxicated dervish who had a good time, even while he was losing his donkey.

"The colonised person can turn into a programmed machine, constantly occupied in tuning themself to the demands of the culture and its customs," Shabe said.

"They stamp out their own freedom to keep others satisfied. This relationship—which is actually covert violence—brings about emotional pressures and psychological problems. We've seen some of the consequences of this widespread abuse, and we see examples of it both in ourselves and among other people."

"Then could you say that the outward I is society's delegate in our skull?"

"Quite right, Soren! And its job is to maintain control over our acts and ideas so as to preserve society's interests. You'll see later, though, that being outward is not something confined to identity. In fact, the outward person lives in a world of imposed beliefs and ideas."

"You could write an entire book about the outward world. And if you do, I'd certainly help," said Soren.

The Tale of the Mud-Eating Man

"With what we've read so far, a question comes to mind," Soren said.

"What's that?"

"Why do people seem oblivious to this situation, despite so much pain and pressure? With such widespread mental and emotional problems, why don't people ever wonder if they can live differently?"

"Good quest—" Shabe began before Tara barked to grab his attention. Shabe laughed. "Oh, sorry, Tara. You're hungry, aren't you?" He turned and said, "Sorry. I'll quickly feed Tara, and I'll be back. But I do have a note on that very question. You're welcome to read it while I sort Tara out."

"Yes, thanks!"

Shabe scanned the contents page and said, "The general reason is habituation. That is, it's routine that prevents people from realising the plague they're going through. Ah, yes. Here it is." Shabe flicked to the page and handed the book to Soren before heading to the kitchen with Tara in tow.

As Soren read, he could almost hear Shabe's voice in his head.

The reason humans usually fail to understand how the imposed world has deprived them of profound joy and serenity is a multilayered one.

First, humans have grown accustomed to being constantly bombarded with suggestions and indoctrination, and now this way of life appears to be normal, despite the inherent pain and conflict.

Second, the nature of the complication is like an epidemic. Because this mindset is so widespread, the value-laden view *has created a cultural and psychological order, which in turn have spawned various establishments that preserve this old system.*

Social institutions such as culture, tradition, custom, language and education are all built upon mental values or shaped by them. These institutions uphold and perpetuate a value-driven culture. This dominant value-centric system, with its epidemic complications, often obscures the suffering that arises from even being noticed.

It made perfect sense to Soren. He remembered that the American historian and philosopher Will Durant had once said that habit made most stupid things seem plausible. He read on.

The third reason is being accustomed to this pain. Humans suffer from chronic distress, but they have lived with it for so long that they just don't notice it. And they have totally forgotten the freedom they enjoyed as a child.

Soren's thoughts drifted back to just a few years before, when his world had seemed so different: peaceful, wondrous and free from stress. He wondered when everything had changed. Had the world shifted, or had he?

Homework wasn't just something to finish anymore; it was pressure. Time spent with friends wasn't simply fun; it had become complicated, full of labels and expectations he never used to think about. When did this weight settle in, and why hadn't he noticed it happening? He continued reading.

The other reason is false pleasures. *We resort to superficial joys, such as building wealth, retail therapy, physical pleasure, and even getting satisfaction from dominance, abuse and revenge. These offer temporary relief, a makeshift treatment for the ongoing discomfort of an empty, superficial life, though they hardly address the deeper suffering beneath.*

We often notice that we're hurting but cannot tell why. We just feel it's something within. Had we tasted the sweetness of liberation, we wouldn't be prepared to step back into this narrow world. Sadly, because we're now used to this suffering, we take living in this cage for granted. It's because we're accustomed to pain that we've given in to this imposed life.

As Rumi says, we have forgotten the taste of sugar and honey and have grown used to eating mud.

Shabe returned, carrying Tara's food bowl.

"Eating mud," Soren said to Shabe. "What a revolting idea!"

Shabe placed the bowl down beside the table. Tara wasted no time digging in. "The term is taken from a story by Mowlana."

"Mowlana?"

"That's the name in Persian."

"Ah, Rumi."

"That story is titled *The Tale of the Mud-Eating Man*."

Soren handed back the book. "Can you tell me about it?"

"Of course." Shabe smiled, as if he'd been hoping Soren would ask. "In the olden days, Rumi says, from childhood, a man was always fed mud instead of food. It was no wonder the man was accustomed to eating it and actually liked it.

"Once, the man went to the grocery shop to buy sugar. He asked the shopkeeper to give him a few stones. The shopkeeper placed a weighing stone onto one of the scales before heading to the back of the shop to fetch the sugar. While he was away, the mud-loving man noticed the weighing stone was made of mud. Glad to see that, he seized the opportunity to eat as much of it as he could. Before long, most of the stone was devoured.

"Meanwhile, the shopkeeper had seen this from behind the curtain and decided to remain quiet because the more mud the man ate, the less sugar the shopkeeper would have to provide."

Shabe glanced at Soren, who was smiling and looking intrigued.

"Quite a thought-provoking story, I think!" said Soren.

"It is," Shabe agreed. "It's significant as it shows how we're so used to a shallow, painful life. It shows how, in our confusion about real happiness, we cling to things that are poisonous and how we increasingly distance ourselves from true peace and tranquillity through the joys of mud-eating."

Soren added, "The sad thing is even when someone tries to free us from the mud-eating life and show us the beautiful taste of sugar, we often resist and insist on lingering in the dark dungeons we're used to living in."

"True, and that's what the story wants to say."

"Interesting. Just like the play *People's Enemy* we read in the literature class. It was fascinating."

"Absolutely, I'm glad it caught your attention. It's a great story, isn't it?"

"It is. I've thought about it often."

"That's why Rumi, in various ways, warns us about illusions. He says you miss great treasures, not because they do not exist or even because you do not try to seek them, but because you are trapped by false treasures.

> 'What you imagine as treasure
> Is but an illusion.
> And it is through illusion
> That you lose the true treasure.'"

The Fundamental Humiliation

Soren nodded thoughtfully.

"Briefly speaking, the main tools of manipulation are comparison, blame, belittlement and praise, which we'll touch upon. But before we go any further, Soren, have you ever thought about what's really behind all this suffering? The wars, the oppression, the way people seem so stuck?"

Soren shifted slightly, his curiosity piqued. "As I see it now, it's about self-loss or searching for value."

Shabe nodded. "Yes, correct, but that's only part of it. What I'm talking about is the root cause. The foundation of all those things. I mean, where do self-loss and value-seeking come from?"

Soren looked puzzled. "Not sure. You'll have to tell me."

"Humiliation," Shabe said. "In its various forms."

Soren looked at him curiously. "Humiliation? I know you've mentioned it before, but I didn't realise it could be behind everything."

Shabe nodded slowly. "Yes, almost everything. Soren, if you want to understand the whole story, just look at everything we have said so far, and everything we say in future, through the lens of humiliation. Only when you have this insight can you adequately appreciate everything."

Soren's brow furrowed. "Like when Hans and Daniel mock others? Is that what you mean?"

Shabe turned to face him. "Humiliation goes much deeper. It's about seeing yourself, or others, as *less*. It's believing, even subconsciously, that humans are not as valuable, not as worthy, as they are. It's when we underestimate the merit of being human. Those obvious insults and mocking that you got from Hans and Daniel are just the tip of the iceberg."

He paused, letting the words sink in. "Take a look at history. Throughout history, humans have been abused, subdued and victimised for all sorts of things—ideologies, faith, land, country, customs, even traditions. And let's not forget the literal sacrifices for imaginary gods, goddesses and so-called holy entities."

Soren's eyes widened. "Yeah, I remember reading about that. The Aztec tribes would sacrifice prisoners to satisfy their gods."

"Right."

"And the Mayans would spill blood for their deities, and the Egyptians even buried slaves alive with the pharaohs for the afterlife. Many people bowed to rocks, hills and statues and worshipped them."

Shabe nodded. "Exactly. You remembered that well. And think about the Crusades. Christians and Muslims slaughtering each other for the sake of saving what they believed was sacred. The medieval church tortured and burned people to preserve the *right* belief. It's all based on the idea that the belief is more important than the lives lost for it. We still see echoes of that today, in different forms."

Soren's face softened. "But aren't things better today? Surely, we've moved on from that kind of thinking."

Shabe sighed. "Yes, things have improved, and we should be thankful for that. But different types of humiliation still exist, often in subtler ways. It's still embedded in our mentality—a subconscious belief that shapes how we act, feel and treat others. It's still very much alive."

Soren raised an eyebrow. "Like what?"

Shabe leaned forward, his voice steady but intense. "If we felt worthy enough, we wouldn't become so oblivious to ourselves and focus entirely on others. We do that because we suppose that others are more important and more influential than us, and that's a sign of self-humiliation. Why does what others think or do, or how good or bad they are, occupy our minds far more than our own role and place? Why do we lose sight of our own lives, worrying about others' opinions or actions? Because of feeling less important and less noticeable."

Soren nodded slowly. "And we search for happiness and success in all the wrong places, right? Like chasing after other people's approval."

Shabe's eyes gleamed. "Exactly! We become dependent and insecure, believing our happiness lies in others' hands. Soren, why do we, instead of valuing our incredible human potential, waste our time on trivial things?

"Why do we get lost in shallow entertainments, pointless debates, and futile activities that don't nourish us? Isn't that all because of an imposed and assumed humiliation? That we don't really believe our being is a most valuable asset and is worth the utmost care and appreciation?

"So we have internalised this humiliation and accepted it as a given, because we are unfamiliar with what a fulfilled and meaningful life truly feels like!"

Soren sighed. "Right. Many people, with so much promise, waste their lives away."

Shabe's voice grew darker. "And, Soren, what drives us to commit ugly, immoral actions despite knowing they're evil? Why do we surrender to injustice, oppression and cruelty and accept them? I know there are times when people are truly helpless or in a desperate situation. But that's not always the case. Most of us feel too small, too powerless to fight back when we actually *do* have the power, and that in itself is a manifestation of humiliation."

Soren sat back, absorbing Shabe's words. "Yes, we just become passive. We give up because we think, 'Who am I to do such a big thing? It's up to greater people to do this!'"

Shabe nodded. "Yes, and like I said, there are many more forms of feeling inferior or humiliated. When we follow without questioning, when we accept something just because the speaker is famous and has lots of followers, and when we don't have the courage to criticise or judge for ourselves. Isn't that because we assume we're too inadequate to make our own choices? And when, instead of working on our inner and personal growth, we sell part of our actual *life* to this company or that business to buy shiny, new things that ultimately do nothing to help us improve, isn't that a sign of self-belittlement?"

Soren stared off into the distance, quiet for a few moments. Then he said, "Very true." He looked at Shabe. "And like you said, it's relying on others for validation. Looks like we need their attention just to feel worthy, to feel like we matter."

"That's exactly it! Every time we surrender our own worth for the sake of other peoples' opinion or a system, or engage in a futile or ugly action, we fall deeper into that humiliation." Shabe paused, then continued. "Even things like law, education and ethics—things that are supposed to help us—have often been turned into levers of control. They exist to serve us, to make life better, not the other way around. If those systems kill our happiness and erase our individuality, then what's the point? It's a contradiction."

Soren's voice was quieter now but clear. "So the key is to break free from that. To stop looking outward for what we already have inside."

Shabe's enigmatic smile returned. "Yes. You know, Soren, many of us do have good intentions to put things right and use sincere efforts to change and reform—which is excellent—but the trouble is, we merely look at the fragmented pieces of the picture, instead of seeing it as a whole. We become busy with parts and pieces, oblivious to the bigger picture. Whatever we do for the betterment of humans, we must do it with an understanding of the whole system.

"It all starts with recognising the system for what it is. It's not an economic or political system. It's much deeper. It's a cultural and psychological one. Humiliation drives it all. And we, Soren, have to wake up!"

Soren shifted, a new intensity in his eyes. "But how? How do we make people see this, Shabe?"

Shabe leaned forward, gaze steady. "Education, Soren. Real education. We need to start teaching self-awareness, and self-care. Not the shallow kind but deep self-care that includes knowing yourself, valuing yourself and understanding how to live consciously and insightfully. We need life philosophy, practical psychology—subjects that teach people how to think, how to deal with their emotions and how to lead an informed life."

Soren nodded slowly. "But it's not enough to teach that in schools, right? It has to go beyond the classroom."

Shabe smiled, impressed with Soren's insight. "Exactly. We need to expand public education and awareness on these topics. Make them part of everyday life. Teach people, young and old, that these are the most crucial topics for life and happiness. We need centres, public programs—places where people can learn these skills and understand how to take control of their own lives."

"So if we want to change the system, we have to start with ourselves. And with the way we teach each other."

Shabe nodded. "Yes, if we want real change, it must start with self-awareness. Once people truly understand themselves, once they start to adequately appreciate their worth and merit, they will stop relying on outward, borrowed things for comfort and validation. They will break free from the cycle of humiliation. That's the only way forward."

"I see," Soren said.

"And, Soren, we should stress that emphasising self-awareness and inner growth doesn't mean being selfish or retreating into self-improvement alone. In fact, empathising with others and offering care and support is part of what makes us human. It fulfils deep emotional needs and is essential to our personal and social development.

"However, meaningful action and lasting social contribution can arise only when we truly know ourselves, when we're clear about our motives, conscious of our needs, and wise enough to act with insight. If we remain unaware of our biases, assumptions, subconscious needs and vulnerabilities, our actions will only cause more misery and suffering."

Comparison

A long pause followed Shabe's last sentence. They both thought for a minute or two.

Finally, Shabe began. "So the first tool for manipulation is blame or reproach. However, as blaming cannot happen without comparison, we'll first attend to comparison."

Shabe adjusted his glasses as Soren refilled his glass of water. Tara had finished eating her food and lay on the vintage Persian rug by their feet, peering up at them both.

"As we've already discussed, it's not fair to judge or compare humans. The obvious reason is that every person is unique. Their emergence and shaping have resulted from numerous historical, geographical, cultural, genetic, familial and environmental factors. That's why they say each person is a singular system, a new world to explore.

"Just as you probably won't find two individuals whose face and body are identical or whose fingerprints are the same, it's unlikely you'll find two persons with the same interests, values, talents and capabilities. Therefore, it's fundamentally unfair to expect a person to be, or behave, just like another person."

Soren thought of his twin cousins, Sam and Ben. They appeared identical, and at times, Soren still confused the two of them with their dark hair, round faces and brown eyes. Yet they had virtually nothing in common.

Sam was an outgoing, talkative boy who enjoyed sports and outdoor activities, and Ben was shy and quiet, preferring to spend his time reading, gaming or playing music. Thankfully, Soren's auntie had rarely pushed them to do any particular things, and each twin pursued his own interests. The blatant difference between the brothers had always surprised everyone, even people who knew them.

But if Auntie Nancy were to compare outgoing Sam with introverted Ben, expecting Sam to act as a child who didn't mind sitting alone, practising music or watching movies, that would make life torturous for him.

Soren was pulled back from this train of thought by Shabe's words.

"Another drawback of comparison is that it disrupts our ability to appreciate a person's unique needs and aptitudes because …" He paused as he noticed Soren smiling. "What's funny?"

"Just imagine a factory where people with all different faces, heights, genders and body types enter at one end, go through a standardisation process, then emerge through the other end in standard shapes, like cubic dolls with identical heights, faces and colours. The Human Corporation Pty. Ltd."

"Absolutely!"

They both laughed, and Shabe continued.

"To help a human develop their potential and flourish, you need to see them exactly as they are. It's illogical to evaluate a person's capacities by comparing them with another person, or to examine them according to your own tastes and expectations. That would involve ignoring that they're human and disregarding their unique capacities. If I expected my child to play music like their classmate does, I'm looking at the classmate's abilities, not my child's. That comparison would deny my child's needs and talents.

"As the children of yesterday, what we should keep in mind is that we're doing the same things to ourselves. Right now, comparing ourselves with others stops us from seeing our own limits and capacities." Shabe stopped. "You know, Soren, wishing to be someone else is a major obstacle to our thriving."

"I agree," Soren said.

Blame

"Let's now turn to blame. You could say it's the mother of most of our suffering." Tara appeared and took a seat beside Shabe on the floor. He peered down at her. "Looks like you're also interested in this discussion!"

"Perhaps she's impatient to see when we start discussing animal rights." Soren laughed, stretching down to pat Tara.

"Could be." Shabe chuckled. "The germination of the vicious entity called ego, or *nafs*, in the Sufi language, is caused by blame and reproach. That's what gives birth to most of our pain and conflict. And as we've seen, blame is based on comparison.

"Let's say I called my daughter, Mary, dull and untalented because her results in maths were lower than Annette's. This means that I actually had my attention on Annette, not Mary. Meanwhile, had I compared Mary to Helen, who scored lower on the test, I would have said Mary was a bright and talented child. See? What it means is that comparison is always a tentative measure, yet we use it as an absolute one, which is evidently unjust.

"The second issue is that the standard for blame is often just the personal taste of the person handing out the blame. Who is the judge of the court that decreed Mary stupid? In whose eyes is she dull or untalented? I determined Mary was stupid because I wanted my child to come first in the class so I could announce proudly, 'My Mary is the best!'

"But, unfortunately for us, children's natural states don't always follow our competitive needs. What happens then is I say to my child, in a disappointed tone, 'You're hopeless' or 'That's not good enough. You'll have to work harder.' I inflict a sense of guilt on the poor child. Why? Because I'm frustrated because I can't boast the way I want to."

Soren said, "Very true."

"So what happens in the act of blaming is I hold a subjective court, where I issue a final verdict, convicting my poor child of stupidity, and that's now stuck on her psyche. And then *she* feels like she has to hide this shameful fact from the rest of the world, merely because of an unjust comparison."

"I never compared Melody with other kids before, but now I'm extra careful not to."

"I'm glad you say that. I wish we could all have useful conversations when we talk so we could lift these burdens off our minds and lives. Unfortunately, many of us are far more interested in the third marriage of an actress or the latest design of pants than discovering what's going on inside us," Shabe said.

"Yes—and among us. I was just thinking the same thing a moment ago! This is the way to a more informed, compassionate and peaceful life: reading, learning, thinking and having constructive conversations." Soren added, "And being kinder to ourselves."

"Of course. That way, the world turns into a better place to live in." Shabe leant back in his chair and sipped his water, his gaze drawn to the sea. He smiled as if he could see this beautiful world right before his eyes. "Soren," Shabe called, sitting up straight again. "Do you go to warehouses often?"

"Yes, I do. I go with Dad sometimes. Why do you ask?"

"Then I'm sure you've seen staff putting price tags on their goods?"

Soren nodded. "Yep. They unpack the items, put them on the shelves and put tags and labels on them."

"Well, the labelling and tagging is a good metaphor for the nature of blame."

"Makes sense because when they blame you, they often give you labels," Soren said.

"They do! Labels that can remain on the forehead of your mind for a long time. And, Soren, when you blame someone, there's pricing and valuation in what you do."

"There's *what*?"

"When I call my child clumsy or hopeless, I'm treating the child and their features like a merchant who places labels on goods of either high or poor quality."

"Or even 'best before,'" Soren interjected, laughing.

"I love your wittiness, Soren! *Best before*. We must add that to the book," Shabe said. "And that is exactly what pricing means, which is a selfish and abusive way to treat a human. Blaming someone is a way of framing them based on our own standards and opinions. And we stick these labels on them—not on their bodies, but on their psyches. This turns humans into submissive slaves whose main goal in life is to carry and protect expected values."

"Psychological slavery!"

"Very well put! As a reaction, I might spend a lifetime proving otherwise, like becoming an influential politician, a wealthy businessman or a celebrity. But the painful labels don't ever completely disappear and won't let me be free to enjoy these things. And that's a true example of profound slavery."

Insult

Shabe scrawled something on the page before flipping it over. "Another method of manipulation is insults, swearing or what we call verbal abuse, to belittle a person to themself, demoralising them."

"Excuse me? You said, 'Belittle them to themself'?" Soren interrupted.

"Yes."

"But when someone is insulted, aren't they also belittled in the eyes of others?"

"I don't think so."

Soren looked puzzled. "Huh? How can that be?"

"Imagine you see me swearing at someone who accidentally cut in front of my car. In your eyes, who is belittled—me, the one swearing, or the person I'm yelling at?"

"That's obvious. You, because your actions show that you're rude."

"Yes. I appear immature and small-minded. And generally, who would you sympathise with? The one insulting or the one being insulted?"

"The one being insulted. You're right. Why didn't I see it like that?"

"Because our minds are filled with certain ideas, and we cannot think critically. The other point is that insulting someone is a futile attempt to diminish them. When I criticise someone with abusive words, all I've really done is sent a bunch of words into their mind.

But words alone can neither take away anything from them nor add anything to them.

"Soren, let's push aside our mental habits for a moment and look clearly at insults and swearing. When I tell you you're stupid, where do my words actually damage you? Your hand? Your legs? Your brain? Your talent? Your money? Do my words really take away your intelligence and make you stupid?"

"Maybe your insult will cause their house's pipe to burst or their car tyre to go flat!" Soren laughed.

Shabe laughed too. "I'm not sure about the pipe, but sometimes, we really do puncture each other's emotional tyres! So that's false language, isn't it? It is tricking you into imagining you've suddenly shrunk into a small or unimportant person merely by uttering a bunch of words."

"A fine example of manipulation!" Soren was awed. "Perhaps I think the insult damages my personality."

"Yes. That's the mistaken idea I'm pointing out here," Shabe answered. "We should ask ourselves, what kind of personality is so easily lifted by one word and yet plunged into despair by another?"

"Why did people invent insults, then? What's their purpose?" Soren asked.

"That's the question that reveals the deceptive nature of insults: what does the person insulting gain from it? For example, let's say I tell you that you're worthless and cheap during an argument. What's my intention? For some reason, I feel small and inferior to you, so I try to bring you down to soothe my own feelings of inadequacy. In other words, because I feel low, I try to lower you to ease my pain."

"But insults aren't just words. There are feelings of hate and enmity behind them," Soren added.

"Look, Soren, let's not stray from the main point. Of course, the drive behind insults and swearing involves hate and anger, as do many other behaviours of people obsessed with *empty values*. But the real question is, what happens when someone tries to belittle another person?"

"Yeah! You're right."

"So belittlement means making something smaller. The word itself reveals the truth—by attempting to belittle someone, I'm admitting to their worth or abilities. Otherwise, why bother trying to make them feel small? Would it make sense to try to shrink something that's already insignificant?"

Soren shook his head.

"We only try to pretend someone is unimportant when you admit their importance, in one way or another. Would you ever insult a child because they're weak or powerless, even if they made you angry?"

"That would be ridiculous! Like if I laughed at Melody just because she can't talk properly. Or tell her she's not big or important."

"It *is* ridiculous," Shabe agreed. "Like I said, the concept of humiliation has vast, profound implications. You could say the entire way society treats the individual is an extensive form of humiliation. Society victimises our thoughts and emotions with the dagger of conformity, self-loss and torment, disguised as rules and values. It brainwashes our minds to believe what really matters is values, not us. And even if you do have worth, it's thanks to the values you obey, implying that you must be victimised for these values to live on. Such a suggestion means social valuations matter to us more than our own common sense.

"Soren, it's difficult to understand those who chant slogans about political freedom, while humans still carry suppression and violence in them as part of their attitudes towards themselves."

After a short pause, Soren said, "It's fascinating …"

"What is?"

"Words," Soren said. "It seems many of the words we considered meaningful have always been untrue and empty. Yet many words are often ignored, while they actually have significant meaning, like the word *humiliation*. I'd always taken it for its superficial meaning, but now I can see the great implications humiliation can have."

"Right. You could be upset about a superficial humiliation, while unaware of the deep one you're going through," Shabe said. "You know, Soren, words are like a small old safe in the corner of our home that's never been opened. You can always see the outside of it and assume you know what's inside. But if you unlock it, you'd find that one has nothing in it, while another might contain an incredible treasure.

"There are many words we use all the time and take their meanings for granted. As soon as we ask ourselves what that word really means, we could discover astonishing facts. Rumi says,

> *'People's bodies are sealed jars.*
> *Look within each jar to see what it holds.*
> *One jar is filled with the water of life.*
> *Another is filled with the poison of death.*
> *If you focus on the contents,*
> *You are a king (of wisdom).*
> *But if you stare at the container,*
> *You are misguided.*
> *Words are like humans' bodies.*
> *Their meanings are like the souls within.'*

"He uses the metaphor of jars to illustrate how external appearances can be deceiving. And a great example of that is words! Words are like jars with lids on. You must take the lid off each jar to see what is really inside. Just as people's bodies contain their souls, words hold deeper meaning within them. If you focus solely on appearances, you'll misunderstand people, and focusing only on the superficial meanings of words will also mislead you."

"Like pearl diving," said Soren. "The deeper you dive, the bigger your pearls."

"A great simile, Soren! Take the words *love, respect, justice, pride, fear, selfishness* and *value*. If you look into them closely, you'll often see incredible things. It's like suddenly turning the light on in a dark room. Everything looks so bright and vivid."

Soren smiled. "And that's the light of inquiry."

Praise and Admiration

Shabe glanced at his watch, surprised to find it was almost half-past five. They'd spent the afternoon attending to the plants and examining the sprouting flowers in Shabe's garden and had become so absorbed in their conversation that the entire afternoon seemed to have slipped by.

"What's this one called?" Soren asked, gently lifting some white bushy petals dangling from a small tree.

"Elderflower," Shabe answered. "It's antiseptic and great for common colds."

"And this one?" Soren pointed to a large shrub sporting purple flowers, attracting a dozen bees.

"Lavender. It can be used as an antiseptic and to ease insomnia and depression."

Soren was fascinated. "It's like nature has an answer for everything!"

Shabe chuckled. "Perhaps that's so."

They now sat on the front veranda sipping iced tea, watching the sun disappear beyond the horizon.

"Well, we'll just read the last part before we close today's court," said Shabe.

"Court?"

"This is a court, isn't it? We're talking about the things we discover in our journey, and we judge the things as good and bad, right and wrong."

"Well, that's what we always do, isn't it?"

"That's right. Everyone is a judge, and their world is their courtroom. We issue the verdicts, deciding things are good, bad or valuable. We must try to be vigilant and fair judges because whatever verdict we issue has a direct effect on our own world, before anyone else's."

"Hear, hear!" Soren exclaimed.

"So, my learned colleague, are you ready to deliberate on the last case?"

"Of course!" Soren said.

"It's about praise and admiration."

"Okay."

"Social interpretations involve a sort of self-interest. Therefore, there's little difference between negative and positive values. In the first chapter, we talked about praise and admiration. Here, I'm going to add a few more points. Doubtless, children's emotional and intellectual growth requires adequate care and attention. However, that's totally different to using subjective, value-laden words to refer to them.

"Whether I say to my child, 'I'm ashamed of you' or 'I'm proud of you,' I'll have evaluated them by *my* personal standards, and thus, I've ignored *their* genuine interests. Take, 'I'm proud of you,' for instance. What does this really mean? Doesn't it mean, 'I'm delighted because, as a way to satisfy my desire to show off, you've done well'? That means I'm more concerned for my *own* status, and being able to boast about everything my child does or doesn't do, than I am for their flourishing."

"Yeah, that makes sense," Soren said.

"Apart from that, what you can see here is the value-oriented person becomes so infatuated by subjective values that they become detached from reality and submerged in the world of their own imagination. They hardly bother to wonder what *pride* is, or what it really means to be proud of someone or something.

"If someone does something remarkable and acquires fame, what does that have to do with me and my character? How would I benefit from linking my personality to their success or status, even though that person is my sister or a fellow countryman?"

"So boasting or being proud of things shows a sort of psychological need?" Soren said.

"Precisely. Boasting and bragging are other inventions of the cunning mind to evade the pain of hollowness. Pride is a form of identification. It's a kind of self-deception employed by the mind to evade a feeling of inferiority." Shabe looked at Soren and said, "I hope you've found today's reflections stimulating."

"Yes, always! I just need to think more about some things, as you said."

"Thinking means exploring new lands. The more new lands you discover, the more your world grows," Shabe said. "By the way, Soren, don't just take in these discussions or my book. I want you to read *more* books, watch good films and go to enlightening lectures and thought-provoking discussions—even those that present opposing views. Awareness is a light. Let's enhance its brightness as much as we can."

"Yeah, okay." Soren said. "But I've found myself thinking a lot about the points you've talked about, and when I talk about these things, a few people are surprised. Some say it's fantasy or that it's unrealistic."

"Of course! It's not surprising when those who can't understand new ideas will often just make fun of them. Until a couple of centuries ago, many believed that diseases were caused by bad air or imbalances in the body. But perceptive people always spot what habit-stricken minds hardly have the power to grasp.

"When the French chemist Louis Pasteur proposed that tiny organisms, which he called *germs*, were responsible for causing diseases, he faced opposition. Some called him misguided because these germs were invisible to the naked eye. However, through experiments and with the help of microscopes, Pasteur and his supporters proved these microorganisms indeed caused illness, which was a big turn in the course of modern medicine. We can all see things vividly; we just need to make use of the microscope in our brains. And that microscope is doubting and questioning."

The Village of the Slaves

"Well, that's all for today," Shabe announced.

"Thank you so much!" Soren said with a smile

"You're most welcome, sir," Shabe said, and they both laughed. He then continued. "If you agree, we'll meet up again next week. I need to sort a few sections first. At least now you'll have time to think and read. But still, make some time for play. Any questions?"

"Not a question, but I do have something for you today." Soren grinned mysteriously.

"You do?" Shabe asked. "Oh, wait. It's your story, isn't it?"

Soren nodded as he removed his notebook from his bag. "It's finished now!"

"Really? That's fantastic, Soren! I'd really like to hear it."

"Can I read some to you now?" Soren asked. "It's called *The Village of the Slaves*."

Shabe stroked his stubble. "Sounds like a profound story coming up."

Soren opened his notebook. "Well, this is the outline. I'm still working on the details. But I thought it would help me to share what I have so far."

"Well, I can't wait anymore."

"The Village of the Slaves," Soren read. "Once upon a time, in a land not too far away, a cunning master owned several slaves. For generations, they'd been born and grew up on the master's farm. Unsurprisingly, they had no ideas about a liberated life or of working for themselves. This farm was all they had ever known, their entire lives.

"This cruel master pushed the poor slaves to work harder and harder, without any rights. The slaves didn't dare make any objections. They even praised their great master, appreciating what few amenities they received, such as food, clothes and somewhere to sleep when they were exhausted at the end of the day. And, above all, he always praised them for their strengths or abilities."

Soren eyed Shabe from time to time to see his reactions; he seemed immersed, so he went on.

"The master would say to one slave, 'You're excellent at sewing. The finest tailor in the world!' To another slave, he'd say, 'You're so tall! You're the perfect height for efficiently picking fruit from the branches!' And then to a third slave, he'd say, 'You're the strongest! You're my best porter!'

"The master would hold contests among the slaves, and these could turn brutal or bloody at times. Winners were awarded medals made from scraps of tin stamped with titles. *The Best Woodworker, The Best Carter, The Best Gardener*, and so on.

"Winners who turned down the work or fell behind in a competition were punished and humiliated by the master, who'd rip the medal from their chest. 'You're absolutely useless!' he'd shout. 'Look at Joe! See how smart and strong he is, you imbecile!' He'd award the medal to someone else.

"So there was constant rivalry among the slaves to obtain their master's approval. Everyone focused on snatching more medals from others. They were constantly anxious about losing the medals they had won.

"The outcome was not difficult to imagine. The poor slaves worked harder and harder for their sadistic master, making his lands prosper and his gardens flourish and keeping his silos filled with grain. Yet the slaves received no more than two stale, unwholesome meals each day and a dark dungeon to sleep in. Despite that, they were quite accustomed to their bleak lives.

"What mattered most to them was gaining medals, so they resorted to fighting, trickery and theft. Enmity, jealousy and distrust prevailed among them. Rarely could anyone spend a night in peaceful sleep, nor did anyone enjoy friendly or healthy relationships. Instead, they were utterly familiar with this pathetic way of life, which offered little more than oppression and suffering.

"Then one day, a traveller passed through their village, sharing the truth of what life could be like beyond the master's control. At first, the slaves couldn't believe what the traveller told them. Could life really be so different?

"The traveller urged them to leave the village and see for themselves. It took a lot of courage to defy the master and his tyranny; however, with this newfound awareness, the slaves began to resist the master and claim their freedom.

"The cunning master tried to suppress them by force, then by temptation and deception. But the slaves were now too aware and empowered to keep accepting abuse and enslavement. Eventually, the master, unable to overpower them, fled and was never seen again.

"With his departure, the slaves were free. As soon as they realised they were in a new world, they came to understand what a liberated life meant and started to enjoy their independent work and life.

"The medal winners threw aside their worthless awards and lived together in peace and friendship from then on. Everyone discovered their likes and interests and pursued them. The people enjoyed their liberty so much that they vowed never to subject themselves to any master, ever after."

Soren closed his book, looked up at Shabe with a smile reflecting life, hope and promise, and his eyes sparkled with warmth.

"Very appealing, indeed, Soren, and inspiring," Shabe said after applauding enthusiastically. "I was sure great things would arise from your gifted mind."

"I'm glad you like it!" Soren answered, delighted.

They continued discussing *The Village of the Slaves*, and Shabe shared some ideas for developing the story and its details.

Finally, an elated Soren said goodbye and headed towards the library. He realised he now had an even stronger thirst for knowledge and wanted to learn more, especially about topics like philosophy and mysticism. He made a mental note to borrow a few of the books Shabe had suggested.

After dinner, Sally asked Soren how his talks with Shabe were going, so he explained the points he now better understood.

"I'm quite intrigued by the things Shabe tells you," Sally said. "I wouldn't mind attending your next discussion, if possible. I have some questions I'd like to ask Shabe. Soren, would you like us to invite Shabe over for lunch sometime soon?"

"Oh, sure. Thank you, Mum!" Soren said. "Just let me know what day is good for you." He leant towards his mother and kissed her on the cheek.

Melody, toddling around the kitchen, clapped her hands and said, "Dat a gweat idea!"

This made Soren and Sally burst into laughter.

CHAPTER SIX

THE CIRCUS

Soren was setting the table while eyeing his little sister in the next room. Melody was muttering softly to herself and playing one of her favourite games: removing items of clothing from the drawer, folding them, putting them back and then pulling them all out again.

"Soren!" Sally called as the bell rang. "Someone's at the door!"

"It's Shabe," Soren called back, quickly straightening the cutlery on the placemat. "I'll get it!"

Soren greeted him and gestured for him to come in. A moment later, Sally appeared, removing her apron.

"Good evening, Shabe," Sally said. "Good to see you! How are you going?"

Soren knew his mother and Shabe would want to catch up, so he closed the front door and led them both to the living room, where they sat on the sofa.

Minutes later, glasses of iced tea appeared on the table in front of them. It was obvious that Soren was excited to see his favourite teacher at their home and how impatient he was for their conversation to begin.

Melody was now in her mum's arms, staring inquisitively at the stranger. Shabe gave her a smile, entertaining her with a few amusing gestures, and she smiled back, gradually making friends with the newcomer.

"So," Sally said, adjusting Melody in her lap. "Soren really enjoys the conversations he's been having with you. You've had quite an impact on him. His father and I are glad about that. I haven't remained unaffected either, to be honest. You probably read *Horizon Weekly*?"

"Yes," Shabe nodded. "I sometimes read it. And I follow some of your topics. I find them thought-provoking."

"Thank you, Shabe. Then you probably remember I write the family column. I answer questions and offer solutions to reader problems as well. I believe the sorts of discussions you and Soren are having would be quite helpful in getting a deeper understanding of the difficulties we all face, one way or another. When Soren told me about your topics, I found them very relevant to the jobs that people like me have. I don't know why they don't include them in the school curriculum."

"I'm glad you're interested! The school pursues its own programs and, unfortunately, topics like self-awareness, the philosophy of life and dealing with fundamental questions about life—which is the most crucial knowledge—have little place in schools. Everybody needs to become aware of their own intents, ideas and roles in society and pursue life in the light of such awareness. I strongly believe our schools ought to offer such important lessons alongside maths, geography and English as an integral part of genuine education. They're by no means less important."

"I do agree, and if taught effectively, students would actually find them very interesting," Sally said. "I'm looking forward to today's discussions."

"Great. Shall we begin?"

"Please. And don't forget your drink! I'll serve lunch soon, but before I do, I have two questions I want the answers for. Is that okay?"

"Of course," Shabe answered.

Sally said, "You've spoken about the authentic self many times. Your main point seems to be that our suffering stems from not having an authentic self and not living an authentic life. Could you provide a clear definition of these concepts? I know you've explained them throughout the discussions, but having a comprehensive definition might be useful."

"That's right! Look. Every human being naturally possesses a set of intrinsic qualities—talents, needs, inclinations, physical and psychological traits and so on. At the same time, part of our life is shaped by deliberate choices—things we thoughtfully and willingly select for ourselves.

"Anything that originates from either of these two sources—our innate nature or our conscious choices—is part of our authentic self. Living authentically means that our thoughts, behaviours, relationships and emotions are guided by our inner qualities and our deliberate choices."

Sally asked, "Hang on a minute. Is this self the way we see ourselves, or is it the way we are?"

"What do you mean, Mum?" asked Soren.

"I mean, in this definition, when we say the authentic self, are we referring to the authentic way of seeing and evaluating ourselves, or are we talking about our pure, authentic being?"

"That's a very subtle question. Thanks for asking! It's both. We are referring to both our genuine being and to seeing and comprehending this being, albeit through a lens of clear, logical reasoning," Shabe said.

"That makes it clearer," Sally said. "So you say anything that doesn't come from within us is inauthentic?"

"Exactly. Anything that isn't a natural need or inclination of yours but has instead been imposed, conditioned, instilled, manipulated or driven by fear is an external influence that distances you from your authentic self. It obstructs the path to ease and genuine growth," Shabe told her. "Similarly, an inauthentic life is one where you are governed by alien and foreign forces—where your efforts are directed towards things that neither stem from your own free will, nor truly serve your growth and wellbeing." Shabe paused a moment and then added, "This is my understanding and my definition, of course, like anything else I have said so far."

Sally looked to be contemplating, weighing the idea in her mind. Then she asked, "But our choices are more or less intertwined with our environment, aren't they? Maybe it's not possible to draw a clear-cut line between the two. What I mean is, it's not always obvious which parts of our life are fully authentic and which parts are shaped by external influences."

Shabe nodded. "You're right. It's relative."

Sally went on. "So having an authentic self and living an authentic life isn't a destination. It's a continuous process, a journey of growth. Isn't it?"

Shabe nodded. "Yes, that's exactly right. It's not about how authentic you are; it's about the direction you are moving in."

"Meaning?"

"Meaning an authentic person isn't someone whose life is completely self-made in every respect. Rather, it's someone who moves *consciously and passionately* towards realising their genuine potential and true needs. And like any other journey, this path includes trial and error, ups and downs and moments of doubt. But what truly matters is that their movement is towards *freedom, self-awareness and fulfilment*."

Sally nodded thoughtfully.

Shabe added, "In short, living authentically is an ongoing process of shedding what has been imposed, and cultivating what is truly yours, consciously, wisely and in alignment with your real contentment and growth."

Sally smiled. "That was a very insightful and inspiring explanation. Thank you."

The Society Within

"My other question is about society," Sally said.

"Sure." Shabe nodded.

"You frequently refer to the concept of society in your explanations. I would like to know, what do you mean by *society*? How do you define it? I think this topic should also be included in the discussion."

Shabe thought for a moment. "Yes, you're right. Thanks for bringing it up. By *society*, we mean the collection of people along with everything they have created or invented, including institutions, organisations and phenomena that have been produced through collective human effort. This includes physical structures such as buildings, churches, mosques, hospitals, roads and factories, as well as intangible elements such as language, culture, science, religion and traditions.

"However, society is not merely an external phenomenon. We also have another type of society, the inner society, or the society within. By this, I mean the society not out there, but in here, within you. The inner society is the mental representation of the external society. This is the society that you carry in your mind and psyche all the time, in building a contented life and a flourishing being, so remaining aware of the inner society is crucial.

"The inner society is that part of our being that results from living among others. If we were completely isolated beings, this part of our mind and behaviour would not exist. For example, if you hadn't grown up among others, you wouldn't learn language, understand concepts like religion, culture or traditions or acquire knowledge and science. Our understanding would be limited to our own individual experiences, and our lives would be reduced to a very primitive state.

"For this reason, all the knowledge, feelings and influences that shape us through interaction with others form part of our inner society. Even our affections, interests, thoughts and self-image, shaped by others' presence or their behaviour and teachings, are aspects of this inner society. In other words, this inner society encompasses all the influences we have absorbed from others, directly or indirectly, and carry within us."

"That's fascinating," Sally remarked.

"It is, and it should be noted that the inner society is no less significant than external society; rather, it represents and mediates our understanding and interaction with external society. We can only comprehend and engage with the external world if we first construct an internal representation of it. Without this internal map, interacting with the outside world would be impossible," said Shabe.

"Take language. As I said, if we did not have a mental representation of the language of our society, including vocabulary, grammar and intonations, we would neither understand it nor be able to communicate."

Soren piped up then. "Just like the jungle boy! He was raised by animals and had never seen a human. He didn't know any human social things."

"Yes. That's what that story pictured very well. So when you reach out to smell a flower, you already have a perception of the plant and its characteristics, and this guides your behaviour. You understand that this is a flower, that flowers are beautiful and normally have a pleasant scent, that they can be smelled and so on.

"Similarly, before you can sit behind the wheel and drive, you must attend several training sessions with an instructor to learn to drive. That means you try to develop a mental image of the characteristics of a car, its functionality and its role within the overall urban and traffic system. You act, based on this acquired knowledge.

"The same is true when you work in an organisation. You either already have or will gradually develop a conceptual map of the office's structure, its functions and the relationships among its components and members. This understanding helps you grasp your own role, responsibilities and position within that system. As a member and an employee, at every moment of your activities, that overall mental map guides your actions and behaviour. If it doesn't, you might be confused, and chances are you'll get in trouble!

"So to engage and cooperate with any structure or system, one must have a mental understanding of its components and their relationships, and act accordingly.

"The same principle applies to people's relationships with various structures, including political systems and governance. For any government or regime to function and govern, individuals must internalise a mental framework of its structure, and envision their own place within its dynamics. As long as people do this, consciously or subconsciously, they'll serve and sustain the system. The system will only collapse when people cease to acknowledge its structure and authority in their minds.

"This principle applies to law, governance, ethics and all other societal structures. To interact with any phenomenon, we must first have an internal understanding of it. What this means is that all social systems and structures are primarily mental and psychological beings," said Shabe.

"After World War II ended in 1945 and countries like Nazi Germany and Imperial Japan were defeated, all military operations ceased," Shabe explained. "However, some individuals continued to follow their wartime orders, believing the conflict was still ongoing. One of the most remarkable examples is Hiroo Onoda, a Japanese intelligence officer who stayed hidden in the jungles of the Philippines for nearly 30 years. Convinced that the war had not ended, he carried out guerrilla activities until 1974, when his former commander travelled to the island to personally relieve him of duty."

"Wow. That's unbelievable," Soren interjected.

"Yes, I have read about him and have seen some of his interviews," Sally added.

"Astounding, isn't it?" Shabe said before going on. "Onoda only surrendered after receiving that direct order. Obviously, such people did that due to the perception that the war process was still in place and had to be served."

Sally nodded musingly.

Shabe added, "This story shows how far our actions are shaped not by what's really there but by what we believe is there. Even if a system is gone, if we still think it's in place, we keep serving it. That's why profound change doesn't happen just because something outside of us collapses. It happens when something inside us shifts—when our understanding changes. This phenomenon applies not only to political or economic structures but to all aspects of our life, including the false language."

Sally interrupted. "Could you explain again what the false language is?"

"Sure!" Shabe replied. "As we discussed earlier, the false language is a means of exchanging baseless values and instilling false notions of superiority and inferiority through words, gestures and behaviour. In this language, people trade things that do not actually exist. Its function is not to exchange knowledge or truth but rather to manipulate and exert psychological and behavioural dominance."

"How fascinating! Please go on."

"So, as we said, the concept of inner society also applies to this deceitful language and its psychological games. You only react to the false language when you have internalised and believed in it. Others' words and games can only cause distress or inferiority if you accept them as real. In fact, the false language is a game where nothing of substance is exchanged. People chase *greatness* or fear *smallness*, but these are only illusions. A wise person knows that when a competition is over nothing, you don't win by being a better player; you win by leaving the game entirely. And that's what most people overlook."

Sally paused, reflecting. "So the solution is to step out of the entire sinister network?"

"Exactly."

"Thanks. I'm all ears."

"Shabe says you should have a head and mouth too, Mum!" Soren said.

"Oh, of course!" Sally said, and they all laughed.

Watching them, Melody joined in, grinning at them and clapping her hands joyfully. That made them all even laugh louder.

After a moment, Shabe reached for his worn leather bag and pulled out a notebook.

"This is the bag I told you about," Soren whispered to his mother.

Sally nodded with a twinkle and a smile.

"Well, I'm guessing Soren's told you what we've discussed so far regarding our inner suffering. We've tried to examine the causes behind these difficulties, which include influences by the environment, and pressures from receiving blame and reproach, all of which are used to preserve society's pseudo-values. And in case you don't know, this term refers to the values that our own interpretative minds deceive us with."

"Oh, yes." Sally smiled, squeezing Soren's knee. "Soren's told me about these."

"Then we turned to the methods used by society to dominate the individual's ideas and emotions. We found such treatments as reproach, belittlement and even praise and admiration can be tools to keep individuals compliant and subdued. This leads to us acquiring baseless values and adopting them as part of who we are, leading to the birth of an alien entity we call ego or the outward I.

"Also, we've tried to vividly define each of the terms we've used, at least to ourselves. They include interpretation, humiliation, false language, values, the outward I, the value-stricken person, the fake personality and the like.

"Despite saying that, I'd stress that we must not overlook the valuable support and services we receive from society, including knowledge, training, care and services. Our goal is not to paint an entirely bleak picture but to uncover the underlying causes of our behavioural and emotional struggles.

"As you mentioned, we seek a deeper understanding of the common roots of human affliction, allowing us as individuals to contextualise our own challenges within this broader perspective. In essence, our inquiry is diagnostic, not dismissive. We do not intend to undermine or deny the help and support provided by society."

"I see. That's very plausible, I think," Sally said.

"And one last point," Shabe continued. "We have emphasised that none of the issues we pinpoint absolve us from *our* responsibilities for an informed, liberated life. We shouldn't assume ourselves as passive, helpless elements at the hands of society. We're all responsible for constructing an examined, authentic life. If we are to shift the responsibility to society, who is supposed to change things? Society is nothing but you and me!"

Sally nodded. "I fully agree. I still have a few questions, though. If you don't mind?"

"Please, go ahead."

"Well, you've talked about reproach and comparison being wrong choices in treating humans, which I think is right and sensible. But what if my child is weak at a subject without any comparison? I mean, objectively behind the standard and needs improvement? Shouldn't I do something to help him improve?"

"Sure." Shabe picked up his iced tea and took a sip. "First, let's bear in mind that measures like school marks or contests are not necessarily precise indicators of the merits and abilities of children. At school, complying with set rules and standards matters far more than children's natural needs for growth and fulfilment. Likewise, tests and scores are designed to evaluate unique, diverse abilities against strict, universal guidelines—which, as you can see, doesn't work!

"Second, it's obvious I need to do everything I can to help my child flourish and improve; however, the question is: how would *blaming* my child help him improve? And even if it does, what's the benefit of such a so-called improvement if it's polluted by self-loathing and anxiety? I can take my child to the doctor or dietician, enrol them in a gym or music course, but what's the use of whipping them with reproach and criticism—other than, perhaps, satisfying my own unresolved, emotional needs?"

Sally nodded thoughtfully. "One more question?"

"Of course."

"From what you've talked about so far, I'd like to know why people have different levels of happiness. Why do some people show higher levels of violence or depression, while some are more confident and happier?"

"In my opinion," Shabe said, "although the outward I does exist in all of us, the issue of being value-stricken doesn't affect everybody equally; rather, it ranges from weakest to strongest among different persons."

"Can you explain?" Sally asked.

"Sure. Think of it this way. The mind is like a space in which various ideas flow, in the form of words and images. In the self-lost person, an appendage named the outward I lurks in the background of this space. This person might rarely pay direct attention to this background; however, this imposed identity always casts a shadow over their mind, giving them a sort of lethargy and heaviness.

"Imagine you've been deported to a remote town you don't like, nor do you feel safe there. In this town, you'll go about your daily life as normal; driving, shopping, walking around and chatting with others. At these moments, you might even forget you're living in an unsafe town; however, you're always subconsciously aware this isn't the environment you'd choose to live in.

"As a result, continual feelings of sorrow and gloom cast shadows over your mind. You experience despair, and its intensity depends on the extent of your hatred for this situation or how depressed you feel in this place. Whenever you hear someone talk about home or about this town, you are reminded of your exiled situation and your reluctance to be there.

"The speed and intensity of these reactions correspond with your level of discontent. By the same token, the issue of egoism does exist in nearly all individuals, but at different degrees, which is why people have various levels of inner peace and happiness."

"Oh, I see." Sally nodded.

"Like I said, when I feel that my pretty mask has been torn off and my unpleasant self is exposed, due to blame or criticism, for example, I have to grapple with shame, anger, and embarrassment," said Shabe. "The more negative my self-image, the faster it surfaces, and my mind tries every trick to cope."

"Interesting explanation," Sally said. "That must be why some people are more touchy or irritable than others."

"True," Shabe agreed. "And we usually adjust our life to the demands of this vulnerable I!"

Melody squirmed in her mother's arms.

Putting her down, Sally asked, "What does that mean?"

"It means we do or avoid many things to alleviate the pain of inferiority it always imposes on us."

"Oh!"

"Well, my last discussion with Soren was about the outward I and its inherent struggles. Today, we'll explore this further."

"Sounds good," Sally said. "But would you like to have lunch first?"

"Sure! I don't think I can resist that appetising smell any longer!"

At lunch, the three of them talked about Soren's writing and Shabe's former job at the circus, which Sally found intriguing. Long after the meal, they were still discussing the literature and mysticism of the East, and Shabe read some poetry of Khayyam and Rumi.

"It looks like what you call self-awareness, or self-knowledge, is a sort of philosophical psychology," Sally mused.

Shabe nodded. "It's both philosophy and psychology and more."

"You mean ..."

"If we agree that a human is part of the totality of the universe, we can also say knowledge of the human is part of the knowledge of the universe. Therefore, any science, from philosophy to biochemistry, from geography to physiology, is an integral part of our knowledge of ourselves."

"Then how do you define self-awareness?" Soren asked.

Shabe paused. "Self-awareness is the attempt to gain insight into ourselves and our world so that we can sensibly and consciously move towards happiness and harmony. But it goes deeper.

"At the heart of everything lies philosophy. Take a look at your feelings, emotions, and actions. They are rooted in concepts like love, justice, and fairness. Every choice you make, from friendships to conflicts, love to hate, fighting for right or what is a happy life for your children, is shaped by philosophical ideas. Even things like employment, marriage, education and motherhood are primarily philosophical notions, all associated with ideas we often take for granted."

Sally raised an eyebrow. "So self-awareness is about questioning everything we assume?"

"Yes, that's an essential part of being self-aware," Shabe said. "Living an informed, liberated life means questioning, deconstructing and redefining these notions. It's through insight and discretion that we achieve peace and harmony, both within us and in relation to the world around us. Rumi says,

> *'Love is the fruit of knowledge.*
> *Who can access this throne falsely?'"*

"Very interesting," Sally said. "I hear mystics generally undermine knowledge and reason, but Rumi clearly says the opposite."

"Yes," Shabe answered. "Many misconceptions go around about Rumi, including this one, but that's utterly wrong. Rumi was a great thinker and philosopher. He was a highly educated man with a great knowledge and reasoning informing his views and teachings, and of course, he condemns oblivion and ignorance most severely throughout his discourses."

After dinner, Shabe returned to his seat in the living room and was entertained by Melody and her playful antics. Soren and Sally cleared the table quickly and also returned.

"Well," Shabe began. "So far, we've covered five chapters together with Soren, and today we'll discuss what chapter six will cover: the consequences of bearing an imposed identity, the outward I. And I'll answer any questions, of course."

"Great, but I would like to read the last discussions. May I do so after it's been written down?" Sally asked.

"I'm writing the sections as we go," Shabe said. "I'll give you a copy as soon as the first draft is complete. That way you can also share any ideas."

"Wonderful!" Sally smiled. "Shall we begin?"

"Today, we're going to explore more of the potential difficulties of a value-oriented life. However, these issues are broad and diverse, and if we want to benefit from these discussions, we each need to identify examples of them in our own lives, feelings and relationships."

"When you look into these issues," Soren said, "it's as if you're taking a tour of your own being."

"It is! As we said in the beginning, this is a journey to the world, full of thrilling discoveries."

The Reed Moans

Shabe cleared his throat. "To begin, I'll read you a few lines of the opening poem of Rumi's masterpiece, *The Masnavi*. It goes:

'Hear this reed, how it laments,
Weaving the tale of separations.
Ever since cut off the reed bed,
Men and women have wept through my breath.
I seek a heart, ruptured by separation.
To share the sorrows of this longing.
He who is torn from his homeland
Yearns for the day of reunion.
My secret is not far from my moans
Yet eyes and ears remain blind to its light'"

Sally leant forward with interest. "Sounds like a significant poem. It's symbolic, of course."

"It is, and metaphorical," Shabe nodded, and went on. "In Eastern lands, crafting a reed flute starts with uprooting it from the reed bed and cutting off its roots. The plant then goes to a workshop where a red-hot metal rod is thrust through its heart, searing away the membranes that block its hollow throat so the musician's breath may flow freely through it.

"Next, with that same rod, holes are drilled into its body, openings that the musician's fingers will cover to create musical notes. Finally, its end is sealed, ensuring that whatever enters it emerges solely through its chest as music. Thus, the reed transforms into a flute only through hardship and refinement. The burns and cuts etched into its body and spirit allow it to create beautiful music."

"What a fascinating story," Sally murmured.

Shabe continued. "Concepts such as separation, authenticity, longing, exile, empathy and shared suffering are frequently repeated in Sufism, and particularly in Rumi's words. This repetition highlights the significance of these meanings in his thoughts. In Rumi's narrative, the reed serves as a metaphor for human beings, torn from their source, estranged from the paradise of unity and thrust into the illusory world of separations and disparities.

"Now, like the reed, we wander alienated in a dim exile, yearning for a lost peace and wholeness we can barely recognise. This separation has created an ever-present void—an unease that lingers, though many people attempt to fill it in misguided ways.

"Every human endeavour, whether kindness or cruelty, creation or destruction, friendship or rivalry, is ultimately an attempt to soothe this inner wound. Some people immerse themselves in success, power and possessions; others in pleasure and indulgence; some in oblivion; some in faith. Yet all that we do reflects a longing to return, to reclaim something lost.

"Fire is both a symbol of unrest and transformation. The reed must endure fire to give voice to its song; without fire, it remains silent. Fire is not merciful. It burns and melts, but it also purifies and transforms. We, too, face trials in life, enduring wounds and healing alike. But these struggles shape us, refine us and allow us to grow. Someone who has never experienced pain or loss is unable to comprehend the suffering of others, or to appreciate blessings, and lacks the longing for awakening and liberation. But the flute stays silent until it finds a companion, someone who understands the sorrow and shares the longing for reunion. Only then does the flute speak, revealing its tale of loss. The seemingly small, silent reed suddenly comes to life in the hands of the flute player. And then, all the vibrant melodies pour forth from its burnt chest as songs of longing and lament, of exile and yearning.

"Rumi's message for us is this: 'If you truly wish to hear these melodies, you must become intimate with secrets. You need to bring a heart torn open by love and desire. If you seek to hear, from the lips of the flute, the mystery of liberation and the song of union, then be the longing musician.'"

Shabe closed the book and laid it on the table in front of him. "As I mentioned, the first consequence of imposed values is the formation of the ego in our minds. When this false identity begins, people accept the illusion of separation and disunity, leading to the creation of all sorts of hate, enmity and struggles."

"That's very thought-provoking," Sally said. "So a human is like a drop that's been flung out of the ocean, separated from the entirety of the universe."

Shabe nodded. "Though, as I mentioned, humans feel separate from the world, rather than being actually detached from it. The ego, or the Nafs in the Sufis' language, is a mental phenomenon, and thus, the separation it causes is also purely mental and illusory.

"The truth is, while the outward person feels lonely, they're in absolute oneness with the universe. But they don't appreciate this unity and suffer from imagined separateness. That's why, as soon as we realise this separation exists only in our mind, we're elated to find that we are really part of the whole being and of humanity."

Self-Alienation

"It's a truly beautiful poem," Sally said.

Shabe smiled and paused for a moment, his gaze drifting, as if listening to an echo only he could hear. Then he turned back to Sally and Soren, his voice lower, more thoughtful.

"Also, consider this: in ancient Iran, and in some other Eastern lands, the pen was also crafted from reeds. They would cut it, shave its tip to the right shape, and dip it into ink to write, unlike in most Western countries, where quill pens were used instead. Just imagine what a second, subtle layer of meaning adds to Rumi's metaphor." He let the words trail off, then added softly, "But this layer of meaning ... I'll leave it to you, to ponder."

Sally's eyes lit up. "Wow. I must read the book."

"I've borrowed it from the library, Mum." Soren smiled. "*Masnavi M'anavi*, it's called. I'll share it with you."

"Lovely!" Sally smiled and kissed Soren on the cheek. "Thank you, sweetie. By the way, what does *Masnavi, M'anavi* mean?" Sally asked, hoping she had said the words correctly.

"*Masnavi* means *couplet*, which is a poetic format, and *Manavi* means *spiritual*. So the title is *The Spiritual Couplets*," Shabe answered and sipped his drink. Then he said, "So the other point is the human's self-alienation."

"Yes, go on," Sally said.

"As children, no sooner have we begun finding ourselves than we are flooded by overwhelming values burying our true selves under their weight. That's why we often don't clearly know who we are or what we want from life. We're estranged from ourselves, which means we're mostly empty of our true essence and full of borrowed thoughts and imposed wants and feelings. And this self-alienation gives us a constant feeling of suspension and insecurity. The self-alienated person is like someone possessed; whatever they say or do is not really willed or decided by themself; instead, it's the possessing forces ruling over their mind and life."

Conflict

"You put that very well," Sally commented.

"Thanks! As I've mentioned, the development of inner conflict is the chief consequence of inconsistent ideas. Conflict is an integral aspect of all mental and emotional complications, which makes it necessary to obtain adequate understanding of this phenomenon."

"True. Psychologists such as Jung and Adler have also addressed the issue of inner conflict." Sally said.

"That's right." Shabe nodded, stroking his chin. "Jung, Adler, Erikson and others had their own way of looking at inner conflict. Jung saw it as the tension between the different parts of the psyche – especially the self we show and the shadow we keep hidden. Adler saw it as that pull between feeling inadequate and trying to grow into someone stronger and more capable. And Erikson described it as the inner tension that appears at every stage of growth."

"Right." Sally nodded.

"All that said, what we aim to do here is to integrate all that precious insight into our own understanding of the bigger picture. Well, the suggestion of blameful values results in the formation of an illusive self-image."

"Pardon," Soren said. "Is that kind of the same as the imposed I?"

Shabe nodded. "Precisely, Soren."

"The imposed I?" Sally asked.

"Yes! An illusive image of yourself means seeing yourself the way others dictate to you, then assuming this really is you."

"Extraordinary!" Sally said.

"Yes! And in an environment where a child is exposed to mental or physical abuse, it's highly likely they'll develop a sense of ongoing insecurity and anxiety. The outcome is that the person, confused about the real meaning of life and distracted from what truly satisfies their needs and faculties, is instead compelled to pretend, constantly. In other words, they decide to collect various signs of power and worth to conceal what they assume as their unpleasant weaknesses. So they put on a mask of the socially promoted values and hide their truth behind it."

"This is a perceived truth, I understand, though?" Sally asked.

"Of course, as this so-called truth is what has been externally imposed," Shabe replied. "What happens in this process is two conflicting Is, or identities, are sprouting in our minds: first, the unpleasant I, which constitutes our current identity, and second, the ideal I, which we aim to achieve. Here is where a big chasm develops in our psyche: the conflict between what we are and what we think we ought to *be*."

"Ahh," Sally said. "But then what becomes of the real or true self?"

"Well," Shabe said. "Our true self is held captive in the process of the struggles between these two alien selves, like a person tied up by burglars in their own home. Mind you, one notable point is that conflict is not simply the outcome of our struggle to obtain the fake values; it lies in the very nature of them."

Sally sipped her juice. "How so?"

"Because fake values are essentially founded on conflicts. Each value can only be envisaged in contrast to its opposite. If you don't contrast fake values, they disappear," Shabe said. "Realising this point can save us from many errors in appreciating our problems. It can keep us from getting trapped in a vicious circle." Shabe glanced at Soren and Sally and added, "Baseless comparisons intensify even objective issues."

"What's an example of this?" Soren asked.

Shabe said, "Well, if I don't compare my disabled leg with your healthy one, being disabled will be less upsetting. Missing your home and family when you're away is a natural feeling, but constantly comparing where you are with where you imagine you'd like to be will only intensify your blue feelings and longing.

"But the point is, real things have their existence independent of comparison; they do exist even without us thinking of them.

"Take honesty. Whether I think about its opposite or not, being honest does leave its positive effects in my personal and social life. Or even if I don't think about theft, trustworthiness still involves real and practical advantages."

Sally said, "Could you explain that a bit more?"

"We don't need to consider honesty and its goodness to appreciate the harm that stealing causes. Stealing does have objective features and impacts, which our minds can believe. Or when you say that cold is annoying, you don't necessarily mean that heat is pleasant because you can feel and understand cold without thinking of heat," said Shabe. "This isn't the case with value concepts. When I consciously think I'm hopeless, I must envisage being powerful or talented to be able to picture being hopeless. Thus, the word hopeless doesn't hold an independent sense and isn't clear on its own. What that means is such concepts as uselessness, hopelessness and even pride-worthiness are merely mental and interpretative. They hold no objective reality."

Soren said, "But it looks to me that hopeless does have a clear meaning. For instance, we call someone hopeless or clumsy if they're not capable of managing their life or organising themself or able to do their jobs."

"Would you call your old, frail grandpa hopeless or clumsy if he had difficulty cleaning his room or doing his own jobs?"

"No, I wouldn't," Soren said.

"Why not?"

"Because hopeless is an insult."

"Right. Such words as hopeless and clumsy hold a negative mass. They contain feelings of anger and reproach. Unlike objective or neutral words, like impotent or weak, which don't necessarily hold such loads. That's why value-laden words, on the social level, cause hatred and enmity and, on the individual level, induce feelings of incompetence and worthlessness. So I reckon it's now clear that subjective values and traits are devoid of meaning. And people usually hate or fight over value-based words, not objective ones.

"To be precise, these values are born only out of comparison and labelling, because you can never imagine one of them alone. As long as I don't give my friend's luxurious car the label of *fashionable*, I can't think of my own car as *useless*. Or if I don't look at your job as *prestigious*, I can hardly look at mine as *lowly*."

Soren and Sally's faces showed great interest in the explanation.

Shabe continued. "So try that, right now! Think of a person or a house or anything else. Give it a value label like *high-profile, fashionable* or *outmoded*, and then try to envisage that characteristic without thinking of its opposite." Shabe paused.

Both Soren and Sally tried to do that.

Sally imagined her friend Martha's house, which she'd always thought of as *luxurious*. She tried hard to understand its luxuriousness without bringing the elements of humility or cheapness to mind, but she failed.

Soren also shut his eyes and tried to picture his dad as a heroic figure without comparing him to Hans's father, but he couldn't. After a few moments, Soren smiled and said, "I give up!"

"Very interesting! It looks like you just can't do that!" Sally said.

Melody, playing with her Legos and apparently trying to build a wall, repeated, "I tan't!"

All three laughed.

A few moments later, Shabe said, "You see how the mind baulks at doing that? This clearly shows these subjective attributes are hollow.

Without comparison, these pseudo-attributes simply disappear, which shows that our minds just made them up. They don't exist!"

Soren said, "That means when we're after values, we're after … nothing?"

"Totally right! The key insight here is that whenever we struggle with a negative trait, it's because we're comparing it to a positive one, and vice versa. Many struggle with inner turmoil because they overlook this. What we see as a *great person* and an *insignificant person* are just two sides of the same coin."

"Sorry. I didn't quite follow." Soren scratched his head.

Shabe answered, "Think of it this way. The *bad me* I try to avoid exists only because I also have an image of a *good me*. But that *good me* is just a reflection of the bad one. They define each other. They can't exist separately. You must've experienced the way our false feelings of pride and ability are contaminated by vague anxiety after we do something we're praised for. You'd have felt your happiness is not pure or light-hearted.

"The reason is that enjoyment comes from a feeling of relief from danger, the enjoyment of an escape! But we wouldn't be so attached to praise if we hadn't felt in danger. We say to ourselves, subconsciously, 'Thank goodness. I dodged it this time. I managed to cover my fears of inferiority with praise and approval; however, I shouldn't feel too much at ease, as danger is always lurking, so I must also be on the alert!'"

Shabe reached for his old bag and pulled a movie out. "Soren, could you put this film on?"

A few moments later, the scene of a massive circus emerged. Perhaps a thousand people of all ages were in the audience, their faces revealing enthusiasm and impatience for the entertainment to start. Red velvet curtains dominated the stage, and the intense lights behind them cast dazzling bright lights through the space.

Long, dark blue curtains divided the front of the stage from the back. After a brief wait, the curtains lifted, revealing the portly showman dressed in a black velvet frock coat, glossy black hat, white shirt with a black bow tie, polished dark shoes and sporting a thin moustache like all circus performers in movies.

After a warm greeting and a few jokes, he announced, "The first one to stun us all with his amazing artistic talents today is Allan Ralph, the master tightrope walker!"

Rapturous applause from the audience.

Allan appeared at the end of a tightrope, holding a long stick in his hands.

Soren and Sally exchanged a smile before looking back at the scene. To Soren, the rope looked over thirty metres high, stretching from side to side across the hall. After greeting the thrilled spectators, Allan started to walk along the rope, stepping with utmost care, holding the stick horizontally for balance. As the camera zoomed in, sweat dripped down his face, his eyebrows furrowed.

A while later, the camera angle changed. Apparently, a small camera was pinned to Allan's chest, showing the scene from the tightrope walker's viewpoint. The scene looked even more exciting—and scary. Allan's feet felt their way along the quivering rope with stunning mastery and artfulness.

Then the perspective shifted to show what Allan saw beneath his feet: spectators gazing up at him, clapping, screaming and whistling. Every now and then, the bright flash of a camera caught the unnerving image of the tightrope walker's scary situation.

Immersed in the scene, Soren and Sally's faces reflected their thrill and their worry with each step the performer took. The journey across the tightrope took several minutes but felt much longer. At the end, applause erupted from the delighted audience.

Shabe paused the video and said, "Well, that was exciting, wasn't it?"

"Yes, it really was!" Soren and Sally said simultaneously.

Soren asked, "Shabe, was that your circus?"

"Yes. Years ago! You know, back then, it felt like my whole world. Life under the big top, crowds cheering, the suspension, the rush of every act. Now, when I look at it, it's like watching a distant dream.

There was always so much going on beneath the surface." He leaned forward, his tone shifting to a more thoughtful one.

"What society does to introduce the outward I to an individual's mind looks exactly like what a circus does when it hires a tightrope walker to entertain people. The entertainer walks along the rope and receives people's applause. In this job, the danger of plunging from a high rope and the pleasure of people's applause are not separable but interdependent, as neither would exist without the other.

"The tightrope walker's goal in endangering himself is to earn people's applause, and people's reason to applaud is his willingness to take risks. Therefore, tightrope walking as a profession inherently involves a continual cycle of applause and danger. If either element were to be removed, the profession would no longer exist. And that's exactly like the process of humiliation and encouragement in creating and maintaining the outward I."

"That's an interesting metaphor, tightrope-walking!" Sally said.

"Yes, but I've spoken to Soren about taking care not to be fooled by examples," Shabe said.

"What do you mean?"

"Just take this example. Tightrope-walking is really a job and a form of art. A tightrope walker is paid for his labour, a real payment. However, the self-lost person jeopardises their life and assets in return for nothing but transient joy and constant worry and suspension.

"Anyway, back to the topic of conflicts. As I said, the *bad I* and the *good I*, one of which we avoid and the other we long for, form the two sides of the same fake coin, called the false personality, or the persona, if you like. The thing is, as our mind focuses on each, at any time, it doesn't notice this oneness. Rumi calls this illusion cross-eyed-ness.

> '*This double vision is the illusion*
> *Of the cross-eyed mind.*
> *Otherwise, the beginning is the end,*
> *And the end is the beginning.*'

"So, in my obsession with prestige, I ignore the fact that the outward character is not something I can grasp; it's the very process of blaming myself. The imposed identity consists of values founded on self-disown and the resultant urge to always be something else. In other words, the ideal personality is not a goal; it's the mindset of constant discontent with oneself and one's situation. Thus, if I become afraid or insecure, the answer isn't to try to grasp more and more values; rather, it's to comprehend the falsehood of the ideal personality. I need to realise my problem is not that I'm weak or inferior; it's that I'm trapped in a vicious circle, rejecting myself and wishing to be someone else. That's the error entangling my mind, turning it into a closed circuit.

"So, as Rumi says, any attempt to achieve a better I is like washing blood with blood. And the way out of this cycle of pain is to become aware of the empty game of the values and lose interest in them. What I need to understand is that my weakness is not being imperfect; it's in rejecting my imperfections. When I finally accept myself as I am, with all my faults and strengths, and stop pressuring my psyche, I'll suffer neither inferiority nor try to attain the ideal character. That is, I'll find peace of mind and being."

Shabe stopped to wait for anything Soren or Sally might have to say.

Sally said, "My query is about growth and perfection. As humans, we're perfection-oriented, after all. We all want to grow and thrive, though some go astray, but how do you define perfection, and is it really achievable?"

Shabe answered, "To me, these two words, *perfection* and *achievement*, are mutually exclusive. Incompatible, if you like."

"How come?"

"We need to clarify a goal for ourselves before we go after it. Very often, we simply invest our life and energy to achieve something, without ever having tried to define what it really is and how it can be reached, if at all. Happiness, success, calm and the good life are only a few examples of such ideals. Likewise, we must have a clear understanding of the concept of perfection to aim for. In fact, perfection is not a destination, it's a continuous journey," said Shabe.

"That sounds very insightful. As one poet said, 'Watch the road closely; there's no destination ...' But there's another question, if you don't mind," Sally said.

"Definitely not."

"If I accept myself as I am, as you suggested, what will motivate me to improve and flourish?"

"I know what you mean. First, let's clarify that. Accepting ourselves doesn't mean doing nothing; it means we shouldn't condemn our situation or blame ourselves. And these are two different attitudes. Obviously, if I abandon my broken car, it won't fix itself. Or, if I'm ill, if I don't think of a treatment or take action, my health might be at risk. However, what I mean is such reactions as blaming, being angry with or rejecting myself only block ways towards sensible and constructive actions.

"Second, in us humans, like in all other creatures, there exist mechanisms of growth and self-protection. For example, we all have curiosity, which is a natural drive for discovering the unknown, acquiring knowledge and building an ever-better life.

"And all people are inclined to love and care, which is a factor in sustaining the family and society, and for cooperation among humans. These intrinsic drives, combined with our powers of thinking and reasoning, keep our lives moving and thriving. However, one thing's for sure: being thrown into self-blame and inner conflicts will hardly help solve any problem."

Soren said, "I was also wondering about something to do with blame."

"Sure," Shabe said.

"Once, my auntie said something about this. Suppose Jess, my cousin, is behind in her studies most of the time because she's naughty and doesn't pay attention. If my auntie didn't tell her off, would she have any motive to change her ways? And if my auntie did and said she was lazy and irresponsible, wouldn't that push her to wake up and do better?"

"The answer is no! It's just the opposite!" Shabe said.

Soren joked. "Excuse me. Would you mind answering yes, for once, for God's sake?" Then he blushed. "You always say, 'Oh, it's just the opposite!'"

Sally and Shabe both laughed.

"Look, when you reproach Jess, the problem doubles," said Shabe. "One, that she's behind in her lessons; two, that she's a lazy and reckless child.

"Being behind in lessons is an external, objective issue, but being a naughty person is an internal and subjective problem, a psychological one, if you like. Labels such as *lazy* and *reckless* stick in our minds, then produce inner problems and psychological pains.

"By reproaching her, what happens is that a realistic problem, such as difficulty with school, gets overshadowed by a more sensitive one, the fear of being a bad person. So she'll just be proving that she's not lazy and reckless. Even if she does study better, that'll be more because she's afraid of blame and accusations, not because she loves learning or wants to gain knowledge."

"My take is the same," Sally said.

Shabe continued. "And, as well as that, experience shows the resentment that teasing and tormenting would trigger in us could rob her of her interest in study or any other useful activity."

Shabe was silent for a few moments, and went on. "In fact, this is a major flaw in the way we approach teaching and education. In the hierarchy of human needs, feeling safe and secure comes before curiosity and discovery. If you're in a threatening situation but also come across something interesting to discover or learn about, naturally, your first instinct will be to protect yourself, not explore. You can only focus on learning once you feel safe.

"But in our education system, students find themselves constantly under pressure, worrying about low grades, attendance penalties or failing a subject. That's a real contradiction. The very system that's supposed to encourage learning disrupts it by creating anxiety, which gets in the way of real understanding and engagement. That's why many people, after they finish school, have no interest in more education or learning. That's not a small problem; it's a tragedy!"

Fear and Insecurity

"Well, that takes us to the next topic," Shabe said. "Other after-effects of labelling someone are fear and lack of confidence. How would you define *fear*, Soren?"

"It's a feeling that danger's nearby."

Sally said, "It can also be a survival mechanism, a means to protect a living thing from danger or harm. If we're not afraid of accidents, we might lose our lives. Or if we aren't afraid of heights, we might fall off a cliff and put our health at risk."

Shabe said, "Yes. Though I don't think it's only fear that drives us to care for our lives or others'. We have other strong motives as well, such as reason, compassion and love. Anyway, I'd add here that, unlike natural fear, the worry that comes out of a value-oriented thought has two sides. First, it's a blind fear of a vague danger, not a sensible, realistic one. And second, it's not a reasoned and short-lived fear, but a persistent one that shows up as habitual worry and anxiety. This person fears they are incapable and worthless.

"Most of the relationships and activities of the self-lost person are various types of fear and fleeing, either directly or indirectly. And if they're constantly thinking about fleeing, they lose any joy in just being alive and waste their precious life in worry and disquiet. One place where this fear can clearly be seen is in relationships. We're afraid of each other, and yet we need each other's approval. So the shadow of worry and caution generally poisons our relationships."

"What's your definition of *self-confidence*?" asked Sally.

"Good question! We should all ask ourselves that question when we think about such ideas as having, or lacking, self-confidence. What is this self in which we can be confident? Should we rely on a trembling and shaky thing? Can a self, whose life and death is up to others, be relied on?

"In the true sense, self-confidence is feeling you can rely on your own powers of thinking and action. This attitude forms the foundation of our calm and happiness. And it's the very opposite of fear and shakiness," said Shabe.

"That's why, if you look closely, you'll see society always targets your confidence to manipulate you. To make you doubt your capabilities. To make you hesitant about your goodness and ability. And this is a trick employed by *all* systems of abuse and exploitation, whether it's political, cultural or economic."

Sally was looking rather disappointed. "So what do you think about methods of boosting confidence?"

"It depends on what you think of as confidence and what method is used. Many imagine that by repeating, 'I'm not afraid of that' or 'I'm a worthy person' fifty times a day, they'll become a self-confident person.

"But self-confidence isn't something you can add on to yourself. Self-confidence means you have no fear, hesitation or shakiness. When you don't have to depend on others' approval for your worth and merits, you'll enjoy profound, inherent confidence, without having to inject confidence into your psyche through slogans and mottos."

Ignorance

"What you're saying sounds absolutely right. We shouldn't easily buy into everything we hear. Many things have lost their true meanings," Sally said.

"As it happens, the next topic we'll discuss is *ignorance*, which comes from imposed, baseless ideas."

"How does this ignorance get into our minds?" Soren asked.

"As children, we're attacked by social brainwashing, which fills up our minds with other people's myths." Shabe looked at Soren and his mum over the rim of his glasses and added, "Like I said, that's apart from the useful guidance we get from our family, teachers or others about hygiene, health and, to some extent, observing others' rights."

He went on. "Ask ten people to define such words as *love, justice, patriotism, respect, personality* and *knowledge*. Everyone thinks they know the meaning of these words, but the ideas they'll give you are vague and contradictory.

"Like I said before, these are the concepts that form the foundations of our thoughts and reasoning. We behave, judge and feel based on these ideas, but surprisingly, we rarely have a clear idea what they are! This way, our outlook on most crucial things is founded on confusing, contradictory thoughts and feelings.

"Hardly anyone tells a child they don't know the meaning of friendship or respect or asks them to think about tradition and justice, then try to define these words for themself. Ever noticed how few ever teach a child the art of discovering something for themself but how everybody tries to put ideas in their mind?

"With this bombardment with the known, the child, who inherently loves learning and discovering, is gradually afflicted by false saturation, and then as an adult, they see little point in trying to think about the meanings of things. So people's minds get crammed with involuntary information, and they mistake this known-ness for knowing.

"Known-ness is the most destructive form of ignorance! It forms a network of oblivion and prejudice, which plays a massive role in the emergence of selfish and ignorant actions," said Shabe.

"Remember how, in our discussions about how we treat children, we talked about an imported self-image that gets shaped by subjective interpretations? I'd like to add this: a world-image also emerges out of the prefabricated conceptions, but it's a vague and contradictory one."

The Remote Control

Shabe paused and sipped his tea.

Sally excused herself to do some tasks. A few minutes later, she came back with Melody and saw a present on the table.

"Mum, Shabe's got something for Melody," said Soren.

Shabe picked up the gift and offered it to her. "Here, darling. Take it. It's yours!"

Melody ran up and grabbed the attractively gift-wrapped present, then sat down and tore the paper off to reveal a beautiful doll with long hair wearing a gorgeous pink-and-blue dress. Melody picked up the doll joyfully and said, "Tank you!"

Shabe smiled and said, "You're welcome, love. I'm glad you like it!"

Sally said, "Oh, it's such a nice dolly, isn't it, Melody? Thanks a lot, Shabe! You really shouldn't have."

"Look how excited she is!" Soren said.

"Now, look at this, Melody!" Shabe said and clapped his hands.

At the sound, the doll also clapped her hands. Melody loved this and laughed.

Then Shabe whistled, and the doll started to laugh. After a few moments, Shabe whistled twice, and the doll started crying.

Soren tested this, and his mum did the same.

All three were cheered by Melody's delight.

Posing like a spokesman, Shabe picked up the notebook and announced, "Well, I now call the meeting to order!"

Soren and his mum laughed.

"Please, go ahead," said Sally.

Shabe said, "The self-lost person's situation is like this remote-control toy. A toy is controlled by one or two persons, but the outwardly person is like a machine with hundreds of remotes, each one in the hand of a different person."

Soren glanced at his mum, and they smiled. Melody was fully occupied with the doll.

Shabe went on. "At any moment, anyone can push a button, if they wish, and the machine has to follow hundreds of commands from many different operators at the same time. And with any one command it obeys, it can't do anything but feel guilty, as it has inevitably disobeyed the other operators. The result is the value-obsessed person is rootless, dragged here and there with every new command.

"A painful consequence of this mentality is over-dependence on others' judgements because, in fact, to the self-lost person, being good is the same as being approved of. Other people must decide if what they do is right and acceptable.

"So the self-lost person has put the lead of their thoughts and feelings into the hands of others. They're like a slave who depends on their master for food, shelter and wellbeing. It is up to the master whether to feed them or leave them starving and, if they're angry, to torture and whip them.

"So the value-driven person must constantly be aware of others' judgements, as they can easily devastate them morally by a tiny amount of approval or disapproval. They could lift this person up as high as the moon or drop them down to the ground.

"Before doing anything, the humiliated person must ask for social permission, often in their own mind, of absent others. It's natural, then, for them to find themself skewered by others' verdicts and feel imprisoned and frustrated, whether they show it or not.

"If you look closely, you'll see this is the story of most of us. We don't have emotional independence. It feels like our hearts are tied with ropes held by several people, who pull from every side and rob us of peace and security. We're mentally and emotionally controlled by others."

Projection

Shabe went on. "The over-dependent person desperately reaches out to others to find cures for the pain they feel inside themselves. This is a greatest obstacle to freedom."

"I reckon we call that *projection*," Sally said.

"Correct! The outwardly person doesn't really understand the nature of their problem and, in fact, doesn't want to! Surprisingly, they'll find it hard to believe the roots of their suffering are inside themself, even when they're told. And unsurprisingly, they tend to blame others for their real or perceived difficulties. This is what makes them more entangled in this complex cobweb.

"Rumi beautifully describes this blind striving to release ourselves.

> *'Someone put a thorn under the donkey's tail.*
> *It doesn't know how to rid itself.*
> *It only jumps up and down.*
> *The more it jumps, the worse the pain.*
> *There needs to be a wise man*
> *To take the thorn off and rid the animal.'"*

Soren laughed. "*Masnavi's* stories are all fascinating!"

Sally agreed. "They're very telling, and I think that's because the examples are so charmingly pictorial."

"I bet if Rumi was here now, he'd use a lot of visual art, especially drama and movies," Soren said.

Shabe smiled. "Yes, I'm sure he'd make engaging action movies that were both profound and thought-provoking."

"And he'd make use of various tricks and techniques in them. Just imagine that!" Soren said.

Sally laughed and asked Shabe, "Who's meant to be the wise person who can help a person to pluck a thorn from their soul? Is it a mentor or a guru? Or something else?"

"That's an important question. You know, when I'm blind because of my own ignorance, how can it help me to follow a sighted person, however wise and knowledgeable, to solve my problems? Really, the only way to light and brightness is to help me open my eyes and enhance my awareness."

"I see," Sally said. "And I suppose that would be through knowledge and intellect."

Shabe continued. "Absolutely. Rumi believed in two levels of reason or intellect in humans, which he called The Universal Intellect and The Partial Intellect . This refers to two types of attitude or comprehension or, let's say, sight and insight.

"The Partial Intellect holds a confined and shallow understanding of things. It can hardly see and grasp the whole picture. Thus, in the context of our discussions, The Partial Intellect is the level of reasoning obsessed with value calculations and achievements. Rather than being aware of its role and place in the network of empty struggles, it surrenders to it and gets absorbed into it.

"But The Universal Intellect is a liberated and realistic way of thinking, one that holds a profound and holistic grasp of things. With such an insightful comprehension, it can well serve our true growth and wellbeing, both physical and moral.

"This Universal Intellect has stepped out of the narrow circle of illusive values and can see truths. It's awake and aware. We need this other level of intelligence to emerge and grow in our being, otherwise we can never break out of the inner prison of delusions brought on by imitative, value-obsessed thought."

"So could we say that the wise person refers to someone who can see the problem with an open mind or, like you said, with a non-interpretive attitude?" Sally asked.

"Right! And such a person can help others understand their problem, rather than struggle in darkness. Though, of course, no one can help anyone change if they don't genuinely want to."

"I agree."

"But most importantly, the wise guide must ultimately be the power of thinking, examining and selecting that's in all of us," Shabe explained. "After all, no one can think or see *for* us. Others, however wise and knowledgeable, can only help and guide us on our way towards growth and enlightenment. We need to see and choose for ourselves."

Running for a Mirage

Shabe had more to say. "One more thing to consider is that subjective values are unreachable. They are not accessible as real objects."

Sally asked, "How come?"

"Just ask yourself: 'Why do I want to gain these values? Why do I long to be someone special?'" Shabe paused to see if Sally and Soren had any suggestions.

Sally said, "Well, I reckon because we feel we're not good enough. We've accepted that we're worthless."

"That's right! And so, whatever level we supposedly reach, we still carry the image of an inferior person in our mind. We cannot help feeling the image we've won is nothing but a mask.

"The reason we often take offence at any little criticism is because we're like a robber carrying a stolen item around under their clothing all the time. They're always worried about disclosure and scandal. This masked person is habitually worried about their *smuggled self*. That's why, when they're criticised, they feel like they've been arrested in the act of smuggling."

"Interesting simile," Sally commented. "So you think the reason for our sensitivity is fear of disgrace?"

"Often, yes. Another reason for the inaccessibility of the outward character is its false and unreal essence. Suppose I felt ashamed because my dad's only a labourer. So I decided to study and get a prestigious job as a professor. But my aim is not to acquire knowledge; it's to rid myself of the inferior label of a labourer and gain the more prestigious status of an academic.

"Now, ask yourself, why is being a labourer shameful? If you put aside your habitual ideas and looked at the facts, you'd see this. A labourer is someone whose job mainly involves physical activity. That's all!

"Where on earth does shame or inferiority come into it? And if it doesn't, where does this inferiority *we* feel come from? Obviously, from our own minds. Surely, *we* are the ones who attach shame and embarrassment to such things as labouring. These attributes don't exist in reality.

"Now ask the same question about being a manager or a boss. Where in this job do you find qualities of being prestigious and high-profile? A manager is simply someone who's studied a subject, worked in it for some time and gained a good level of skill. They use these skills and earn corresponding money for what they do.

"These are the facts about this job, detached from any illusive, imaginary values. So where in this job do pride or prestige lie? Why should a manager need to brag about this career or feel superior to others?" Shabe said.

"Well, I think a boss or manager has trained and learned a lot of skills, so that must be a difference from someone with little knowledge or ability," Soren suggested.

"Yes. It does make a difference. This person, ideally, has studied and trained for years and is therefore enjoying an easier job with more advantages and is being paid for having higher skills. But why would they also need to boast or imagine themself more worthy or important than others?"

Sally said, "I think that does make sense, Soren."

"Remember, we agreed to cast aside our mental conventions and look at things with fresh eyes. Is it clear now why the outward character is something unreachable? Because these are imaginary things, not real! So they can never be gained or lost.

"The question is, what are you trying to gain? Something of your own imagination? What are you going to get rid of? Your mental illusions?"

"Hafiz beautifully describes this futile struggle. He says,

'Tell the tradesmen of the world of delusions.
Lessen your merchandise,
As profit and loss are the same.'"

Sally said, "I like that. A trade of delusions! It means buying and selling fantasies!"

"That's right," Shabe said. "Now, suppose an old friend suddenly showed up and said, 'How's the poor labourer going?' How would I feel?" he asked.

"Ashamed and embarrassed, for sure," Soren said.

"Well, wouldn't that be the same feeling I suffered before I became a boss? If that prestige was real, why did it disappear? What have I been collecting all these years, then? Something that vanishes with a puff?" Shabe asked.

Sally said, "Yes, good question!"

"Here's another one. Don't worry; it's an easy one! Suppose I'd worked hard for years and saved two hundred thousand dollars, and then someone said, 'You're poor. You have no money!' Would my money disappear? Would I feel poor because of their words?"

Soren said, "Of course not!"

"Why? Because what I'd obtained was real. But why should I feel inferior with just a few words by another person? Doesn't that mean the status I think I've won is a fantasy? If I thought about that question, I wouldn't have wasted precious days of my life going after something imaginary," Shabe said.

"I remember your saying once that, sometimes, a few moments thinking can change a whole life," Soren said.

Sally followed up. "But why is that? I mean, I'm still not clear why personality is something unreal or, as you say, imagined."

"Look, as I said, what we're talking about is not our real personality. It's the false mask, which relies on approvals and affirmations, and naturally fluctuates with them.

"It's like a Lego house that children build," said Shabe. "Each child contributes a Lego piece until a whole house is formed. If any child takes any brick off, the building will lose a piece somewhere. Or if they change their mind about any piece, they tamper with the shape or colour of the house. Similarly, the showy character is like a shaky Lego shelter. But we don't have to take refuge in such an insecure shelter. Once we get out of it, we'll live free from fear and stress."

"How can we move out from under this shelter?" Sally asked.

"Well, the outward I is a creature that lives within us, but it's imposed by others. Looking at it from that angle, we'd lose our interest in it. So the fewer our concerns for it, the deeper our serenity."

Shabe then opened his notebook and wrote. "At this moment, little Melody is sitting on the carpeted floor, busy playing with her toys, free from all these fusses, in absolute joy and light-heartedness …"

The Doubled Pains

A few moments later, Shabe asked, "If you're not tired, let's move to the next topic."

"I'm not tired at all. I'm enjoying it," Soren said.

Sally nodded with a smile. "We've set aside our whole day for this. Please go ahead," she said.

So Shabe did. "Being value-obsessed often aggravates our pain. If you look closely, you'll see that this mentality adds a second layer of emotional suffering to the actual, practical problems."

Sally said, "I can guess why …"

"Suppose I couldn't earn decent money to provide my family with a convenient life. Poverty is a real hardship that needs to be dealt with by all possible means.

"So the healthier my physique is and the stronger my morale is, the more effectively I can face challenges like this and get them sorted out. But, if I had a value-occupied attitude, I'd be far more concerned about how I'm regarded in society than how to find solutions to the practical problems of my life.

"I'd be more concerned by the idea of being pitied and called a poor thing, and that would torment me more than my down-at-heel shoes would. The reason is clear. Psychological pains are always more overwhelming than physical ones to us humans. And, as value-related issues tend to be more urgent to us, my energy would mainly be sucked up by those concerns, stopping me from freely attending to real, practical problems."

"Makes sense," Sally murmured.

Shabe added, "And let's not forget that many of the secondary issues of poverty, such as emotional difficulties, violence, crime and addiction, are caused by feelings of worthlessness, rather than poverty itself."

Sally said, "But I think you mentioned we're social beings. We need to belong, to feel accepted and loved. It seems natural for us to seek that connection."

"You're absolutely right. It is natural to like being accepted and to enjoy the support and admiration of others. But there's a difference between appreciating those things and becoming dependent on them.

"Enjoying or valuing something is one thing, but feeling over-dependent on it—needing it as if it's a vital necessity—is something else. It's fine to value approval, but the real issue comes when our sense of self-worth hinges on it. When not getting approval sends someone spiralling into despair or when they feel like they're nothing without constant praise. That's where the real problem lies."

"I'm getting it, I guess," Sally said.

Shabe continued. "For example, as a director, I'm naturally pleased when I see the audience enjoying my drama or when they tell me they found it artistic and impressive. Or when readers praise my book and find it thought-provoking, it feels rewarding to witness the positive impact of my work.

"However, why should I plunge into despair or feel worthless if I don't receive that approval for any reason? Why should my sense of worth and confidence be tied to others' opinions or actions?"

"That's because of identification, I suppose; they take everything personally as they identify themselves with it. Is that it?" Soren asked, his hands under his chin, looking at Shabe over the edge of his glasses.

"Well done, Soren. Precisely so. You've grasped things very well," Shabe answered.

Sally gave Soren an encouraging smile, raising her eyebrows in praise.

Shabe went on. "Any natural need or desire can turn into an excessive or unhealthy dependency. Take our need for food and drink or the need for safety and wellbeing. These are natural and necessary at a healthy level.

"But if we become excessively fixated on them, they can turn into unhealthy compulsions, resulting in obesity, blood-sugar issues and indigestion or obsessive fear and unhealthy overprotection. In these cases, they end up disrupting our wellbeing instead of serving it."

"Sounds right," Sally said.

Conditioning

Shabe looked at his watch and said, "Well, do you want to see a bit more of the circus?"

"Oh, yes! Why not?" Sally said.

Shabe pushed the button of the player, and a new scene appeared.

The ringmaster came on stage again and announced, "Ladies and gentlemen, Joe Z and his extraordinary dog, Alex, will perform the next item on the program today. Alex is a genius dog whose astounding abilities will leave you speechless!"

A few seconds later, the ringmaster stepped aside as another circus man entered with a little black, fluffy dog. He had thick, wavy hair and wore a loose blouse of shiny fabric with full sleeves, along with tight trousers and white, pointed shoes. The dog had black, wavy hair, just like its master, and wore a tiny white waistcoat and a gold necklace, looking cheerful and energetic, eager to start the show.

Joe Z gave a bow to the impatient audience, and after hugging and stroking Alex, they started the show. First, the band played slow music, and Alex danced to it. As the music played, the dog lifted one back leg and then the other, then its front feet, one by one. Then it began walking on its hind legs, wagging its tail. As soon as the music stopped, Alex did too.

Multiple flashing cameras from the audience members cast a bright light on the scene, washing over the entire hall for a second.

Upbeat Spanish music came next, and the dog followed the lively rhythm. The audience, thrilled by Alex's amusing moves, cheered him on with whistles, screams and applause.

Soren and his mum were clearly enjoying the performance too.

When it was time for numbers and leaps, Joe brought in some numbered cubes and set them on the stage. The show involved him calling out, "What's five plus five?"

Alex jumped to the corresponding number as if to say, "This is the answer." This trick was repeated several times.

Next, Joe asked the spectators to call out a simple addition, which they did. Amid their laughter and applause, Alex jumped on different cubes. The little dog performed a few more tricks. He climbed onto a box; Joe held a ring in front of him, and the dog leapt through it. Each ring was soon replaced by a smaller one. The smaller the ring, the louder the audience's applause for the intelligent dog.

Finally, Joe stood in the middle of the scene, bowing and saying goodbye to the audience. Alex stood on his hind legs, wagging his tail and clapping his paws. Then both left the stage to the audience's rowdy applause.

Soren and Sally also laughed and gave a few claps.

Shabe stopped the film and looked at Soren and his mother for their reactions.

"That was really exciting!" Sally said.

"Yes, it was! I'd love to go to the circus again and watch things closely. We've only had the circus visit once, and I was really little."

"And I was in it," Shabe said, winking with a smile.

"You're kidding?!" Soren exclaimed, staring at Shabe in shock.

"Really?" Sally asked. "That's amazing! I remember it was a very exciting one. So professional. Good job!"

"Thanks. Perhaps it was a good job, but a change of job felt better." Shabe said with a chuckle.

"I do agree," Soren said, also laughing.

They discussed some of the memories they all had from the circus.

"So, you already knew our town when you moved here as a teacher, didn't you?" Sally said.

"I did, like I told Soren. And I'd met many of the people, though no one could remember me for obvious reasons," Shabe said smilingly.

"For the mask!" Soren commented, menacingly.

They all laughed and then Sally turned to Shabe. "I bet that video is the introduction to another riveting discussion?"

"You win!" Shabe said. "A symptom of self-loss is being programmed. Or brainwashed. This isn't a minor issue. It robs us of the power of free thought and turns us into automatic, compulsive beings."

"Just like Alex! Poor dog!" Soren said.

"That's right. A *reactionary* being." Shabe pushed his glasses back up his nose. "It's impossible to arrive at a sound understanding of our problem without proper appreciation of what it means to be programmed. The human mind can be trained and conditioned, just like an animal's. You can feed your beliefs and behaviours into people's minds by suggestion and indoctrination. We can be trained to recognise particular *goods* and *bads*.

"We've already been conditioned, psychologically and behaviourally, by our environment to act and react in certain ways. But as you saw, social indoctrination starts in childhood. That's when our inexperienced minds are like a blank sheet of paper, ready to be written on when we can hardly make decisions or judge things wisely.

"But as adults, we don't have to rely on others for our survival as much as we did as children. An adult has the power of analysis and judgement. But the problem is that social indoctrination has been so powerful that it's gradually shaped our entire outlook, beliefs and attitudes in its own desired ways.

"Obviously, as an adult, I don't need others to make judgements for me or to tell me what kind of person I am. Yet I keep criticising myself according to other people's standards. When I look at it properly, I know this spoils my life. Even when no one's around to judge me, I judge myself by these learned standards.

"Thirty years ago, my dad said, 'You're such a disappointment!' Today, I still see myself as that disappointing boy. For thirty years, I've been desperately acting so people will confirm I'm a valuable person, even though I've become rich, famous and socially acclaimed. Yet I still feel the old wound from that word—*hopeless*—stamped on my soul."

Sally was following these explanations and reviewing her own experience. She realised most of those who contacted the *Weekly's* office had issues of the same sort. She wondered how she could put this insight to use in her own profession.

Shabe said, "If you pay attention, you'll see how strong an influence others have over how we feel about ourselves. Even when they're absent! Isn't that unnatural? Why should others dictate how I must feel about my worth, actions or rightness? It's like they've implanted a mental chip into our minds!

"As a result of conditioning, our actions and reactions are nearly always the same, and we have little control over them. They're strongly habitual. For example, if we're praised, we can get boastful and ecstatic. If we're criticised, we lose ourselves. If we're ignored, we get sad and offended. If we receive attention, we think we don't really deserve it. We can hardly change the ways we think and behave!

"One further point. Here, and in many other things in life, our scale for judgement is I—the outward I, in fact. Have you noticed that if this I is given what it wants, the world seems a great place, and the person who's given you that is the best one ever! But, if this I is denied what it wants, it feels like life is dark and gloomy and the person denying you is the worst human ever! You see how stupid and short-sighted this I is? And how this selfish being has shortened our sight and narrowed the way we see the world?

"I see things from the tiny window of my own interests. I lack the insight to see things in a broader way. For example, I don't care that you're a kind and caring wife to your husband, an efficient counsellor to your clients or a valuable member of society. I only care about what you think about me and what you can do for me.

"Then, if you don't give me the attention I want or don't like me for any reason, I see your whole being as *bad* and think, *She's an idiot!* And of course, the other way around. Our anger, joy, peace or unhappiness follow our own selfish standards.

"Thinking logically, your criticism doesn't do any harm to me; it could even help me improve myself and my work. But when it comes to practice, I find myself getting angry or offended with any criticism or disapproval."

Sally asked, "But why?"

"Because I've been trained to believe deeply and subconsciously that the only good thing for me is praise and approval, and that criticism means rejection of my character. As a programmed person, my feelings follow social indoctrinations, rather than my reason."

"So what should we do? You know, I often come to this same question."

Shabe said, "I reckon we should first ask why, Sally. Why has our being turned into a nest of festering feelings, all beyond our own will? Why, indeed, should we have things going on in us that we've never wanted or chosen?"

Sally nodded.

Shabe continued, "If I look at what's going on in my life, I'll see I'm doing the same thing to myself that others once did to me. I evaluate myself by the same biased measures and expect different results!

"My dad once compared me to my cousin and said, 'You're so stupid!' Today, unbelievably, I still keep comparing myself to my cousin and think, *I'm stupid!* My big brother saw me a hero, and I've grown up with this burdening belief that I always have to be perfect. I've been programmed by these beliefs!"

Sally remarked, "That means today, the problem is *us*."

"Understanding that truth is critical. Society—that is, Mum, Dad, Uncle and Auntie—have gone, long ago, but we're still holding ourselves up to their expectations, even in private, just like a loyal slave! That's conditioning.

"You'll have heard of Pavlov, the Russian scientist, and Skinner, the American psychologist? Yes? They clearly demonstrated the phenomenon of conditioning. Pavlov's dog heard a bell each time it was going to be fed. Interestingly, after a lot of repetition, the animal started drooling when the bell rang because its digestive system had been programmed by its ringing, even when there was no food around.

"Skinner conducted a similar test with a pigeon. The bird was in a cage with a hatch. Grains of wheat would show up each time the pigeon touched the hatch with its beak. The bird had been trained to do this whenever it was shown a card that said 'eat.' And to turn around whenever it was shown another card saying 'turn around.' Obviously, the bird couldn't read the cards, but it followed the commands automatically because of training and conditioning. In these tests, both the dog and the pigeon lost their usual sense of judgement.

"Excuse me," Soren said. "Does that mean humans are another species of animal or …?"

"We're not debating whether humans are also animals or are higher than them," Shabe said. "The point is, in us humans there exists a capability called *conditioning*. We must clearly recognise and remember this, and other mechanical features of our mind.

"You've heard me say that our minds are malleable and suggestible things, which can be an advantage, but if this works in a blind way, that can be a grave disadvantage to our freedom and tranquillity.

"The conditioned person is not free but a programmed robot—a compulsive machine that's been wound up then placed on certain rails, which it follows from then on. There's little choice about what they do, think or feel, let alone their friendships, enmities and efforts. What they call *choosing* or *deciding* is little more than pressing one of the buttons on a machine. It's not a real choice or will." Shabe paused, waiting for reactions.

Sally said, "Very interesting topics and vivid examples, but you referred to poverty. I think about that a lot. I believe poverty and deprivation are among the most fundamental of human problems.

"As I see it, they're caused by the greed of some and the submissiveness of others. Therefore, they need to be dealt with by serious, comprehensive actions. We shouldn't remain indifferent towards them."

Shabe answered, "Let me emphasise again that our attention to self-flourishing and the inner world is not synonymous with denying other factors such as politics, economy and the like. These are all important and necessary.

"But the essential point is that the roots of everything we do are within *us*. Hence, without empowering *ourselves* with self-belief, knowledge and insight, no action can be really fruitful and effectual.

"Yes, poverty is a serious problem, and indifference to it is an illogical and inhumane attitude. But I'd like to highlight a few points about this. First, contrary to what we might think, fighting poverty or engaging in any social action isn't synonymous with violence or rage. Second, being happy and joyful, despite these issues, doesn't equate to being indifferent or cold-hearted."

"Obviously, you and I must take individual as well as social action to solve any problems, including poverty and injustice, but what's wrong with doing that in a peaceful and cheerful manner? We can combine raising social awareness and building common knowledge with peace and care.

"Instead of creating further difficulties by triggering hate and anger and depreciating our capacities, which only benefits the forces of poverty and oppression, we can use our resources wisely and effectually to solve the problem. That will let us reach our goals more easily and effectively."

"That sounds very plausible. But to be honest, it's difficult to imagine coping with such problems as destitution or illness, yet simultaneously keeping a strong morale and being free from worry and fear," Sally said.

"We should understand that worry, fear or hate have hardly helped solve any problem; they only make matters worse," Shabe said. "If we cannot control ourselves and our reactions, how can we control things? We'll discuss that further.

"So here's a very general but significant point. All along, our environment has treated our minds like warehouses for leftovers. Parents, aunties, teachers, television and newspapers have filled up our minds however they liked with undigested beliefs, blind habits and baseless fears.

"No wonder our minds are now like a shed full of shabby, messy clutter! Nothing's in its right place. Many extra things are simply occupying our space and need to be cleared away. Many other things we don't really recognise, and still others we simply haven't decided what to do with."

Soren laughed. "Hey! That's like our shed. It's been in a mess for ages, and Dad keeps saying he'll tidy it up at the weekend, but he never gets around to doing it!"

Sally frowned at Soren, then burst out laughing.

"Good example," Shabe said. "Now, just imagine all that stuff is sitting in the middle of your living room, right now. And how hard that would make life!

"That's exactly how our minds are going at the moment, like a house chock-full of clutter! If we wanted to live in this house and have a convenient life, we must tidy it up. We'd need to look at each thing carefully and identify it. We'd have to throw out the unnecessary things. We'd need to prioritise the remaining things then make a place to put them in for easy access."

"So that's like what we call *mind management*. I think this is an important thing to do," Sally said.

"And the most pressing! Thought is the commander of our lives. It governs all our decisions and behaviours. How is it that when we open a small business, we try to find the most experienced manager to run it, yet we have so little concern for our minds and thought when *these* manage our whole life?"

"Yes!" Sally agreed. "I wrote an article on just that topic in our *Weekly*. I reckon it was issue 146 …"

"Yes," Shabe said. "I read that article! You developed the topic very well there."

"Thank you, and please help yourself to a snack." She picked up Melody's bowl to feed her.

Shabe took some grapes and started to eat.

Soren was glad to see his mum was so interested in the discussions, but couldn't help thinking, *I wish Dad was interested in these talks. It's a shame he's so obsessed with work all the time.*"

On the Bolting Horse

"I believe what we just discussed is actually closely related to the issue of aimless rumination or intruding thoughts," Sally remarked.

"That's correct," Shabe replied. "And that's what I was just going to touch upon. I call it mental revolt or thoughts going wild and unruly. As I've discussed with Soren, one of our difficulties is that instead of our thoughts serving us, we're at their mercy. We passively follow and obey them."

"Completely right," Sally agreed.

"Now stop. Just focus on the flow of your thoughts a few moments. Imagine it's a charming evening on a beautiful day, and you're sitting in the park, relaxing. But will your thoughts allow you to rest and relax?

"No! You'll be thinking about your cousin and the maths you help him with. Then you'll remember being hit by a classmate as a child. Then you'll review the rubbish talk that politician gave last night. And then your thoughts fly home, worrying about what the kids are up to …"

"See? Your thoughts keep wandering aimlessly, nosing here and there, and they bring to mind hundreds of ideas and memories, both sweet and bitter. Trouble is, each idea makes your blood pressure go up and down. You're like a helpless spectator sitting in front of a cinema's screen, watching various scenes—true and untrue, sad and exciting, real or fictional—and you have to follow all these, going through so many different, ever-changing feelings like sadness, joy, anger, frustration …"

Soren could picture what Shabe was describing. How often had he been upset when recalling his classmates' teasing and bullying? How often had he pictured the scene of that fight, so full of hate and anger? How often each day did he remember how his classmates made fun of his lack of height? These futile ideas would crowd his mind and sweep him away like the irresistible flow of floodwaters.

When he thought about it, he could see many sweet memories from the past too, so why did the bitter ones tend to be more persistent?

"Why is that?" Shabe went on. "Because all this time, your thoughts have been riding *you!* You've actually been on a compulsory mental journey. Even back in the day, Rumi knew all about this.

> *'The soul is every day trampled upon by imagination,*
> *By pictures of losses, benefits and fears of annihilation.*
> *Thus, it is robbed of purity, gladness or glory.*
> *It can't find any paths to heaven.'"*

Sally, also deep in thought, remembered how bittersweet memories plagued her frequently. The phrase 'trampled upon by imagination' sounded like a precise description to her. Her cousin Rosa had used to make fun of her freckles. More recently, in an office, the clerk had insulted and embarrassed her by shouting, "Listen! I'm not going to attend to your job!"

She recalled the day at school when her friend Flora had won the first pianist prize, while she'd come fourth despite all the hard work she'd put in. Flora's dad, Mr Stern, the wealthy estate owner, had bought her an expensive new piano and hired a private teacher for his daughter, but Sally's family hadn't been able to afford that. She could only rehearse on an old piano that had belonged to her late mother.

She could see clearly those sad experiences whizzing about like bees in a beehive, robbing her of peace of mind, and now she realised what a huge portion of her life had been squandered in mental sorrow and how she'd ignored this important reality.

Shabe spoke. "Don't you think it's worth asking why we're at the mercy of our own thoughts? This skull belongs to us, so why do intrusive thoughts and racing ideas flood our minds all the time?"

Soren said, "As you say, we must stop identifying with our thoughts."

Sally added, "That sounds accurate. I suppose the best way to manage that is through mindfulness. Don't you agree?"

"Yes and no," Shabe said.

"You mean …" Sally said.

"Mindfulness is valuable," Shabe continued. "It helps regulate the flow of thoughts and creates space between us and the mental noise. We should all practise it. But there's a deeper issue that many overlook. Calming the mind alone won't solve everything.

"You see, it's not just about stopping intrusive thoughts. What truly shapes our lives are the *ways* we think: our expectations, judgements and our perspectives on ourselves and the world. These form the foundation of our emotions and behaviours.

"How can I expect peace if I believe life is a race to stay ahead of others? If I think what I own or how I look is what gives me value? If

I carry jealousy, confusion or resentment, and have no clear, examined philosophy about life, self-worth or the place of others? Living in a vague, imposed framework of ideas naturally leads to inner conflict, including the constant surge of unwanted thoughts. Without examining our deeper beliefs, no technique, however calming, can bring lasting change."

"That sounds very true," Sally said. "As you said earlier, this is the critical aspect of the matter which is often ignored or undermined."

The Treadmill

Shabe said, "Well, so far, we've dwelt on several issues that arise from value-obsession. Now let's turn to what can be called the time-stricken condition."

"What does that mean?" Soren asked.

"Yes, that's probably a new word for you. But, before we go further, here's a tale from a children's book to introduce our next discussion."

Soren said, "I'd kill for tales!"

Feeding Melody, Sally said, "I'm listening too. Please go ahead."

"I'm reading from *The Tale of Baker Hani.*

"In a lively, beautiful town, there was a kind and hardworking shopkeeper called Baker Hani. People were very happy with the bread and cakes he provided, so his shop had many customers.

"But one day, Hani was ill and couldn't go to work, so, he nailed a sign above the shop door. 'Closed Today. Please Come Back Tomorrow.' A few days on, Hani was well again and opened the shop. But days passed, and there was not one customer.

"That seemed weird. So after a while, Hani decided to attract customers by other means.

"First, he thought perhaps other shops offered better bread and cakes or had better service, so he tried to outdo the rivals. He provided even better

breads, more delicious cakes and cookies. He also renovated his shop and offered a discount on his products, but he had no luck.

"Hani, mystified, feeling sad and disappointed, sat in his shop as he watched the street and the people passing by.

"A long time went by until, one day, a severe storm blew up. Hani was going to take shelter inside his shop, when suddenly something heavy dropped loudly, just in front of his feet from above his head. A piece of timber had hit the ground and shattered.

"Hani was surprised to see it was the 'closed' sign, which the gale had loosened. He had forgotten about this sign. As he swept up the debris, it suddenly hit him like a light bulb switching on. He realised this was exactly why he hadn't had any customers in so long, and why all his efforts to bring them back had achieved nothing.

"Hani laughed as he threw the shattered sign into the garbage tin, and had a fresh sign made. 'The Shop IS Open Now!' Soon, Hani's business was up and running well, as it had been before."

Shabe closed the book.

"That's a beautiful story," Sally said.

"And must have a beautiful meaning, no doubt," Soren said.

"This apparently simple story demonstrates a critical problem in how we feel about life. That problem can be called the time-stricken condition.

"Like I said, subjective values, even though they look different, all give us the same message. You must be something else! In other words, you're always imperfect and guilty, so you must always be unhappy with yourself!

"So we make the mistake of believing we need to be something or someone other than who we are, to get rid of the imperfection we feel. And if we do, we imagine we'll be good enough and, hence, happy.

"However, that imperfection doesn't lie *in* us, but in the standards we judge ourselves by. These are founded on never-reaching and always-being-unhappy principles."

"Fascinating!" Soren said. "Just like the sign on Hani's shop. Leave today; come back tomorrow!"

Shabe said, "That's right. Or like a treadmill. Built to walk on but not to reach anywhere."

Sally said, "Yeah, right! Treadmills never reach anything. Obviously, you need to get off the treadmill, not run faster and faster!"

Soren suddenly pictured Mr Stern, the stout, irritable estate owner, jogging on a treadmill in sports clothes, drenched in sweat, his tongue sticking out. In front of him was an image of a safe brimming with gold coins, gleaming gems and bundles of money.

Soren stifled a laugh and thought, *Well, at least that might help him shed a few pounds!* A minute later, he thought, *That wasn't very kind of me. I'm judging him, after all.*

Shabe's voice pulled Soren from his thoughts. "This kind of thinking keeps us focused on another place and another situation. Because we often see ourselves as imperfect, we carry an ideal self in our minds, one we believe we'll reach in some vague but significant future, causing us to undervalue the trivial and unimportant present. But it's clear that life is always unfolding in the *now,* and what we call the *future* is just a collection of images in our own heads."

"So one whose mind is absent from the present, is absent from life," Sally added.

"Exactly. Have you noticed how our mind struggles to evade where we actually *are* and yearns to go somewhere else or longs for another moment to come? When we're at home, we want to go out; when we're out, we can't wait to reach the shop. But then we get tired of the shop and cannot wait to go to the park. In the park, the same thing; we long to go back home!

"Our mind is always obsessed with somewhere else or something else. That means we never taste true delight and satisfaction, despite all our efforts. And that keeps going until our last moment in this universe. And that means losing life.

"The time-troubled person's problem isn't not having or not being; it's not seeing. Rumi says that all that restlessness comes from the tyrannical, insatiable ego. As he puts it,

> *'He drinks up all the seven seas,*
> *Yet that doesn't quench the thirst*
> *Of this people-burning monster.'"*

"What does he mean by 'people-burning monster' here?" Soren asked.

"I suppose Rumi is being ambiguous. In one sense, it means that the ego is a monster that burns the people who submit to it and carry it within them all the time.

"The other meaning is people who are occupied by this alien will sacrifice everything, including others' lives and happiness, to try to quench the insatiable thirst of this oppressive enemy. That's exactly what you can see going on in the world around us."

"So insightful, really," Sally said.

Shabe went on. "Going back to our discussions, if this restless person looks into themselves, they'll find out those same feelings of guilt and apprehension are still there, even five or fifty years of struggle later. The problem comes from an unending comparison of this situation with another situation, this place with another place and this life with someone else's life."

"Excuse me," Sally said, "I've also heard that contentment is the key to happiness. That's a general approach in the Eastern philosophies, as far as I know. I assume they suggest you should avoid greediness and instead appreciate what you have."

"Mm. Though *contentment* has a much more profound meaning. At the moral level, contentment means appreciating the present, ourselves and the world, just as they are. It means a life without craving; embracing what is. Accepting people the way they are.

"At the practical level, that shouldn't mean submission or indifference. We must make every attempt to improve our society and material life, and these two attitudes aren't contradictory."

"Yes, I think I know what you mean," Sally said.

"Have you ever tried saying, sincerely, 'Today, I'm completely delighted and satisfied. At this moment, I don't want anything more to be happy, and, right here and now, I am faultless, peaceful and delighted.'"

Sally was silent, thinking.

"Try it!" Shabe urged. "You'll see how difficult that is because our minds are not familiar with being satisfied. As soon as we want to do that, our ever-whingey mind starts to nag: 'But you have piles of unsolved problems and unanswered needs! You're flawed and imperfect. How can you be content and happy?'"

"You're right," Sally said.

Shabe said, "Isn't it ridiculous that we don't dare be happy and serene for fear of our own minds? Being happy is our natural mode of being. It means being healthy and being kind to oneself, as well as to the world.

"And being happy is a right, a perpetual and unconditional one—just like the right to life and fresh air. Nothing should take that away from us. It's also obvious that sadness or guilt have never really helped solve any problem."

Sally and Soren were silent, thinking about what they'd heard.

"In several spots, Rumi considers the source of our hardship and pain is our mind's entanglement in the trap of time. So the key to a happy and delighted life is the mind's release from these ties. He says,

Your mind is obsessed,
with the past and the present.
When it gets freed from the two,
the problem is solved.

"What that means is, as soon as the mind stops wandering aimlessly and remains in the here and now, a great deal of self-generated problems cease to exist. Reflecting on this point lets you grasp its depth. The time-stricken condition is but one of the burdens on our lives through self-loss. Life refreshes itself every moment, but we keep living in the same dark mental cave."

"But thinking about the past and future is necessary, isn't it? Otherwise, how can we plan and organise our life?" Sally asked.

"Obviously," Shabe replied. "We must use our memory and refer to our learned information so we can think about things, make decisions, communicate with each other and even recognise people and objects. We have to consider the future to plan for tomorrow and organise our life, as well, just like you said.

"The point is, conscious and useful thinking is deliberate and constructive, very different from aimless and futile wandering of the mind, which is fruitless and disturbing. This is what we are opposed to, and this is what we need to get rid of for a wise, peaceful life. We'll discuss imposing ideas shortly."

"Makes great sense. Thank you." Sally said. "But how can we get relief from so much inner struggle? Is there a way out?"

Soren spoke up: "There must be, but to be honest, I have the same question. I'd really like to know how to free ourselves from so many complications."

Sally said, "From what we've heard so far, it seems a very complex issue. I hope there's a solution in your theory. Some things are easier said than done."

"Soren and I have already talked about that. The answer usually is, particularly with inner issues, that understanding the problem and remedying it are more or less the same. The more we gain insight into the essence of our problems, the more the issue fades away, despite its apparently complicated nature."

"How come?"

Soren said, "I read somewhere, 'Happiness is like a butterfly. The more you run towards it to grab it, the further away you'll push it. You need to sit quietly and calmly so the butterfly comes and sits on your shoulder.'"

Sally smiled. "Beautifully said. I believe, though, this applies to blind, self-defeating struggles, not informed, constructive effort."

Shabe agreed. "That's completely right! In one sense, happiness and liberation are matters of passivity rather than activity. In the other sense, they're matters of activity and effort."

"I can't quite get that! Would you elaborate a little?" Sally asked.

Shabe said, "The problem is like having an unwelcome guest in your home. This guest is the ego, or in Sufis' language, the Nafs. It's very natural to go through pain and conflict as long as this intruding guest is there.

"So, what we need to do first is to distinguish and differentiate between this alien self and our genuine self. Next, put all our efforts into cultivating and satisfying our genuine self rather than this imposed stranger. So the solution is to ignore this intruder and cultivate our true, genuine being."

"Got it. Makes sense, really," Sally said. "It means nursing and cultivating your genuine being rather than feeding an intrusive alien or parasite."

"Yes," Shabe said and went on. "If we sit and reflect on the ways our beloved enemy has been putting us through dismay and distress, we'll give up our interest in it, and we'll get free of its merciless shackles and enjoy true peace of mind for the first time."

Melody started hitting her food bowl with a wooden spoon, enjoying the sound it made.

Shabe pointed at Melody. He smiled and said, "Yes, that sort of joy and happiness! We usually only have pale memories of it from our own childhood."

"So the solution is knowledge or awareness? Is that what you mean?" Sally asked.

"Correct. And attending to your genuine needs and endowments, rather than working for fake wants or indoctrinated needs.

"Look, our main problem is thoughts. We'd have no problem without extra, unneeded thoughts around such compulsive, constant ideas as 'How can I prove myself to Nancy? Why didn't Joe or Richard like me? Why did I appear so timid at the gathering?' And thousands of other useless ideas.

"So the first step is to stop useless ideas, altogether. I'm not referring to objective, independent evaluations of our own qualities and abilities. We need them to improve and flourish. And we need to listen to others' viewpoints and take advantage of their ideas and even criticisms. But the way we look at ourselves mustn't be dictated by others. We always need to preserve and cherish our independence and authenticity.

"Neither am I referring to thoughts about the material, practical side of life. What I'm talking about is useless concern about fake values that keep assessing us by social wants and standards. This sort of thought upsets our peace of mind.

"It's like drinking salty water to quench our thirst, or as Rumi puts it, 'Washing blood away with blood is impossible.' The solution is to stop the thought and realise its futility and instead take advantage of our unique faculties for creating our own thriving, fulfilled being."

Soren and Sally were silent, thinking.

A moment later, Sally went off to get refreshments and came back with a tray of tea and fruit. Minutes passed in silence as they reflected.

Then Sally said, "A question often occurs to me, particularly in my work, but I haven't been able to find a satisfying answer."

"Tell us!" Shabe said. "I'm sure I'll learn from this too."

"What's the reason for the difference we can see among outward people, as you call them? What causes the difference between their conditions?"

While Shabe considered this, he wiped his glasses with a tissue, then put them back on and moved them up his nose. "In general, it could be said that self-loss, as an affliction, is informed by two factors: type and intensity. Like I said, the means of control include belittlement, praise and intimidation.

"So the extent to which a person fears social judgement depends on how intense the pressure is. The stronger the pressure, the harder one will work to satisfy others, which leads to the persistence of the imposed identity. However, this can also be influenced by factors such as genetics, education and life experiences."

Sally asked, "I suppose we should also add neglect and lack of affection, especially in childhood. They can be important factors also."

Shabe nodded thoughtfully and paused. "That's a good point, Sally. Neglect and lack of affection, especially early on, can definitely shape someone's sense of self and their need for approval. I hadn't fully considered that angle, but it makes sense. There's so much we're still learning together. I appreciate you bringing that up."

A small smile crept onto Sally's face. She wasn't expecting him to be so receptive and open to new ideas. She thought a while, then asked, "So the intensity of the disorder depends on the intensity of the pressure, and the type of disorder depends on the type of pressure?"

"Yes. Someone who's been ignored, or as you said, neglected, as a child, usually resorts to pretence and attention-seeking behaviour. Someone who's been humiliated or insulted typically adopts anger and aggression. And someone who's been censored, controlled and suppressed can develop baseless fears, shyness and self-censorship. Mind you, in the outward person, all these symptoms usually exist together, but normally, one is more prominent."

CHAPTER SEVEN

THE RECLINING CHAIR

Shabe barely heard the phone ringing as he was hammering a nail to fix his old chair. He enjoyed handiwork. It kept his hands busy while his mind relaxed. What was more, he liked to know everything in the house stayed secure and reliable. Most evenings, he sat in this reclining chair on the terrace, reading or thinking. Usually, he kept a pencil handy for any insights that came to him.

He often watched the sunrise or the effortless flight of the seagulls. Or he might gaze at the dew-covered flowers or at the grass being combed by the early morning breeze. He found the mixed smells of grass, sea and forest intoxicating and enjoyed the feathery brush of the breeze on his skin.

He cherished this chair, as he'd inherited it from his grandmother. When he was a child, Grandma Sara had sat in it and told him stories—tales of jinn and fairies, the princess and the poor lover, ancient warriors and their daring feats. Sometimes, she'd recited poetry too. All her stories came from the East, wrapped in the fragrances of a distant, exotic world. Often, she'd shared memories from her own childhood or youth. For inquisitive little Shabe, who was always full of questions, Grandma's stories had always conjured up an atmosphere of awe, beauty and engaging mystery.

Shabe picked up the phone. "Hello."

"Good day, Shabe."

"Sally! How are you going?"

"Very well, thank you. What are you up to right now?"

"I was just fixing my rocking chair," Shabe said. "Do you have a reclining chair at home, Sally?"

"What do you mean?"

"One to relax in and just listen to the birds singing?"

Oh, typical Shabe, Sally thought, laughing. "Yes, we do have one, but …"

"Great! Do enjoy it. But make sure the legs are firm and secure."

"Okay," Sally said. "But I'm calling about your book."

"Yes?"

"Today, I told our editor, Mr Neil, about it and the discussions we've had. He showed a lot of interest and wondered if he could read a copy when it's ready? We'd like to publish it in the *Weekly* with a bit of adaptation and summarisation. Say, one title or one section a week."

Shabe smiled to himself. "You'd be more than welcome. No problem at all."

"Oh, thank you so much!"

"No need to thank me," Shabe said. "I'm writing it for people to read, so I definitely want it to reach more people. If the audience shared their feedback and suggestions, it may help me clarify a few things, help to improve the book."

"I see what you mean. When do you think the draft will be ready?"

"I need a few more days. If you like, get Soren to pick up a copy on Thursday."

"I will. Thanks again."

"Just two things …" Shabe said.

"Yes?"

"First, if you need to change anything, would you please check with me first?"

"Certainly."

"The other thing is that the last chapter of the book isn't finished yet. I'll have that to you in about two or three weeks."

"Oh, so the book is not finished yet? I thought you said it was complete?"

"Well, this book is mine *and* Soren's, after all. We began this journey together and promised to finish it together. The last chapter is practically complete, but Soren hasn't read it yet."

"Oh, I see," Sally said. "Thank you for all the care and attention you've given him. I'll be happy to wait for the last chapter to be completed, and I'll get it from you then. Bye for now."

"Goodbye, Sally."

Who Is I?

Shabe was getting ready when Tara ran up to the gate, jumped up against it and barked at their guest.

"Hey, Tara," Soren said across the fence. "How're you going?" Then, glancing at his watch, he muttered, "Hope I'm not too early."

The cool breeze brushed his face. Seagulls screeched as they soared into the blue sky, circling above or swooping in search of prey.

Soren stared at them. *Do these birds think of themselves as individuals with a distinct I or character? Or as part of their flock? Do they think, 'This is mine, not his' or feel anger or even jealousy towards each other? Obviously, they sometimes fight over food or squawk at each other. But how do they truly see themselves?*

A sudden movement caught his eye—a clown emerging from behind the fence, walking with an exaggerated, theatrical gait. Dressed in a crisp white shirt under bright red suspenders, and wearing mismatched striped socks, oversized red shoes, a bulbous red nose and a wild mop of curly carroty hair, the figure was an absurd spectacle.

With a playful croak, the clown swung the gate open and beamed. "Heeelloooo, Soren! Step right in, won't you?" Then, as if struck by an unexpected revelation, he added dramatically, "Oh! How terribly rude of me! I forgot to introduce myself. I'm the clown!"

Soren laughed. "Yes, I can see that!"

"How do you do? You're ten minutes early today, but it's okay—good, actually. Well, let's go inside, shall we?"

Everything was ready. On the table were fruit, tea and biscuits, popcorn and dark chocolate. Soren pounced on some chocolate as he waited for Shabe to start.

"Well, how are you?" Shabe asked.

Soren laughed, unable to take his eyes away from Shabe's ball-shaped nose. "I'm well, thank you."

"Tea?" Shabe asked.

"Yes, thank you," Soren said, "By the way, have you read the *Weekly*? Two chapters of your book have been published so far. It's started a lot of talk in town. I've heard many compliments but some criticism too. Yesterday, on the bus, I saw two people with the *Weekly* on them, but they were making fun of your points about education."

Pouring the tea, Shabe said, "That's how publishing is. Writing a book is like planting a tree. It produces fruit only after it's read, and these discussions are part of the fruit."

"Mmm." Soren was thoughtful. Or eggs unhatched, just like *The Ugly Duckling*. He laughed and then asked, "So you already knew all that?"

"Yes, I read the *Weekly*," Shabe said. "I got a couple of phone calls and letters as well. I'll attend to them later. Well, now, have some tea and let's start because today's our last day, and we've got a lot to do."

"So we won't be meeting anymore?" Soren sounded gloomy.

Shabe smiled. "Of course we will! What I mean is that today is the last day of us reading the book. Our first topic today is this. Who Am I?"

Soren rubbed his hands together. "I'm ready. Today, everything will become clear, won't it?"

"Many things have already become clear, haven't they?"

"They have," Soren agreed. "But I mean the riddle of who we are is solved and bang! We're released!"

"Soren." Shabe chuckled. "It sounds like you read too many detective stories! Though it could certainly be put like that. But we've been getting to know ourselves, step by step, through what we've been reading. Learning so many things about ourselves means knowing ourselves, doesn't it? But you could say that today, we're attacking the focal core of the problem."

"'Hooray!" Soren shouted. "Ready for a pincer attack! Let's go!'"

Shabe laughed. Then he removed the red ball from his face and rubbed his nose.

"Can I borrow that?" Soren asked.

"Of course," Shabe answered.

Soren grabbed the ball, examined it, then put it on his nose and made a few silly faces.

They both laughed, and Shabe said, "It really suits you."

"I know. Thank you!" Soren removed the red ball and put it back on the table.

Shabe said, "Here, we come to a fundamental question in self-discovery. Its answer will clarify a lot of other things and help untie many other knots. In fact, if it's not answered, this question will leave the main core of the problem in the dark. And that question is, what is I?"

"What is I?" Soren repeated. "I think that's an interesting, fascinating, enlightening, enthralling, eng—"

"Soren!" Shabe barked and paused for a few seconds, trying not to laugh. "Spiritual teachers say a proper comprehension of who you are is an essential part of self-liberation and growth.

"And that makes perfect sense, Soren. If you're not sure who you really are, and if you can't tell your true being from other imposed or illusive things, how can you invest in your growth and happiness? How would you make sure you're not spending your precious life on something that is a stranger?"

"A stranger? Very interesting."

"Well, let's put I under a magnifying glass and try to identify it. Nearly everyone, at some moment in their life, has asked themselves, 'Who am I, really? Who is this being who's sitting in me, talking, thinking, feeling sad or happy? Who's this person who worries and becomes angry, enjoys or suffers, whose presence I feel in me at every moment?'"

Soren nodded. "I've been there. When you ask yourself that, it's like there are two persons inside us: the I who's asking the question, and the other I who's being asked the question."

"And that makes the matter more mysterious," Shabe added.

"I love mysteries!" Soren said.

A slight smile crept across Shabe's lips as he stared out to the horizon. As if talking to himself, he said, "Perhaps Hafiz experienced this sheer wonder when he wrote,

> *'I wonder who it is, in my restless heart*
> *Who is in uproar and commotion,*
> *While I am silent.'*

And Rumi, when he wondered,

> *'Who is the ear, who hears my songs?*
> *Who is the one who puts the words in my mouth?*
> *Who is the one who looks out through my eyes?*
> *And which soul is it, for whom I am but a dress..?'"*

Shabe slowly turned his gaze to Soren and went on, "The interesting point is perhaps few people can give a lucid and satisfying answer—at least to themselves—to the question of *Who am I?*"

"Just think about it, Soren! In ourselves, we possess something we call I. We love this I and care for it. We even see ourselves as it, but surprisingly, we have no idea who this I is, nor its nature. We can hardly see or define this I, the way we see and identify our hands, our shoes or a friend."

Soren said, half-jokingly, "It seems like our troubles are never going to end."

"What do you mean?"

"We haven't even recognised our true self yet, and we don't know who we are. Then we have to find and identify that false self. After that, we'll need to resolve the conflict between the two. In short, we've got quite the mess to deal with."

Shabe laughed and said, "No, it all comes down to one thing. Once you know your true self, you'll be able to distinguish it from anything false. Including a false self. That's when the false self will fade in your mind. In fact, you'll see it as a stranger, and you won't work for it anymore."

"So interesting! It's kind of like a horror movie! You know the feeling you get in that moment when the kind, innocent character takes off their mask, and we see they're really a gruesome, scary monster."

"Soren, I told you not to watch so many horror movies!" Shabe chuckled. He paused for a moment, gazing into the distance, then went on. "But you're right. All of a sudden, your interest in that creature turns into hate and horror. That's also how things are with the ego. As we discussed before, the ego lives entirely through our interest in it."

"A wrong interest."

"Exactly. So, when we realise how evil and ugly it is, it loses its worth in our eyes, and the outward I collapses. When that occurs, our concern-laden, agonising thoughts just vanish. The mind becomes like a bright, cloudless sky, calm and peaceful."

"Yes, I can imagine that."

"All right. Let's return to the main question: Who am I? We've already talked about this I extensively. And now we are ready to feel and experience this being in ourselves. We want to vividly see who and what this I is. Is this I the same as the ego? Or is it possible that more than one I lives within us?"

"How awesome. And how terrifying!" Soren said.

Shabe smiled. "Indeed. We want to try and dissect the nature of this entity, one that's closer to us than anything else yet so unknown."

"Isn't this the same question Mum asked about our true self and false self?"

"Yes," Shabe replied. "And remember how we said that the genuine self is not only about who you truly are but also about seeing and understanding yourself in an authentic way and that these two questions are intertwined?"

"Yes, I remember."

"Now, we're going to explore how we can perceive ourselves as we really are, through an unclouded lens, free from confusing masks."

"I see. That's really interesting."

"And Soren," Shabe continued, "this isn't just theory. It's essential for your happiness and growth. If you mistake yourself for a stranger, you might end up devoting your entire life to serving and satisfying an imposter, instead of your real self. And in the end, you're left drained, impoverished and unfulfilled, with all your gifts and potential wasted on something that was never truly yours. That's why you can see so many people, despite their apparent success, feel lost, anxious or depressed."

Soren involuntarily thought of Mr Stern, the grumpy estate owner. Everybody knew he was wealthy from his extravagant clothes, grand house and lavish lifestyle. And everybody knew how irritable and intolerant he was.

Soren shuddered. "That's kind of eerie, but yes, really true."

"Indeed," Shabe replied. "Soren, what would be a good answer to the question of 'who am I'? Something straightforward we could just move on from?"

"Well, like saying, I'm Soren Dustin, a teenager, a student, a boy who lives in the town of …"

"That's absolutely right. But it doesn't seem like the kind of answer we're after, does it? Those are just labels—names and identifiers that distinguish us as individuals in society. We are not looking at our physical characteristics or the names given to us by our parents or the details registered about your birth."

"And that's why simple answers can be misleading."

"Good point, Soren. What we're searching for is the essence of the I, especially its place within our being—the I that speaks inside us, sees, feels and exists moment by moment. And particularly, we want to explore how we perceive this I and what standards we use to judge and evaluate it."

Soren thought for a moment. *Really, what is I? Is I my personality? My experiences? My feelings? None of that seems right. After all, I assign all these things to I, so I must be something else and other than all these ...* "To be honest, I'm not sure," he said.

"Well, one way to be saved from endless theorising and find a satisfying answer is to pay attention to the characteristics of the I."

"You mean ..."

"I mean if we try to understand I through its traits, we might be able to uncover its nature. So let's start with a few simple and clear questions."

"Okay."

"The first question is, when we say 'I,' what do we really mean? In other words, how are we using the word 'I'?"

"Well, to refer to ourselves," Soren answered.

"Right. But there are different ways of referring to oneself. For instance, I might say, 'I am Shabe Ashton, a man, forty years old, 170 cm tall, 70 kg in weight, born in New York, a human with two hands and two feet ...'"

"Like the answer I gave earlier."

Shabe nodded. "Now, the question I need to ask myself is this. What place does this I hold in my mind? Because the way my mind perceives this I can shed light on its position within me. In particular, the subconscious reactions I have towards this concept are some of the best clues for identifying its place in my mind."

"So we're looking into the psychological nature of I. Is that right?" Soren asked.

"Yes. Well done! We've talked extensively about this I in theory, and now we're going to identify the place and significance of I as a mental and emotional being. And at the same time, we must consider that our feelings and emotions about everything are deeply tied to our moral and conscientious views of it."

"Got it. Thanks."

"And the method we're going to use for this purpose now is called *introspection*."

"I've heard that word before, but I'm not entirely sure what it means."

"Introspection means paying close attention to your inner experiences, the ongoing states and behaviours of your mind and psyche," explained Shabe. "It's about observing what's happening within your mental and emotional world."

"I see."

"Through this introspective view, we can focus on the characteristics of I in ways that make sense to us. We will also piece together everything we have learned so far."

"Cool."

"Now, Soren, let's take this introspective view and look at the characteristics of the I as we're discussing it. For example, if someone, say Ms Grant, were to tell you, 'You're not Soren Dustin; you're George Farlen,' how would you react? Would you get angry or upset?"

"Of course not. I'd just say, 'No. My name is Soren Dustin.'"

Shabe nodded. "Right. Similarly, if a colleague said to me, 'You're a bicycle!' or 'Your hands are two metres long,' I wouldn't feel particularly affected, would I?"

Soren laughed. "No, I don't think so. You'd probably snigger at such a ridiculous comment or doubt if they're in their right mind."

"Correct," Shabe said. "At most, I'd call out their mistake. But why? Because I know that statements like 'You have six hands!' don't change any of my actual characteristics. The reason I remain calm in the face of such remarks is because I know my name, gender and other traits are fixed realities, unaffected by what others say."

"Right," Soren agreed.

"But there's another way we use the word I. Or, more precisely, we view the I another way: through the lens of social values that we've mostly absorbed from our environment.

"So we call your self-image the outward I when you see yourself with the labels you have borrowed from others, which are, as Socrates said, unexamined. Here, it's natural that your feelings towards yourself are also dependent on others' opinions."

Soren, now immersed in this explanation, nodded and said, "Yeah. That makes sense."

"So in this sense, if a classmate says, 'You're a mean person' or 'You're an idiot,' how would you react?"

"Hmm. I'd probably get angry. Or dislike them. Basically, I'd feel upset."

"I can imagine. Do you know why?"

Soren considered this for a moment before shrugging.

Shabe answered the question. "Because you feel as though the person is stripping you of your goodness. It's like they're tearing away a piece of your psychological self, and that kind of separation is painful. That's why you immediately experience feelings like anger and resentment."

"Absolutely! I've actually felt that way myself," Soren admitted.

"I know, and that's also why you might often try to retaliate with a counter-insult. Something like, 'You're the idiot!' In doing so, you're trying to tear away a piece of the other person's valued traits, making them feel the same pain you did. It's a way of soothing your own hurt."

Soren thought for a moment, then said, "Interesting. And if the guy who insulted you apologises or takes back what they said, it's like the anger suddenly fades, replaced by relief—like that stolen piece has been returned to you."

"Very true! And that's when you realise your honour has been restored, meaning the good qualities of your I have been returned to you."

"Yeah, that makes sense. It's something everyone can relate to."

"Well, I'm glad we're on the same page so far. Now, isn't that really because this I is made of words and thoughts?" Shabe waited a beat. "Soren, think about what goes on in you when this I is attacked or threatened. What do you experience in your mind and feelings? You probably feel sad and anxious when you hear harsh words but happy and secure when you hear kind ones. So what is this thing that shrinks with criticism and swells with praise?" Then he simply waited.

Soren sank into thought, his usual faint frown intensified by concentration. Two minutes passed before he finally said, "I think you're right. I can feel it in myself. I can vividly see it."

"Well done! So that which we have talked about before we can observe in ourselves now. If we spend some time reflecting on this, we'll realise that this I can only be made up of words and images."

"A very interesting experiment!" Soren said.

"So we can see that the outward I is a collection of thoughts about ourselves that reside in our minds, naturally accompanied by feelings—pleasant or unpleasant, uplifting or distressing. In this sense, the I is a thought. That's why it feels empowered when it hears kind words and shamed when it hears cruel ones."

"Like those fairy tales where wizards turn people into frogs with a simple magic spell!"

"Absolutely! Of course, words themselves can't directly affect anything. Words can only introduce a bundle of thoughts and images into our minds. If something's nature can change through words, it must be nothing more than thought and imagination. The words of others bring positive or negative images into our minds, about things and about ourselves."

"I see."

"That's why the outward I can shift so easily based on someone's comments. What makes us happy or sad isn't the words themselves but the change in images within us. You could say that what swaps our joy with sorrow, or vice versa, is simply the replacement of one thought with another."

"Wow! So we are really dependent on just a bunch of words?"

"Sometimes, yes. Remember at the start of our conversation, we said that the comments others make about a child gradually shape the sense of self in their mind, a sense they accept as their identity or I?"

"Yes, I remember."

"The outward I is made up of those very impressions—impressions dictated to us by society, which we accept as our identity and carry in our minds."

"So, you mean …"

"I mean, these reflections once more show what lives within us as the outward I is a picture of ourselves, as seen through the eyes of others.

"Soren, from the moment we begin to recognise ourselves, society provides us with a pair of glasses, and we soon learn to view the world through their lenses. As a result, we gradually learn to judge ourselves—and everything else—based on imposed standards. And this way of seeing ourselves and the world becomes completely normal to us."

"Invisible glasses!"

"Exactly. And of course, since a specific emotion accompanies every value-laden image, the thoughts or images related to the outward I are inevitably tied to feelings of embarrassment, pride, sadness or worry."

"So would it be correct to say the inward I is our personal traits and the outward I is our social behaviours?"

"No, Soren. That's not quite it. These two I's are actually two ways of looking at things. If we want to define them, we'd say the outward I is seeing ourselves and the world through borrowed lenses, while the inward I is seeing ourselves and the world through our own eyes. So the difference lies in the perspective, not in what we're looking at."

"Wow! A change in perspective!" said Soren.

"Correct," Shabe replied. "You can look at anything—yourself, your traits, your beliefs, even your clothes, home, family, nationality or the whole world—from either an inner perspective or an outward perspective. You can view it independently or through the lens of outward influence, see it through your own eyes or through the eyes of others.

"Take something as simple as your height and weight. Even these, you can see through the value-based judgements of others, leading to joy or disappointment. For instance, when the kids used to call you 'shorty.' Pardon me …"

Soren smiled and waved the apology away. "Oh, it's fine. It doesn't matter to me anymore."

"I'm glad to hear that. You see, that mocking expression was an attempt to impose a hurtful perspective on your mind about yourself. When the kids said those words, what caused you the pain wasn't your actual height but seeing yourself through the lens of their taunts."

"That's true."

"And why are you free from that pain now? Because you no longer fall for those words. You have realised their hollow and deceitful nature. You no longer believe in an imposed view of yourself."

Soren's eyes lit up. "I can feel it now! Woohoo!!" He paused, then asked, "But one question comes to mind."

"Yes."

"Could we say the inward I is also an idea or an image? I mean we also see the inward I as an image or group of ideas anyway, don't we? So what's the difference?"

"That's right, Soren. Anything we envisage, we eventually see as an image or idea. But there's a difference between being a realistic image—that is, the picture of something actual and a borrowed, empty image with no actual reality. In other words, sometimes, what you imagine has no real-world essence or existence."

"Just like a unicorn or Spiderman!"

"Right. Let me tell you about a concept in social psychology called the *looking-glass self or mirror self*, which was first introduced in 1902 by the American sociologist Charles Horton Cooley."

"Sounds thought-provoking."

"It is. The looking glass self refers to the image we hold in our mind of how others perceive us. In simpler terms, it is the reflection of ourselves that we see in the mirror of others' perceptions. Cooley states, 'I am not who I think I am, nor am I who you think I am. I am who I think you think I am.'"

"Wait a second!" Soren struggled to focus on the idea. "So I'm not who I think I am, and I'm not who you think I am. But I am who …"

"I think you think I am," Shabe completed Soren's sentence.

"Oh, I got it! Interesting!"

"Through this statement," Shabe continued, "Cooley emphasises that what we see as our identity is a social construct shaped by our understanding of how we believe others see us. For instance, you may perceive, accurately or not, that your friends, family or society view you as a weak and timid boy. Or you might believe others see you as a capable and significant person."

"So when Cooley calls it a perception, he means this image is only a perception, and so it can be right or wrong?" Soren asked.

"Exactly. Basically, the looking-glass self has two main points. First, that how we see ourselves is shaped by what we think others think of us. People tend to see themselves through the filter of how they suppose others judge them. In other words, a person takes on others' view of them as their actual identity. This means that how someone understands their own worth and abilities is more or less influenced by what they assume others believe."

Soren nodded.

"Take your friend, Joanne, for example. She's really good at art, right? But if enough classmates kept telling her she wasn't or if her family ignored her drawings, she might start thinking she's not very talented—even though we know she is. On the flip side, your classmate Ali might believe he's hilarious just because everyone laughs at his jokes, even when they're not all that funny."

Soren smirked.

"Second, this idea leads people to constantly try to match up with what other people expect. Based on feedback from others, or what they think others are saying, they try to create an image of themselves that will be seen in an approvable and desired way.

"Think about Madhuri," said Soren. "Do you remember how she used to love answering questions in class? But after Julia and Christie rolled their eyes at her a couple of times, she started keeping quiet."

"Great example. She adjusted how she behaved, just to fit in. I'm trying to help her with that, though," said Shabe.

"By convincing her she shouldn't stop just because of others' opinions, right?"

"Correct. Bravo! Well, Cooley's definition shows how social norms decide what's good or bad and how people rely on approval from others to feel like they matter. Obviously, this can really hold back independent thinking and creativity. As we've seen, a lot of psychological struggles come from this kind of pattern. When people depend on others to define their worth, they can get stuck in a cycle of validation-seeking, which makes it hard to truly express themselves and leads to inner conflict."

"So the outward I is the same as the looking-glass self, right?"

"True."

"Got it. Thanks."

Shabe paused for a moment before continuing. "When you see things through the eyes of others, it's as though they're sitting inside you, looking at the world on your behalf! Could there be any deeper form of captivity than that?"

"No way!"

"The inner perspective is conscious and grounded, a solid and authentic view. In contrast, the outward perspective is borrowed and imposed, a foreign picture. The first is rooted and self-sufficient, while the second is insecure and dependent. That's why, to maintain this outward *I*, being good isn't enough. In fact, often, it's not even necessary! What matters is being *seen* as good or great. This I is an image painted by society, a mental mask placed on your face by others."

"A mask! This game keeps getting stranger! What a fabulous journey! Woohoo!" Soren shouted.

Shabe laughed. "I'm glad you're enjoying it. He went on. "Let me give you another example. Let's say you have a rare talent and play the piano brilliantly."

"All right."

"Now, you can view your musical ability from two perspectives. First, from the outward perspective. You evaluate yourself using outward or societal standards. You might think, 'I'm an accomplished and renowned musician' or 'My art is a source of pride.' But if you look at your music through the internal perspective—through independent and personal criteria—you might think, 'I enjoy playing music' or 'I want to improve my skills' or even 'I take pleasure in developing myself.'

"In the first case, your motivation is recognition, while in the second, your motivation is personal satisfaction. See the difference? Titles like 'renowned musician' or 'source of pride' are judgements you've adopted from others' perspectives. And vice versa! Others can take them back from you, leaving you feeling dejected."

At this, Soren thought of Steve, the butcher who had dismissed him. "What a clumsy boy …" Aloud, he muttered, "And they often do just that."

"Of course they do," Shabe said. "And when that happens, others drag you from the heights of pride and joy to the depths of anguish and humiliation."

"Yes."

"But when what motivates you is your own satisfaction and the growth of your abilities, no one can take that from you. Because having these things means you aren't relying on anyone else's opinions or approval. So you remain calm and confident."

"Got it." Soren nodded. "Cheers! But I do have one question."

"Go ahead."

"Even if I don't accept these outward standards to myself, other people might still do so. For instance, the boys might say, 'Soren, you really nailed that music!' Or newspapers might write, 'Soren Dustin, the country's number one musician, will deliver a spectacular piano recital tonight at Central Hall.' What then? I'm still seen and judged from this outward perspective. What do I do about that?"

"You're right," Shabe said. "But if you have an internal view of yourself or if you hold an authentic and independent outlook, these words wouldn't matter much to you. If your goal is your own joy and growth, you won't care about what's said. Instead, you'll calmly play your music and hold your concert. The applause of your fans or the criticism of your rivals won't intoxicate or intimidate you. Better yet, you'll neither rely on applause nor feel troubled by criticisms. As a result, your art will be more genuine and fulfilling, and you'll have peace of mind. You won't feel anxious or vulnerable."

"Hmm, I get it now. Two perspectives: the outward and the inward. But what about other people?"

"What do you mean?"

"I mean, how do these two perspectives affect my relationships with others?"

"That's a great question. Do you remember what overwhelmed you the most during that fight the other day?"

"Yeah. Hearing all those conflicting reactions from those three people. I was stunned! I couldn't figure out who was right. Was I useless? Polite? Aggressive? I wondered, 'Whose tune am I supposed to dance to?'"

"I see. Society's colourful labels left you dizzy. Because each person gave you their own version of who you are—a version that was different from the others. And none of them was actually your own version of yourself. It was all someone else's interpretation."

"Exactly. Three forced images!"

"And that's why you felt trapped and confused. That was the outward perspective you were questioning. You realised how confusing and contradictory it was. Society was trying to dictate how you should see yourself, and for the first time, you noticed the contradictions in its commands."

"That's absolutely spot on!"

Shabe laughed.

Soren continued. "So if I had looked at getting beaten up from an internal perspective, how would I have seen it?"

"In that case, you would have told yourself, 'In this fight, I didn't have the physical strength to take on those two, and they hurt me.' That's it! No blaming yourself, no shame, no inner conflict."

Soren thought for a moment and then said, "Wow! That's such a liberating way to look at things!"

"What is the difference?"

"That it's not hurtful."

"Exactly. It doesn't carry any value judgements or blame, so it's free from emotional strain. It's *your* understanding, not someone else's. And it's a judgement that comes from your own reasoning, making it confident and independent."

Soren added, "And it's not contradictory."

"Absolutely right. There's no confusion or contradiction in it, and these are not small things. These qualities form the foundation of wise thinking, one that frees you from the emotional and mental captivity of others, releasing you from being an anxious follower and bringing you to a state of calm and self-sufficiency."

Soren drank in the meaning of every single word, paused, then said, "But I have another question!"

"Go ahead."

"If this I is just a thought or, as you say, an image, why don't we realise it is? I mean, why don't we feel that the outward I is nothing more than a bunch of ideas?"

"Well, we do realise it to some extent, but this image or thought is ever-present in the back of our minds. Remember the metaphor of the exile town?"

Soren nodded.

"The outward I is like that, a collection of value-laden images we hold of ourselves. This I comes from constantly reviewing these images. Since these values aren't our traits but just words and thoughts, the reality of our being doesn't change when different words are said."

"Then why do we get upset?"

"Because we overlook the simple fact that others' words have no effect on our goodness or badness."

"It's actually calming to think about that."

"Through repeated suggestions, we've been conditioned to equate others' opinions with our traits. All our suffering stems from this habit! If we try to understand this point deeply, our anxieties will fade, and a sense of calm and lightness will take its place."

Soren punched the air. "You're right. I can feel it! Like a big heavy chain is cut off your brain."

"It's not just that." Shabe smiled.

"What do you mean?"

"The desires and interests of these two selves—that is, the outward and the inward—are different and often in conflict."

"For example?"

"There are countless examples. The outward self is obsessed with blind imitation and outward appearances, while the inward self focuses on inner growth and peace.

"The outward self demands that you invest your time and energy in various meaningless things to win others' approval, while the inward self asks you to invest your effort in growth and inner harmony. The outward self commands, 'Deny your mistakes to protect your image!' The inward self suggests, 'Make use of criticisms to improve yourself.' The outward self insists, 'Pretend you know so you don't look ignorant,' while the inward self says, 'Admit you don't know so you can learn and grow.' In all these situations, following the outward self leads to shallowness and stagnation, while focusing on the inward self furthers growth and richness."

"That's so real!" Soren exclaimed.

"There are a couple more points that would help you."

"Like what?"

"Well, the ability to see yourself as others see you isn't a bad thing. In fact, it's a useful and important skill. It helps us understand how others perceive our behaviour and traits, and how they reflect in society. This is essential for human relationships, especially for understanding others' views and feelings."

"Then where's the problem?"

"This arises when we mistake this social self for our *real* self, when we start believing we are who others say we are or that we should become what others want us to be."

"Oh, I see. You mean confusing the outward self with the inward self?"

"Exactly! You've hit the nail on the head. That confusion is what leads to emptiness and self-alienation, mistaking our outward image for our actual reality."

"I think I'm starting to get it!"

"As we said, the outward self is an infiltrator, and it is society's greatest tool for controlling you and me. It's no surprise that society implants this alien entity into our minds and insists that we carry its burden in our psyche. Why? To strengthen the leverage it has over us."

"Oh, an infiltrator! This could make a great spy movie!" Soren laughed.

Shabe chuckled too. "Soren, the environment has conditioned you to believe that who you truly are or want to be doesn't matter much. Instead, you're taught to obsess over the image society has of you. This social image has been planted in your mind as your self. You've welcomed this uninvited guest into the house of your being and pledged to serve it for the rest of your life."

"'An uninvited guest in the house.' That's so true!" Soren said after reflecting briefly.

"And if you're not careful, society will exploit your attachment to this installed agent. Sometimes, it will blackmail you, and other times, it will take you hostage to force your obedience. Insults, humiliation, ridicule—and even praise and flattery—all are tactics people use for this purpose."

"What a dirty trick!"

"Yes! This outward self is the ego, the alien dictator that lives within you and causes you so much pain."

"Ah, so the inward self is our true self, and the outward self is the same as the ego? What a scoundrel!"

"Correct. And recognising this grand deception and refusing to feed this alien is the key to freedom and peace."

Soren shouted, "Eureka! So this is the key to the peace we were talking about!"

Shabe chuckled. "That's right."

"But it's so hard! How can we even begin to do that?"

"As Rumi says, the ego is like a seven-headed dragon. Since all its traits are interconnected, striking any of its heads paralyses the entire beast. What can suffocate this monster is attacking its vital veins. By realising it's a foreigner, letting go of needless comparisons, refusing to blame anyone, understanding that values are just illusions, freeing yourself from the approvals trap or ceasing to identify yourself with outward things. If even one of these happens, the ego's back will break!"

"So they're all related …"

"Yes, they're essentially different aspects of the same process or mentality. That's why shaking any one of these traits will also weaken the ego, if not kill it. And this, of course, is the core message of mysticism."

Soren nodded thoughtfully and asked, "By the way, you promised to explain how the outward self, the ego and character are the same thing."

"I haven't forgotten. But let's have something to eat first."

"That sounds perfect!"

Shabe chose some fruit, while Soren popped a chocolate into his mouth. Both sank into silence, lost in thought. Shabe occasionally glanced at Soren, staring off into the distance. Shabe had requested a snack break to allow Soren to silently digest what they had discussed. Although Shabe believed Soren was a bright and enthusiastic young learner, he knew processing topics like these would naturally require time, contemplation and guidance—especially for a teenager.

Soren's behaviour suggested something profound was happening within him. Shabe had noticed this for some time and felt a quiet sense of joy. One sign was the thoughtful questions Soren asked with such genuine curiosity. These showed how seriously he sought the truth.

Another was the deeply reflective story Soren had recently written. Such understanding and passion, especially in a teenager, were rare and valuable. Hearts like Soren's kept the light of awareness burning brightly among humanity, he mused.

Meanwhile, Soren was mentally comparing Shabe's words with events in his life and the thoughts flowing through his mind. With each moment, he discovered something new within himself, marvelling at the revelations.

Eventually, Shabe broke the silence. "Now, another way to approach this subject is by defining the self as character."

Soren was pulled out of his thoughts to listen to what Shabe now shared.

Shabe continued. "But first, we need to understand what character is. We know that character refers to the traits, habits and consistent characteristics of an individual."

"Yes," Soren agreed.

"But we also often use the word with a more or less different meaning—to refer to someone's social face, the image they project to others. In this sense, character is more about how others see a person, not necessarily about how they actually are. People often evaluate your traits and behaviours and even assign you a score, sometimes low, sometimes high. This is our outward image, of which each of us has a perception and we call it my character."

"That's where character and the outward self become the same," Soren said.

"Right. For example, when you say, 'That person damaged my character' or 'My parents respect my character,' you're referring to this social concept of your identity."

"I agree," Soren said.

"So your actual character is something that exists regardless of whether people recognise or approve of it. It's an objective thing, you could say. But character, in the second sense, is relative and dependent. It's an objective concept. It derives its value from the level of societal approvals."

"And that is what we need to be aware of," Soren finished.

"Precisely. Character, in this sense, isn't a thing. It's merely our perception of how we are seen by others. There's no independent entity called character. If it exists, tell me, exactly where in us does character reside? In our head? Our feet? Our hands? Or maybe our neck?"

"That's so funny! Imagine someone's character being in their big toe!"

They both burst out laughing.

After a moment, Soren said, "You're right. It's impossible to say what or where the character is."

"So like we said, character is a thought or a perception. Now, you tell me, what does it even mean to insult thoughts or harm perceptions?

Does it make sense to worry about a thought being hurt? Is it rational to fight with others over a perception?"

"It does sound ridiculous!" Soren said, grinning.

"The fact that people like or dislike our character is entirely subjective. It depends on the culture, morals and preferences of society. One society might frown upon an action that is quite sensible and right, while another might celebrate the exact same behaviour. So if we tie our happiness to the approval of our character by others, it's only natural that we'll end up anxious and insecure."

"So character is not a bad thing."

"Right. Character itself isn't inherently good or bad. Character simply refers to someone's traits and temperaments. What creates problems for us isn't our character; it's the subjective, value-laden judgements about it."

"You mean people's opinions?"

"Yes. The thing is, society's norms and expectations rarely accept a person's nature as it is. Instead, it judges it based on its own preferences. And society often tries to mould a person's character to fit their desired standards. What creates conflict within us is mistaking the reality of who we are for society's judgements and perceptions of us."

Soren gazed at him intensely, as though watching a scene unfold on a cinema screen. He recalled the rows and fights with Hans and Daniel and the insults they had hurled at him and his father. A faint smile crossed his face.

Shabe set his notebook down, removed his glasses and rubbed his eyes for a moment before saying, "Well, Soren, our journey has reached its end. I'd like to say that I've thoroughly enjoyed your company on this exploratory trip. I hope you've found it enjoyable too and that what you've discovered will be meaningful and enriching."

When Shabe said that sentence, all the memories of their long, delightful journey flashed before Soren's eyes like scenes on a cinema screen – from the moment Shabe reached out his hand to lift him off the ground, all the way to this very second, when he was declaring the journey's end: the tale of The Donkey's Gone, the wildlife adventure, their meetings at Shabe's place, in the park, and at home, Superman, the sunglasses, the suggestible lion, the parable of the mud-eating man, the moan of the reed flute, the remote control, the treadmill, the opium, and the lessons about fear, anger, blame, envy, pride, and humiliation… all swept through his mind at once.

"Thank you as well," Soren said. "I've learned so much. I don't think I'm the same person I was before we took this journey."

"Glad to hear that! I had no doubt you would feel like that."

"By the way, when will the book be published? I'd love to read it from the start to the end. Also, I want to buy a few copies to give to people I know who have questions like mine."

"I wish people were always as curious about meaningful questions. Anyway, with this final chapter, the book is complete. It'll be published soon, but I'll need a few weeks to polish the content."

"What will you call it?"

"How about *The Tightrope Walker*?"

Soren paused for a moment, picturing the long, taut rope, the performer's tense and sweat-covered face, the audience's excitement and their loud cheers. He smiled and said, "*The Tightrope Walker*! It's perfect." He laughed. "By the way, what sort of cover design will you choose? I'd use a mysterious design or even a scary one. That'd be so cool."

"Okay. Let me know what ideas you have, and we can think about it together."

"Sure! I can't wait to see the book and hold it in my hands," Soren said.

"You will do so in no time." Shabe laughed and asked, "By the way, what name should we use for you in the book?"

"Soren! I like that name."

"All right. By the way, do you know when the Save Our Youth from Addiction seminar is happening? Let me check …" Shabe pulled a small calendar from his pocket and flipped through it. "Yes, it's in about two months."

"Why do you ask?"

"Since most town members will be at the seminar, I'm going to suggest a Q&A session during the event. I think it would be a great opportunity to discuss these topics with the audience and the *Weekly* readers and to answer questions. A few friends of mine also suggested this. What do you think?"

"Great idea," Soren said. "I guess you'll announce it in the paper so interested people can attend."

"Definitely! I will also talk to your mother about it."

"I'm sure she'd be happy to help."

"Oh, and Soren …"

"Yes?"

"I have an idea about *The Village of the Slaves*."

"You mean my story?"

"Yes, I'd like to hear your thoughts about my idea."

"Really? What's the idea?"

"I'll tell you …"

An hour later, Soren left Shabe's place, heading home with a head full of new thoughts.

The Opium

A crowd of people were seated in the town hall auditorium, with several familiar faces among the audience, including Bill Stern, Steve, Joe, and of course, Ms Grant. Many parents were also present, including Hans and Daniel's fathers. Dave and Sally had arrived early for the event.

Shabe was seated in the front row among a few colleagues, the principal and teachers of the town's only large school, plus several city officials and executives, as well as professors, lecturers and students from the town's university.

The mayor opened with the importance of paying attention to the youth, their health and their physical and emotional wellbeing. The principal shared points on the same topic, giving examples from his own professional experience. Then Mr Manson, the CEO of the Office for Prevention and Treatment of Addiction, spoke about addiction being a complex and sensitive social issue, before elaborating on actions taken by his office and plans for the future.

It was then Mr. Neil's turn to begin with sharing his newspaper's goals and activities. "Our *Weekly* has been publishing a series of articles titled *Talks on Self-Awareness*, written by Shabe Ashton, the philosophy teacher at St Patrick's School. We've received many calls, emails and letters regarding these articles from our readers, with both positive feedback and criticism.

"All in all, we, along with Mr Ashton, considered this event a good opportunity for him to talk to you and answer any queries, as much as time allows. Thank you to those who accepted our invitation and came here today to participate in these discussions. For myself, I'd also like to thank you for your interest in our newspaper. Well, I invite Mr Ashton to come up and speak to you."

The audience applauded as Shabe climbed the stairs and took the microphone. Next to his hand was a recorder belonging to Sally, who was expecting to create a spectacular report of the event for the *Weekly*.

Shabe cleared his throat and looked at the audience. He smiled and began. "Good day, everyone, and thank you for coming today. Mr Manson talked about addiction and shared excellent points on this topic. Well, today is Saving Our Youth from Addiction Day. The question I'd like to start with is, how can we define addiction? You must have also heard it called the black disaster. But what does it mean to be addicted?"

His gaze moved over the sea of quiet, contemplative faces. After a pause, he continued. "I think addiction, as we commonly understand it, is the unhealthy attachment of the living organism to something foreign or extra. When addicted, our body stops being self-sufficient and becomes dependent on something external, simply to continue functioning. This dependency can grow so strong that it endangers the health and life of the organism. In alcoholism, after chronic use, the body and the nervous system become so dependent on alcohol that without it, the person is extremely restless and desperate."

Some of the audience nodded in response to Shabe's remarks.

He went on. "But, the first question is: why is addiction so bad? Why do we all loathe it? Feel frightened by it? And why have we all come together today to discuss prevention strategies and remedies for addiction?

"I think the answer is simply this: addiction takes your freedom away. Addiction makes your body rely on external or alien substances. And what are they, exactly? Poisonous sedative substances like alcohol, marijuana or heroin? Yes. Or addiction can be a destructive habit, such as gambling.

"What's worse, the addict puts the foundation of their happiness into the hands of others, drug traffickers. Addiction can become so severe that a person is willing to do whatever it takes to obtain and use the substance. It can crush a person's ability to think and judge rationally.

"But there's another side. The addict feels unhappy with themself; they'd like to escape from themselves because they live with constant guilt. It's a truly painful predicament; you suffer deeply and for a long time to free yourself, but you find yourself helpless in the shackles of a ruthless monster, one that's nowhere but inside yourself.

"No one ever could even imagine finding their child in such a situation. But today, I want to share another warning with you. We ourselves can be the ones who make our kids addicted!"

A buzz started up throughout the hall. People exchanged wary looks with each other.

"Again!" Joe, the carpenter, grumbled to the woman beside him. "Always with those weird remarks!"

The woman nodded earnestly. Others muttered words of dismay.

The students seemed to have different reactions. They sat up straighter in their chairs, their eyes widening at Shabe.

The hall fell quiet again.

"We all know that prevention is better than a cure, so let's first try to answer this question. What happens when a healthy person turns into an addict? Why would a person resort to sedative substances?"

Shabe paused, looking around. "Would anyone like to answer that question?"

Ms Grant, the tailor, sighed heavily and stood. "I believe addiction is rooted in a dysfunctional family. And it's most common among the children of divorce."

Steve, the butcher, damp with sweat, raised his hand and went ahead with his high-pitched voice, familiar to all the townspeople. "Lack of a decent upbringing. I mean, a good parent or teacher can save you from falling into many miseries like addiction, theft and immoral stuff."

Listening with great curiosity, Sally was the last to answer Shabe's question. "I think, in a nutshell, the root cause of addiction is psychical unease, and this can come from emotional pressures, such as deep anger, chronic resentment and feelings of worry or depression."

"Thank you," Shabe said. "That's right. The factors pushing a person towards addiction are usually inner suffering and psychological disorders, along with general unhappiness and depression. The victim just wants to numb their mind, to get rid of the wounds caused by torment, blame and negligence. They resort to drugs for relief from self-pity and pain. They anaesthetise themself. But the crucial question is: what brings such heavy pressures on to our being?"

One of the university professors, a middle-aged man with grey, thinning hair who wore a neat blue suit, raised his hand. His face showed deep interest, one eyebrow quirked.

"Yes?" Shabe said, gesturing for the man to speak.

"I think you're right. I teach social services, and I've worked with an anti-addiction organisation as a consultant and researcher for quite some time. I've dealt with numerous cases and various types of addiction and SUD—substance use disorder, that is—and have written a couple of articles on this."

"Great! Sounds like you're well suited to contribute to our discussions. Please go ahead."

"Thank you." The man went on. "I believe one main cause of addiction is being exposed to negligence, violence and being in a dysfunctional family. In truth, most addicts suffer from abuse, humiliation and lack of attention. To deal with this issue, we need to consider an addict's emotional needs and problems."

"Yes," Shabe said. "I agree. Feelings of not being good enough and abandonment result from blame and torment, which can propel a person to resort to all sorts of addictions in their wake. Addiction is one of the devastating outcomes of unkind and reproachful treatment. As humans, we need love and care from others and ourselves.

"However, being frequently reproached and dismissed can bring on feelings of insecurity and abandonment, which then trigger a need for refuge to various self-numbing methods.

"But I'd like to talk about another kind of addiction—one even more insidious than alcohol or drugs," Shabe said. "These addicts do not use any sedative substances, yet there is an even more destructive addiction that threatens them: the addiction to approval, to egoism, to an empty and superficial life. Where does this addiction come from? It stems from a loss of self-reliance, inner emptiness and an unhealthy need for external validation."

Shabe said, "And, as I mentioned, tragically, it might be us who unknowingly plant the seed of this addiction in our own children. We do this by committing a number of significant mistakes in relation to children—faults and flaws that are so chronic and widespread that, unfortunately, they are often taken for granted." Shabe paused to let the audience process his words, then went on.

"Our first mistake is wiping out creativity and suppressing and subjugating individuality. Every human being is a singular creation, entering this world with a universe of untapped talents and unknown potentials. These abilities, if discovered and nurtured, can transform them into extraordinary and impactful individuals. But what do we do with this inherent brilliance?

"We mould children's minds and behaviours, forcing them to think and live in ways that conform to what we deem acceptable. We place them, with their distinct personalities, talents and needs, into schools and classrooms that are governed by identical rules, subjects, clothes and behaviours.

"Cancelling out human individuality suppresses people's identity and robs them of their authenticity, turning them into an army of programmed and standardised workers destined to squander their lives fuelling the machinery of production, consumption and commerce. When humans are stripped of their ability to discern and question, they become susceptible to blindly joining cults, following charismatic figures or joining ideological armies. Cultism, idolatry and devastating wars are born from this emptiness.

"The second major mistake lies inn misunderstanding the meaning and purpose of education. Children come into this world with an innate and profound love for discovery and learning. Just look at their eager eyes, relentless curiosity, endless questioning and nonstop efforts to find out and discover!

"The primary purpose of education is not to transfer knowledge or information; it is to nurture people's love for learning, for exploring the world, life and oneself. If you extinguish curiosity and replace it with a fixed set of information, you'll create an army of prerecorded disks with static information and no further learning or growth.

"But if you inspire a passion for learning and exploration, even if you impart less knowledge, those you educate will never stop wondering, growing and seeking understanding.

"We impose unengaging lessons, administer stressful exams and heavy assignments, and enforce rigid rules, late notes and disciplinary measures on children. Instead of focusing on nurturing their growth and flourishing, our education methods are obsessed more with measuring progress through grades, rankings and certificates than teaching children how to think. Instead, we impose on them what to think."

Sally listened to Shabe's speech attentively, occasionally glancing around to watch others' reactions. Her husband, David, also appeared to be concentrating on Shabe's remarks. Sally was also mindful of the recording that promised a great upcoming article for the *Weekly*.

Feeling her gaze on him, David glanced back at Sally and shot her a smile.

"Dave," Sally whispered. "It's quite stimulating, isn't it?"

He nodded enthusiastically before returning his attention to the speaker.

"The other shortcoming is the glaring absence of essential and important subjects in our curriculum. Fundamental topics such as philosophy, ethics, self-awareness and self-care are largely neglected, even though they are the cornerstones of a wise and purposeful life. What could be more important than nurturing individuals to understand their place in the world, define the meaning of things for themselves, ask questions, analyse answers and make their own judgements?

"Our approach robs children of the opportunity to learn the fundamental skills necessary for an authentic and joyful life. Instead, we reduce them to carriers of a predetermined load of often irrelevant and useless information! As a result, we leave them with unanswered questions while burdening them with mountains of un-asked-for answers," said Shabe.

"Another major problem is sacrificing happiness on the altar of success. From the earliest years of life, we project our borrowed and vague definitions of the good life onto children's minds. Through various methods—grades, passes and fails, criticism and even praise and awards—we overtly or unknowingly compel them into comparison and competition, assuming that social values are the most crucial thing to seek and achieve in life. We implant the belief that being first and shining are synonymous with happiness and success."

Shabe continued. "By the way, have we ever paused to ask ourselves what success truly means? What is more successful than living a happy life? I'd like to ask everyone a simple question: when we take away children's peace and happiness, what do we give them in return?"

A heavy silence dominated the entire space, as if only Shabe was in the hall. The audience seemed to be all eyes and ears, their undivided attention on the chain of Shabe's unprecedented remarks.

Surveying his audience, he went on. "When you lose yourself to trends and mobs, you start to believe everything must have approval or else you'll be worthless and excluded. Inevitably, you'll have to wear some sort of mask to be accepted and feel secure. I call this emotional addiction.

"The self-lost person is also an addict, a slave whose health and happiness are in the hands of the drug trafficker who provides the pleasant opium of 'Well done!' and 'Nice work!' This trafficker is society, which can—and will—take the drug all back, leaving the addict ruined and devastated.

"Our current approach turns children into programmed machines who equate the meaning of life with buying more, consuming more, wearing brands and driving luxury cars. To attain social approval, they devalue their precious lives in the confusing vortex of possession and consumption, endlessly enriching exploitative businesses and corporations. And in their pursuit of this manufactured version of success, they unknowingly contribute to the destruction of the environment, polluting the air, seas and forests.

"Instead of nurturing wisdom and self-actualisation, schools often produce submissive workers for a blind cycle of production and consumption. Have you ever wondered why our children, especially in affluent societies, suffer from emotional and behavioural struggles, despite having access to every possible comfort and luxury?

"By suppressing fundamental questions, encouraging fabricated needs and fostering dependence on external approval, we create a population prone to depression, anxiety and a pervasive sense of emptiness. True growth requires shifting our focus from material wealth to intellectual, personal and spiritual development.

"These mistakes turn our children into dependent, vulnerable beings—addicts who cannot survive emotionally or mentally without the opium of validation and recognition. Thus, they become easy prey to feelings of emptiness and insignificance, forever chasing an elusive sense of purpose and self-worth."

Shabe paused as he spotted a woman in her sixties, wearing dark clothes and large glasses, raising her hand from a seat near the back of the hall. Her grey, curly hair was gathered loosely at the back of her head. Shabe recognised her immediately as Mrs Delia, a former teacher at the school where Shabe worked, with a reputation for being a kind and dedicated individual who deeply loved children. Her smile radiated approval and contentment.

Shabe invited her to speak.

"Thank you," Mrs Delia began. "I've enjoyed your talk, and I've read all the articles in the *Weekly*. I appreciate having a thoughtful and compassionate teacher like you join our community."

Shabe smiled and inclined his head to thank her for the comment.

She went on. "I personally agree with most of your points and views. But I do have a question. If you hold such strong criticisms of the education system, why did you choose to become a teacher yourself? Forgive me if this question feels a bit personal, but I think many might be curious about it."

Several people in the audience smiled at the question, nodding in agreement, their eyes turning back to Shabe, awaiting his response.

Shabe replied, "That's a fair question. First, let me clarify. I'm not here to dismiss the education system entirely, nor do I intend to paint it in a wholly negative light. I believe that, despite its shortcomings, our education system still has many positive aspects. My critiques are about shedding light on their flaws, so we can recognise them and work towards meaningful improvement. But to answer your question about why I became a teacher …"

Mr Stern suddenly interrupted. "After leaving the circus, of course!" His voice was poisoned with sarcasm and frustration.

Shabe smiled and said, "I believe everyone must leave the circus if they want to be free from the circle of a dark, repetitious and confined world."

Confused by Shabe's answer, Mr Stern shifted in his chair with a thunderous face, trying to avoid direct eye contact with Shabe, as he had done all through his talk.

Shabe continued. "I've always believed that children are the most sensitive and pivotal part of any society. I've always loved spending time with this beautiful and inspiring generation. And the only place where I could directly work with children was within the school environment.

My goal has always been to help children and young adults to foster their awareness and growth, while at the same time striving to rebuild and revitalise the education system from within.

"For instance, you may know that it was through my persistence that philosophy was added to our school curriculum. That was the first significant step I managed to accomplish in our institution, and I appreciate our school for accepting that. I hope, with the support of thoughtful and dedicated colleagues like you, Mrs Delia, we can continue to make even more constructive progress."

Mrs Delia smiled warmly and replied, "Mr Ashton, I completely understand your perspective because I've experienced something similar myself. Years ago, I had a sixth-grade student named Ulka. She struggled in many of her subjects, and she would always sit on the sidelines in class.

"One day, I decided to talk to her and figure out what was wrong. During our conversation, I discovered that Ulka loved music. Learning music was her strongest love and passion. But she had been told that music wasn't something she could build her future on. As we spoke, she asked me a question that shook me to my core. 'Miss, why do I have to study so many things that I don't care about? I just want to play like Beethoven one day.' That one sentence changed everything for me.

"I decided to help her. Even though our school didn't include music in its curriculum, I allowed her to spend some time in class talking about music and great composers and even playing her flute, the instrument she loved. From that moment, I saw a sparkle in her eyes, and her confidence began to grow. She was even doing better at school overall. Today, Ulka is a professional composer, performing her music at various festivals. As teachers, we often have the power to change the course of a student's life with a single decision. Perhaps it's these small differences that lead to great transformations."

Shabe smiled warmly. "Yes, definitely. Thanks for sharing, Mrs Delia. That's a beautiful story, and you're completely right. All it takes is for us to remove the lens of habit and see the world through fresh eyes, so we can notice new possibilities and take meaningful action. Thank you for sharing your incredible experience."

Mrs Delia smiled and closed her eyes in appreciation.

Shabe paused, drank a few sips of water and then went on. "Well, let me offer a few suggestions. Of course, these are just the broad outlines. For specifics, we need planning, detailed designs and focused implementation. Others may have even better ideas, and through collaboration, we can achieve much greater results. What I'm presenting today is simply based on my own knowledge and ability.

"The first step is to revise the curriculum. We need to introduce subjects like philosophy, ethics and self-awareness. These subjects help children develop critical thinking skills, better understand their place in the world, recognise the true importance of things and become independent and self-aware individuals. Mind you, ethics as a branch of philosophy is not just about what behaviour is right or wrong. It's much broader. It involves questions about relationships, the meaning of life, preserving our globe and leading a responsible and informed life.

"Second, the evaluation system needs to change. Why shouldn't we replace rigid, competitive exams with projects and activities that highlight students' creativity, interests and abilities?

"Third, instead of imposing a one-size-fits-all curriculum, we should have proper tools and methods to discover and appreciate each student's particular needs and callings. We must give teachers more freedom to adapt educational programs to the specific needs of their students. Clearly, if teachers have the right tools and authority, they can play a much more effective role in fostering individual and social growth and helping students flourish.

"Finally, we must create an environment where children feel heard and understood. We need to pay attention to their questions and show them that asking, exploring and even making mistakes are natural and essential parts of learning.

"I firmly believe that if all of us—teachers, administrators, parents and students themselves—seek improvement rather than simply accepting the status quo, we can transform the educational system from within and build a brighter future for the next generation.

"As George Bernard Shaw put it, we shouldn't merely look at what exists and ask 'Why?' Rather, we should envision what doesn't yet exist and ask, 'Why not?'"

Shabe paused, his gaze sweeping across the audience. "But there's one final point, perhaps the most important of all. Before we can change the education system or the future of children, we, the adults, must change ourselves. As teachers, parents and grownups, we must become more aware of our roles, of who we are and what we do. Perhaps, if we look into ourselves with a fresh approach, we might also find that we too can be addicted to the opium of showing off, of egoism."

The last sentences stirred a loud buzz among the audience. Many looked at each other in confusion or surprise, only to find out the other person was just as puzzled.

As the buzz subsided, Shabe continued. "After all, we've been exposed to the same treatments as children. It's a great pity that we tend to repeat the same things with our children. I have tried to show in my writing that ego, just like a drug, is something external, an enjoyable and addictive thing. Ego is a kind of opium that leaves us dependent on it, to the extent that our mental and even physiological organism can hardly function without it. My main point is that emotional and intellectual addiction are no less addicting than alcohol or drugs.

"So we need to ask ourselves: Are we the role models we expect children to look up to? Do we ourselves possess the insight, authenticity and examined life, as Socrates put it, that we wish for our children to have and do?"

"We must learn to question, to challenge the status quo and to seek better answers. The end of school should not be the end of education and learning. It should be a wonderful beginning to it. We must continuously read and study, not just to collect information but to deepen our understanding of life, the world and, of course, ourselves.

"Studying philosophy, history, ethics and self-awareness helps us live more wisely, recognise our place in the world and protect our freedom and consciousness from being sold to anyone or anything. Only then can we pass this perspective on to children.

"We need to understand that growth and flourishing are not the same as income, consumption and material wealth. Comfort and convenience are necessary but cannot replace happiness, wisdom or a meaningful life. If we fail to grasp this difference, how can we guide children towards a better path?

"Instead of blindly joining the aimless currents of a conformist mob, let us choose a different way. Remember, children learn more from our actions than from our words. If they see us practising critical thinking, if they observe us striving for growth and learning, and if they realise we live with a clear, independent purpose, they will naturally follow our example. And if we don't, how can we help children do that?"

Shabe paused again, then continued more firmly. "The law of life is simple. The tomorrow we dream of is built on the decisions we make today. Thank you."

The audience erupted into thunderous applause, then a standing ovation. Many of the greatest supporters were young students, energised and inspired by Shabe's words.

As the applause subsided, a man raised his hand. He was there with his young daughter, who Sally recognised as a classmate of Soren's. The man appeared to be around Shabe's age. From his appearance, he seemed to be a person of wealth.

Shabe turned to him and, raising his eyebrows. "Yes? Please go ahead."

The man said, "Thank you. I've heard you are against the practice of taking attendance numbers in class and that you yourself don't take attendance. I've also heard this has caused disagreements with school administrators. May I ask why you've adopted this approach?"

Shabe smiled and replied, "Sure. The reason is clear. If we can inspire students to eagerly attend class through our engaging lessons and approach, then attendance becomes irrelevant. And if we cannot engage and inspire them, forcing them to attend through markdowns and roll calls won't teach them much anyway, except resulting in their hating and disliking school, even learning, altogether."

At this moment, Sally turned her eyes to the man. Across the audience, in a voice loud enough for everyone to hear, she added, "And, as everyone knows, Mr Ashton's class is nevertheless one of the most popular with students. Rarely does he have any absences, and his students achieve great results."

Shabe thanked Sally with a nod and turned to the man again.

The man asked, "But how can we ensure that students have actually learned the material being taught?"

Shabe replied, "Why, then, do you conduct tests? Why are there exams and evaluations? Isn't that their purpose?"

The students, still hanging on to Shabe's every word, all rose to their feet, offering another standing ovation.

Mr Stern snorted to the teacher beside him. "These remarks aren't just utter nonsense. They're also harmful. Destructive!" He raised his eyebrows with the last phrase to emphasise his point. "The decision to allow such people to teach ought to be revised."

The teacher smiled politely before turning her attention back to Shabe, waiting for him to continue.

As if he'd heard Stern's remarks, Shabe said, "These points might sound upsetting to us, but agreeable points are not necessarily beneficial—just as drugs may be pleasant but not beneficial."

Stern's mouth tightened. He shouted, "These remarks are offensive! You're insulting people and values and everything!"

Shabe said mildly, "Mr Stern, the truth is indifferent to insult or praise; you must accept it as is."

Rob, the local grocer, who had read the first few issues of the *Weekly* and found Shabe's articles oblique and nonsensical, felt this gathering was an excellent opportunity to tell Shabe this, along with everyone else. "Mr Ashton," he said. "Don't you think these criticisms can cause disorder and doubt? You're questioning the educational and cultural ways of society. You're attacking everything."

"Rob," Shabe began. "If our ways and beliefs are so shaky and feeble that we feel threatened by reading an article or going to a lecture, let us feel so. Maybe that unpleasant feeling can motivate us to revisit such timid, flimsy beliefs. Only then can we achieve certainty.

"But I have to ask you. What's wrong with questioning? If you think about it, you'll find that asking questions is actually very fruitful and enlightening. If no one ever asked questions, there would've been no progress or advancements, nor would anything have been discovered, and nothing would've been corrected.

"We shouldn't be afraid of questions or being questioned, rather, we should be afraid of sheepish followership and the resultant stagnation. If there are any faults with our ways, it's only through questioning that they'll show up. Only with questions can everything progress and improve. And if there are no faults with how we're doing things, how could we possibly be harmed by a few simple questions? If you think I'm wrong, please correct me."

Rob, red-faced, glanced nervously around the hall.

The audience's eyes were on him, waiting to see how he'd respond.

Adjusting his position in his chair, he answered, "Well, before I accept what you say, I must know who you are. Who are you to condemn society with such a huge and established system so forcefully?"

"Well, that's exactly the point. It doesn't matter who I am; what's important is who you are, what you are after," Shabe said. "Ask yourself: what am I looking for? Make it clear to yourself. Will you follow people or truths? Facts or personalities? Who do you think I need to be for you to listen to what I have to say? A man with prestige? A person with name and fame and thousands of fans and followers? Or someone who's been awarded a bunch of medals and titles? Are you a truth-seeker or a medal-seeker? What do you mean by asking, 'who are you?'"

Rob didn't answer. He simply stared back at Shabe.

"The other question is, does being old or huge equal being right or correct?" Shabe asked. "Remember when humans believed the earth was the centre of the universe. Due to their limited knowledge, they imagined the sun and billions of stars and planets and the entire sky moved around them and their planet. Can you see how selfish and ignorant humans can be? That idea lasted for thousands of years! And was it true?

"If so, why did we stop believing that and accept Copernicus and Galileo's ideas? Think. Until only a century ago, if someone claimed that humans would fly even as high as a metre, everyone would have laughed at them. They'd have been called mad. But was the entire world or was that one person right? Just about a hundred years ago, slavery was an acceptable or even legal practice in many places across the world. But today, we have difficulty even believing humans used to be bought and sold, let alone accepting it. Which one was right?

"As you can see, being old or ordinary is not proof that anything is true or legitimate—whether we're talking about a custom, an idea, a way of life or anything else. The truth of everything must be proven via research, logic and reason. And if relevant, through tests, trial and experimentation, rather than mere age, tradition or the number of followers."

A faint hum started up in the hall as the audience murmured to each other.

Shabe waited for another question or interjection. None came. After a minute, he said, "Ladies and gentlemen, if you have any comments or queries about the articles and their contents, I'm here to listen and answer them."

At this moment, several people stood up, letting their chairs scrape noisily on the floor. They made angry, offended comments as they left the hall. But most stayed seated.

The first question about the book came from a young man Shabe had seen around town. He was wearing a pair of jeans, a pink shirt and a white cap. Shabe knew he was the parent of one of the students.

"You said it," the man began. "Even today, our joy and happiness depend on this addictive thing that is the ego. It's quite a profound idea, but if we're not kids anymore, and therefore don't have to rely on our parents, why do we still feel dependant on others? I've read some articles about this, but I couldn't find an answer to that."

"That's an excellent question. Thank you. You know, in many countries where opium is readily available, when someone gets ill with a painful sickness, they often turn to opium to soothe the pain. However, repeated use gradually makes their body addicted. Yes, little by little, that person can become ill with a bigger pain: the pain of addiction. Today, that person's illness might have completely healed and disappeared. When you look, you can't see any signs of the ailment that made the person use opium in the first place. Still, they're now reliant.

"Likewise, those who once used to torment us are not around anymore or may not have the same power over us. Nevertheless, because of the chronic use of this unhealthy medicine, we can hardly live without it."

Mr Kenzie, Daniel's father, was the second person in the audience to raise a hand. Well-groomed, dressed in a smart casual suit, he appeared to be in good spirits.

Shabe invited him to speak.

"Thanks for all your effort to enlighten our children and our community, Mr. Ashton. I'm glad we have such a great teacher in town. I have read all your articles in the *Weekly*. It seems to me that your theory presents three key factors as the main sources of human suffering: humiliation, ignorance and self-loss. My question is: which of these three is the root cause?"

"Yes, thank you. In fact, all three. The fact that we highlight one of them at a time does not mean there is a contradiction. The issue is that we are discussing a complex, multifaceted being called the human. Naturally, deep human issues possess multiple dimensions and characteristics simultaneously. The variety of terms we use serves to highlight different aspects of the same issue, not to suggest that these concepts are separate or distinct.

"For instance, when we talk about humiliation, we are referring to the mentality of smallness and worthlessness, a perception reinforced and reciprocated between individual and society. If a person truly values and respects their own existence, they will not degrade their being with unethical or disgraceful behaviour, nor waste their time in empty distractions and regrettable idleness. Instead of exhausting their talents by following others blindly, they will dedicate themselves to growth and personal flourishing.

"A self-confident person does not see their own intellect and judgement as inferior to those of others. While benefiting from different perspectives and approaches, they analyse, discern and make their own choices. Someone who does this will also treat others with respect and dignity. And if they don't, it is because of deeply ingrained humiliation, a condition that has led them to see not only themselves but also humanity as a whole as lowly and insignificant."

"But what about self-loss? As you mentioned, self-loss means seeing oneself as weak and incapable, lacking the courage to express one's own opinions and surrendering one's inner being to the dictates of others. It means that instead of living within my own existence, my mind and soul become occupied by the insults of my aunt, the methods of my uncle and the propaganda of the TV. It means that, without realising it, I spend my entire life following a path laid out by others, feeling sorrow and joy based on borrowed emotions. It means that I perceive the meaning and significance of things only in the way others have always seen them, rather than how they truly are or could be seen. In this sense, you can see that self-loss is simply another face of humiliation—it is when, in thought, feeling and action, we become occupied and directed by others in a way that belittles us.

"Understanding how these two concepts connect to ignorance shouldn't be difficult. All of these phenomena unfold in the shadow of ignorance and unawareness. Ignorance makes us perceive ourselves as worthless and insignificant. It causes us to regard our own judgement as inadequate. A lack of awareness leads us to sacrifice our peace for competition, or to seek gratification in humiliation, self-proving and exploitation. It causes us to confuse happiness with shopping and consumption. Furthermore, it convinces us this unfortunate state of affairs is normal and inevitable.

"In this sense, concepts such as ignorance, humiliation and self-loss are not separate or distinct; they are interconnected. Discussing one of them inevitably points to the others. All that said, I still believe that the best concept to illustrate this situation is humiliation, for the reasons explained in my writings."

Mr. Kenzie shifted slightly in his chair and said, "That was an excellent explanation. Thank you very much."

Steve, the butcher, rose to his feet. Clearing his throat, he said, "Mr Ashton, I haven't read more than a few articles of yours, but from what I understand, you say we shouldn't care about others' opinions. Well, I just don't think it's proper to ignore others and their views. We live with these people, and we're in constant give and take with them. It's obvious their ideas are important and play a role in our lives."

"I'm glad you brought up this question." Shabe said. "Please note that I don't say we should ignore others or be indifferent to their views; what I say is that we shouldn't fear social judgements. We shouldn't feel lost and overwhelmed by them. I say we shouldn't blindly follow others' steps but ought to have our own clear and well-defined principles for our deeds and judgements and how we live.

"There's a big difference between listening to and taking advantage of others' views and copying or fearing them. There can be two scenarios: in the first one, you listen to what I have to say, check it out with your reason—just as you've done right now—and then decide for yourself if you'll accept it or discard it. It is you who'll decide if my views are right or wrong. In this case, you're not anxious about my idea, nor do you feel compelled to follow it.

"But what I am sincerely opposed to is following an idea without really understanding it. In this situation, we don't critique others' opinions; we fear them. We're afraid society will take our good reputation away from us, or attach a bad one to us. That, I call self-loss, which is because our reason and judgement has been belittled and, worse, we have come to believe that belittlement. The self-lost person unquestioningly follows whatever is common in society. They submit to acts and behaviours they're unsure about, that they haven't even chosen. It's natural then for them to feel enslaved and frustrated. That is what can ruin our peace and freedom.

"Interestingly, we're seriously concerned about social and political freedom, we say we want suffrage and freedom of expression, yet we hardly consider we might be a helpless captive who doesn't allow ourself to think and choose. Mind you, habit has normalised this slave-like behaviour. But intellectual captivity is the most horrendous kind of slavery, because it's profound and hidden. This is our discretion via inner and outer authorities that we always regard as greater and more important than us.

"And who are these authorities? Custom. Tradition. Upbringing. Inherited beliefs. Adverts and media. Prevailing norms and trends. These are what have shaped the ways we think and judge and feel, ever since we were children! So that's what we need to replace with informed choice. Because if we lack emotional and intellectual freedom, reaching inner peace and happiness is an impossible dream."

At this point, a man from the student section raised his hand.

"Yes! What are you studying?" Shabe asked.

"I study psychology." The man looked to be in his early twenties and was in smart-casual dress. The combination of his friendly smile and his serious demeanour conveyed a sincere desire to discover the truth.

"I'm glad to see your interest—and that of the other students—in these matters," said Shabe. "Go ahead, please."

"Thank you. You talk about liberating yourself from others' perspectives, and you say our peace depends on getting rid of interpretive values."

"Yes."

"Well, if I did free myself from society's expectations and, as you put it, the outward I, I'd still have some sort of image of myself and who I am. I can't say I wouldn't have any image or understanding of my identity or even my social status. So in that case, what image would I have?"

"That's right," Shabe took a quick sip of water. "When empty valuations lose their worth in your eyes, the outward I or the mask-personality gives up its importance. In that case, you just wouldn't worry about people's likes. As a result, you'd remove the constant concern for getting others' approval, whether that's from your parents, colleagues, boss or relatives. That's not to say there won't be a public image of I; such an image will always be there.

"However, a great change occurs when concern for how you look is replaced by love for who you are. And this change unlocks the handcuffs from your thoughts and feelings; peace and light-heartedness replace anxiety and pressure. When that happens, you possess an I, but you don't fret about it. You do have a public image but aren't too concerned about how your image looks to others. That image will not be polluted by fear, longing and self-blame.

"You'll see yourself as you are, not through the standards of your dad, auntie, teacher or fashions and trends. Any futile struggles you've had to prove yourself to others will be replaced by the profound joy and contentment of cultivating your true being."

Shabe linked his fingers as he looked out to the audience with a subtle smile. "Let me tell you a parable from ancient Iran."

Several people pricked their ears at the mention of an upcoming story, keen to hear it.

"One day, a renowned, revered mystic was lying on the grass in a meadow, resting. His horse was roped to a stake. A man who'd heard a lot about mystics and their thrifty ways of life knew this mystic was walking by. He noticed, to his surprise, that the stake the mystic used to tether his horse to was made of gold.

"Taken aback, the man went up to the sage and asked, 'I've always heard that mystics are known for their thrifty life and modesty, but I can see that your horse's stake is made of gold. That doesn't look like thrift to me.'

"The sage responded tranquilly, 'As you can see, I've nailed the stake into the mud, not into my heart.'"

Audiences laughed at that, and Shabe went on.

"What that answer means is contentment doesn't involve not possessing, despite what Diogenes and the Cynics thought; it means not being attached. The liberated person is not devoid of identity. They still hold a picture of themself, but this picture brings them neither worry nor doubt because it's authentic and independent. They don't mistake themselves or their value for others' images or judgements of them. They've realised the shaky and unreliable nature of external validations and thus have little concern or sensitivity about it. A wise person stops playing the futile games of society, and lives an unshaken, liberated life. They may own a gold stake, but they've put it into mud, not into their heart."

A young woman, dressed in business attire with a neat ponytail, raised her hand.

Shabe nodded at her.

"I just wanted to say that what you say sounds great and rather beautiful, but I think it isn't feasible," she said. "Sounds more idealistic than practical, if you ask me."

Shabe smiled as if he'd expected this rebuttal. "I understand. By ideal, you mean something unreachable, and being an idealist means going after unreachable things; wishful thinking, if you like. On the opposite side, there's reality and thinking realistically. Am I right?"

The woman furrowed her brow. "Well, yeah."

"Okay, but which one is really idealistic: what I am saying or what most of us do? What I say is that fake values are full of inconsistencies. Holding on to them is like trying to solve an unsolvable question.

"I say, let's not go after imaginary values. Let's not try to become a flawless character. Let's accept ourselves as we are, live by our natural needs and express our authentic feelings. Let's be ourselves; use our own reason and discretion, and not identify with a thousand things that aren't relevant to us. Let's not compare ourselves to others or try to avoid ourselves. Let's not identify with labels printed by society. Let's remove the fear of losing some imaginary status.

"If people lived with the truth—that is, if they accepted themselves and others as they are—would so much hate and pain emerge? Now tell me, is what I say idealistic? Or are these practices, which are unexamined and taken for granted, realistic?"

Silence.

Shabe continued. "Mind you, this matter can be considered from another angle as well. When people like me talk about human suffering or deal with the social, historical and philosophical roots of the problem, many think we want to change the world into a new, flawless one, a utopia. So they accuse us of idealism or wishful thinking. But I don't see how that could be interpreted if you really think about it.

"Ever wondered what the greatest cause of our ignorance is? Labelling, instead of looking! We don't like changing our opinions. We prefer to live in a fixed, static world with all its convenient names and labels.

Whatever we see, we'll pull out a familiar label from memory and stick it on it, whether it's a person, a practice or an idea. We can then say, 'Okay, it's settled; I don't need to think about it or analyse it.' This habit is like a dam in the way of our growth, preventing us from seeing new horizons.

"Obviously, solving the problems of the whole world is within neither my nor your power as individuals, and we don't have the time. However, what we're after is to work out our own problems. If everybody deals with their own problems while helping and sympathising with others, the world's problems will inevitably be solved.

"Think about this: As recently as forty or fifty years ago, if anyone talked about our duty to preserve the seas and rivers or avoid polluting the air or the earth's atmosphere, many would frown and accuse the speaker of idealism, even fanaticism.

"Meanwhile, today, preserving our globe is accepted as common sense, and it's now everyone's responsibility to do so. They say that anyone who wants themself and their family to live in a clean, healthy world, must be careful about how they treat their world's environment. They say, 'Think globally; act locally,' which is a consequence of arriving at this insight and the understanding that we're part of this world and what goes on in it.

"Whether we realise it or not, we play a role with our acts and attitudes. Therefore, if we are to recognise our place in this structure and make sure our actions don't increase the misery and ignorance, we certainly need to know more about this system. Short-sightedness and merely seeing how we can benefit personally, isn't realism; it's foolishness! Most of the world's tragedies are created by those who aren't aware of their own roles in the social structure or underestimate them. Thus, being aware of our role and committed to playing it wisely isn't idealism; it's realism.

"The same thing applies to our sufferings, too. We tend to seek prescriptions to instantly cure our ailments. Quick fixes, if you like. We're blind to the fact that an individual's problems aren't separable from those of the society but are part of its totality. We can't tackle a problem with complex social, intellectual and cultural problems by merely looking no farther than our nose!

"Each of us is the result of centuries of thoughts, acts and experiences throughout human history. Our psychical makeup is shaped by our society's cultural, ideological and psychological structure. What we suffer from is also an offshoot of a huge problem of humanity.

"We can hardly solve our problem as an individual if we fail to identify this wider problem and comprehend it in its entirety. If we opened our eyes, we'd see that the outward world we've built reflects the inner world within us. What goes on in society is connected to how every one of us thinks, feels and behaves.

"This means you and me, mentally and emotionally hassling one another by our groundless judgements. We goad one another towards perfectionism by our irrational labelling and unfair expectations and set off all sorts of painful feelings such as guilt, frustration and inadequacy, followed by hate, misery, addiction and suicide, not to mention heart attacks and nervous system disorders.

"We like to show how happy we are, which makes others feel inadequate and deficient. I know a woman who spent the price of an apartment merely on wedding jewellery. She took every opportunity to boast. I later found that the wedding party had cost as much as the jewellery.

"Anyway, when one person spends enough money to buy several apartments, merely to boast and brag, God only knows how many simple people are tempted to enter the competition and abuse themselves, then leave themselves open to heart and nerve-related illnesses.

"This woman is so elated by showing off that she hardly realises how her bad example could lead so many to steal or commit other misdeeds to catch up. Interestingly, this same lady will go to fundraisers and weep for poverty-stricken, hungry kids.

"Yes! There are ridiculous contradictions in how we think and act. So feeling responsible for our deed's impact on society is not idealistic; it's absolutely essential and humanistic. And the outcome of such awareness is being a sensible human and living a conscious life. And the fruit of that is living in a healthy, wealthy society, not an ugly world where some undergo surgery to remove accumulated fat as others suffer from starvation. Failing to see such a blatant connection is either because of ignorance and self-deceit, or heartlessness and indifference."

What is the Truth?

A university professor around Shabe's age raised his hand.

Shabe smiled. "A question from a professor! Go ahead, please."

The man coughed and said, "You've often used the word 'truth' in your remarks—seeking the truth, arriving at the truth or realising the truth. Others use that word frequently too. Doctrines, schools, faiths, religions, sects and spiritual leaders also talk about the truth. Would you please explain clearly what you mean by truth? How do you define the word?"

"To me," Shabe answered, "the truth means everything as it is. Seeing the truth refers to the ability to see things just the way they are. It refers to seeing the world and its phenomena without prejudice, agenda, fantasy or illusion. These are the things that form the barriers to our reason, obscure our sight and represent things to us in a misleading, distorted way.

"I appreciate your question. It sounds astonishing that such a simple thing is so difficult, that it has stirred up so much debate, disunity and enmity, and has led to the emergence of so many faiths and sects and cults and ..."

Shabe paused and stroked his chin as he contemplated his next words. "Many philosophers, gurus and prophets have come to show the truth or, more precisely, to teach the right way of seeing things. Throughout history, human sight has been obscured by various feelings, wants, needs and fears. These feelings have put a solid wall in the way of our seeing the truth of things.

"The issue is so prevalent that in seeking the truth, your efforts involve finding out what the truth is *not*, rather than what it is! However, it's important to keep in mind that this thick cover has not disguised the truth; it's merely masked our sight because the truth can't be concealed with any veil.

"Thus, seeking the truth means removing the blockage in front of our own eyes. Two people might look at a thing without prejudgement or bias and still see different pictures. However, this difference doesn't necessarily lead to hostility because a wise person is always willing to consider different outlooks and experiences to enhance their own.

"In fact, peoples' fights are not because of differences but intolerance of differences. The reason for so much divergence is that we humans are not unbiased in how we look at the world. So we tend to see what we would rather see, not what's really there.

"Let me share a memory with you. A critic reviewing a film said, 'I was there to hate' after realising the movie he'd seen had actually been a good one, contrary to his prior expectation. This sentence, 'I was there to hate,' aptly expresses our mind's inclinations in seeing and judging the world.

"This critic, as he admitted, had attended the screening with an already-negative mentality. Had he not been a critic, had he not had a critical mind, he'd have seen only the drawbacks of the movie and overlooked the strengths. His mind would've provided him with the evidence he needed to reject the film as worthless. And this is what so often happens in how we see ourselves, others and life. Rumi advises,

'A seeker of anything, my friend,
Sees nothing but what he's seeking.'

And, on the influence our feelings have on our judgements, he says,

As inclinations come in,
the truth is shielded.
Hundreds of veils move
from the heart towards the eyes.

What he's trying to convey here is that our reason is often eclipsed by our emotions. In fact, we could say all these discussions aim to show what tends to prevent us from seeing the truths of things.

"Here, I've tried to show what happens to us from the moment we step into the world as humans. Our fresh outlook is polluted by ignorance, self-deceit and unhealthy demands. It robs us of the potential to see the world clearly.

"As I've tried to show you, humans' suffering grows from seeing ourselves and our world erroneously. Clearly, that doesn't refer to innocent children or those who are unjustly abused and oppressed. Rather, I speak of those who deliberately oppress or, whether through ignorance or self-interest, enable the insidious cycle of injustice and exploitation. The moral cancer of humanity is ignorance and prejudice. To see the truth, we need to identify these veils and pull them off. Peace and serenity are the fruits of submission to the truth."

An elderly man seated at the back of the hall attempted to speak, though the distance made him rather inaudible.

"Sorry, sir," Shabe said. "Would you like to come up to the microphone?"

The man walked up to the podium.

Shabe held out the microphone to him.

"Thanks," the man said. "I read your articles. You make some pretty good points. But you say the cause of all our troubles comes from fake evaluations. Many of our problems are from other stuff, too, like poverty. Financial pressures put a lot of strain on parents, which can explain their irritability with their kids, even to the extent of abuse and belittlement."

He handed back the microphone to Shabe, who said, "Thank you very much for raising that point."

The man walked back to his seat.

"First, please note, I don't say all of our problems arise from false values. You can't claim that incurable diseases or natural disasters do. What I say, rather, is that most of our emotional and behavioural sufferings stem from false values and baseless evaluations. Mind you, if we weren't afflicted by self-loss and selfishness, a legion of disorders that come from abusing ourselves or mistreating others, such as heart disease or addiction, wouldn't happen, or they'd have a far more limited lifespan and happen less. Neither would even many calamities such as environmental destruction and pollution take place, which are outcomes of our blind demand to buy and consume and show off and call it happiness.

"However, my point is that outward issues by themselves can hardly create psychological suffering—at least not with the spread and intensity we see now. Most emotional pains aren't because of objective problems such as poverty and illness; they're because of the wrong, illusive ways of understanding and treating them, including the value-laden judgements."

"I have a question," said a young girl from the student section.

Shabe noticed her colourful dress style, and she spoke with an accent, suggesting she'd come from some distance away for her studies.

"Before we go further," she said. "I have a problem right there. What do you mean by accepting the problems? Shouldn't we do anything?"

"Just the opposite," Shabe replied. "I mean, we must act more effectively. Our pain comes from comparing an unpleasant situation to a perfect one and condemning it as hateful. In fact, most suffering comes from baseless comparison! In one way or another, almost any emotional problem has its root in comparison and reproach.

"Now, accepting an issue as a fact means neither denying it, nor comparing it to an ideal situation. It means trying to find a solution in a logical manner. That's productive and effective. But rejection involves overlooking the problem; it involves deceiving ourselves or facing the issue with denial or frustration. That's futile and unhelpful.

"Why? Because the first step in solving a problem is seeing it! When you look at a problem without making groundless comparisons, you can probe it correctly. And then in dealing with it, you're acting smartly and effectively.

"However, when you reject a problem or hate it, you move the issue from outside to inside yourself. As a result, the issue hurts you on the inside. Here's an example. When you see your car has a technical issue, you see it as it is; you diagnose the fault and get it fixed. You don't suffer mental pain.

"But when you say to yourself, 'This battered vehicle is an embarrassment,' you're adding a personal and internal aspect to the physical issue of the car's breakdown. Here, you're linking 'the battered vehicle' to your identity; that is, you're identifying yourself with your problem. You're adding that emotional pain to the objective, physical issue of the faulty car.

"The hate and anger of the father who hits and abuses his child because of poverty, as you said, is not due to his financial pressure; it's due to the pressure he feels from the value-laden images of *poor man*, and a *failure*, which he associates with himself and his situation. If he could see his financial problem as it is—that is, if he did not look at himself through the labels society has imposed on his mind—his situation would remain at the level of a real one. It would also be much easier to sort out.

"I never meant poverty isn't a significant issue or that it doesn't matter if you don't have enough money. On the contrary! Poverty is a very serious concern, and likewise, to tackle it, intense individual and social actions need to be taken. However, what I say is, poverty is poverty, and inferiority is inferiority. The first thing is objective and real; the second thing is mental and imaginary.

"Unlike exterior problems, our inner feelings depend primarily on the ways we see and judge things. A single event might seem ordinary to one person, but absolutely dismaying to a second one, and even enjoyable to a third! The reason is, these three each hold their own outlooks on that occurrence.

"Let me give you an example. Suppose John, Matt and Fred travel to our town, all at the same time and by the same train. However, during the journey, John is excited to see the city, while Matt looks sad, and Fred seems indifferent.

"When you ask why, you find John's been to the town before and holds pleasant memories of that journey, because he met his spouse here.

"Matt's had a bitter experience, as he fell sick here on his last trip."

Suddenly Joe, the carpenter, burst out with, "Hopefully, Matt hadn't eaten meat from Steve, the butcher!" He was overcome with amusement.

Turning their heads to Joe and Steve, who were sitting near each other, everyone else burst into laughter, even Steve, who showed a mix of mirth and embarrassment at his friend's joke. The hall was full of loud hilarity for several moments.

Shabe, who was also laughing, continued when the noise subsided. "And the third traveller, Fred, is totally new to the town and has no background about it. Here, you have three people in a single, identical situation but with three different feelings. Clearly, these attitudes arise from different mentalities and have nothing to do with the trip itself.

"In fact, our feelings and behaviours are not determined by what's going on around us. They are determined by our understanding and interpretation of them.

"Note that this statement does not mean external events or situations are inherently all good or even neutral, nor does it mean we should not oppose what we see as wrong or unfair; rather, it means that, inevitably, our emotions and actions primarily follow our judgements, rather than following actual facts or events. In other words, this statement does not prescribe anything. It describes the actual psychological mechanism.

"You can see the same difference in the example of the three fellow travellers in the ways people act and feel at the social level. In some societies, where what is called poverty by our standards is commonplace. You see people barefoot, in shabby clothes, and families living in hut-like houses as you walk through the streets. Some of them even live on the streets.

"However, when you talk to them, you find them very laidback and welcoming. You're surprised to see these people have little complaint, despite their hard and relatively low-quality conditions. As you get to know more about their culture and social interactions, you find few traces of hate or anger in their morale or behaviour. These people rarely compare their lives with one another, so they don't condemn it, don't crave a better situation or suffer inner conflict.

"I repeat: this is not to say poverty and homelessness don't matter; the very thing I want to get across is poverty and material hardships, of themselves, cannot create psychological complications—unless perhaps in an extreme form. Whether we suffer or not mainly depends on the ways we think, expect and judge.

"On the other hand, in many idyllic, affluent societies, you often find many rich families who are absolutely miserable, and their emotional lives are such a mess. So are many of their personal and family relationships. Many even suffer profound mental issues; they take anti-depressive medication and seek expensive counselling from psychologists.

"If you look closely, you'll find the reason is these well-to-do folks, instead of appreciating what they have and enjoy in life, tend to compare their life with others' or with an ideal situation and are obsessed with what they think they must have but don't yet.

"In these examples and numerous others, our feelings would follow our judgement regarding the situation we found ourselves in. Understanding that, you'll realise what a massive role your own mind always plays in how you see yourself and judge the world.

"When you discover this determining role, you'd probably rely on outward factors far less than before. And instead of running towards happiness, you'd try to rip out unhappiness from within. And the inner sources of unhappiness are ignorance, self-loss and egoism. Rumi says, in this regard,

> *'The road to happiness lies within; not without.*
> *It's foolish to seek palaces and castles.*
> *See this one, joyful and happy in the corner of a mosque.*
> *Watch the other, sad and disheartened, in the pretty garden*
> *So, ruin the body. The palace is nothing, my friend.*
> *The treasure lies in ruins.*
> *Don't you see that, in the wine party,*
> *The drunk gets joyous only when he gets ruined.'"*

David turned to Sally, eyebrows raised, taken aback by Shabe's words.

She whispered, "Remember how I said Shabe is a researcher of Middle Eastern literature, particularly Persian poetry and mysticism?"

David nodded musingly, turning his attention back to Shabe. Then Mr Neil raised his hand.

"Yes?" Shabe said.

"I hear mystics usually promote strict abstinence, including testing your body by imposing hunger, harsh, uncomfortable clothes and fewer physical pleasures. Is that what Rumi recommends here?"

"No, it's not, and I was just going to elaborate on that."

"Oh, okay. Thanks," Mr Neil said.

"We should bear in mind," Shabe continued, "that Sufism has its own language and expressions, which are often poetic and allegorical. What you've said is generally right about many mystic schools, but it doesn't apply to Rumi's view and teaching. The body here refers to the ego and egoism, which distorts and obscures our understanding. Rumi advises to free yourself from this 'cross-eyedness' to see that outward factors can do little to bring you enduring happiness. The drunk man here alludes to the liberated person and self refers to the ego. Just think and you'll find the profound meaning.

"I'll share one further point: the difference between happiness with enjoyment and happiness with wealth. We often mistake these for each other," said Shabe. "Wealth and welfare are related to physical comfort. They're about corporal provisions. They involve such things as enjoying a decent income as well as good food, clothing, housing and so on.

"But happiness refers to inner satisfaction, to emotional peace and moral contentment. And we all know being wealthy doesn't necessarily mean being happy. Wealth is about what you possess; happiness is about how you feel. You might have great resources but little peace of mind. That's why you often see wealthy people who possess all sorts of material goods but enjoy little inner peace. Of course, we witness the opposite too. Many not-so-wealthy people enjoy deep gratification about life and have rich, flourishing work activities and relationships.

"No doubt, enjoying physical health and having access to material resources are the primary and essential rights of every human. All the same, we need to note that wealth isn't happiness. So to be happy, it's a futile effort to keep striving for more money and more pleasure. What Rumi suggests by 'ruining the body' is the realisation of the futility of this greedy struggle, one which mistakes physical pleasure for inner serenity."

The Chance to Be Present

A middle-aged woman raised her hand. She was attending the event with her grandson, a jubilant, bright-eyed, energetic teenager with a curious look on his face.

Shabe nodded to her. "Go ahead, please."

"Thank you for sharing your ideas. I personally find them absolutely riveting, and I believe it would be extremely beneficial for young people to know about them and use this wisdom in their future," said the woman.

Shabe smiled. "I agree."

"Pardon the obscurity of my question," the woman continued. "But what do you believe is the meaning of life? Why do we live in the first place?"

Shabe adjusted the glasses again as he considered. "I think we first need to ask ourselves what has caused us to look for a meaning to life?

"Life is a short opportunity to be here. Life is not something to translate; it's something to live. I don't mean we shouldn't ask for the meaning of life; I mean the meaning of life is inherent in itself, with all fruitful and enjoyable activities making it rich and worthy to live. You'd be thrilled if you visited a beautiful garden and had the chance to prune and water the plants; your presence and contribution to the flourishing of the trees and flowers would fill you with joy and wonder. That is the meaning of that.

"Of course, the richer and more prosperous we make our lives, the more meaning and purpose we will experience. And vice versa. If we waste our days in futile fights or purposeless wanderings, we will likely wonder why and what can come of so much struggle. The one who breaks rocks in prison will question what they gain from such misery, while the person strolling through a magnificent garden hardly asks themselves why."

Shabe took a glance at the hall's vintage clock. "Well," he said. "It looks like our time is over. I'd like to sincerely thank you all for coming today and participating in these discussions. I'd also like to announce that the articles published in the *Weekly* have been compiled into a novel titled *The Tightrope Walker*."

Whispers could be heard across the hall, with many people echoing the title.

"I'd like to sincerely thank my dear friend Soren Dustin, who was by my side all the way through reading and writing this book. His sincere comments and precious insights contributed significantly to the richness and improvement of the book."

The audience gave a loud clap at the last sentence. Amid the applause, Sally and Dave looked at each other and exchanged delighted smiles.

"When the book is out, I'll donate a copy to our school library and the town libraries," Shabe said. "I'd be glad to hear any feedback, points, criticism and comments. I hope we can all contribute to the growth of one another's awareness by continuing to partake in such useful events as this one. I also hope that the indecent sentence—'that's not my problem'—vanishes from all languages of the world.

"The last point I'd share is this. As far as I am concerned, the real outcome of such discussions is not necessarily coming to an agreement on particular points but coming to the agreement that we all need to read, ask and think," said Shabe.

Shabe left the podium during the applause. In the half-hour tea break that followed, heated discussions erupted, with attendees sharing their takes and opinions on the matter, a mix of support and opposition arising in response to Shabe's ideas.

When the audience returned for the last part of the event, Mr Neil, the editor of the *Weekly*, climbed to the podium. "Well, we have prepared a fantastic closure for this event. We will now watch a performance titled *The Village of the Slaves*, written and performed by the talented people of our school's drama department."

As the applause wound down, gentle music began. The audience became silent, their eyes fixed on the stage's red velvet curtain. Among the eager faces were Sally, David, and Hans and Daniel's fathers.

The music faded, and the curtains swept aside, the spotlight revealing a slave in the middle of the otherwise dark stage. Dressed in a ragged costume and scruffy shoes, he sat leaning on his palm, apparently deep in thought. Under his dishevelled hair, his face appeared troubled, almost exhausted. Around his neck, a tin plaque hung with the words 'BEST GOOSE WALKER' engraved on it.

Beside him stood two other slaves in conversation, their costumes identical to the first slave, except for their colours. They each wore a rusty plaque around their necks. Engraved on one was the title 'BEST CARTER,' while 'BEST WOODCUTTER' appeared on the other.

In the corner stood a middle-aged man with an arrogant smile, wearing a shiny gold medal with 'GREAT MASTER' carved on it. His clothes were pristine: a white suit and velvet waistcoat with a yellow hat and brown shoes. Holding a cigar in his left hand and a lash in his right, the master raked the slaves with his antagonising gaze. He let out a loud, cackling howl of laughter.

Sally and David reached for each other's hands, enthralled.

As the curtains reopened, the audience cheered as Shabe, Soren, Hans, and Daniel smiled and bowed on the stage. Hans and Daniel's fathers clapped enthusiastically among the spectators.

A few minutes after the attendees left the hall, Shabe, Soren, Sally, and Dave gathered in the foyer.

"Thank you, Soren," Shabe said, patting Soren on the back. "In fact, our book was completed today. It feels great, doesn't it?" he asked.

Grinning wide, Soren answered, "It really does. Thank you!"

Dave and Sally watched the two talking, contented smiles on their faces.

Shabe didn't miss the bright gleam of hope shining in their eager eyes as they dreamed of their son's future. "Do come around anytime for a chat, whenever you feel like it, and let's enjoy the fresh look," Shabe said.

"You missed the word '*miracle.*' The miracle of the fresh look!" Soren grinned.

"Of course!"

With his notebook in hand, Soren sat on a smooth rock at the beach. There, the dancing waves, having travelled thousands of kilometres, finally met the hot pebbles of the shore. His trousers were rolled up to his knees, and his legs were submerged in the cool water that swished through his toes, a relief from the sultry summer weather.

He opened the notebook, pulling the pencil from behind his ear and slowly turning the pages. On the first page, in his handwriting, he wrote: '*The Serendipity.*' He turned the page. There, he scribbled: '*Story Summary: First Draft.*'

> *The man had been travelling for a long time. He hadn't kept track of time, nor how he had ended up so far from familiar places. All he knew was that he had been walking for what felt like years, along a narrow, winding path, silent and mostly untouched, a trail more than a road, one that seemingly few others ever dared to take.*
>
> *He was hungry and worn out, searching for a small pouch of coins he had lost long ago. But perhaps, without quite realising it, he had also been searching for something else. Something deeper. When all familiar places had failed him, he turned to the unknown.*
>
> *A heavy backpack weighed him down, and he couldn't remember when it had first been placed there or by whom. Inside it were useful things, useless things and many strange objects whose meanings or uses he didn't understand, but he never dared to throw*

any of them away. He had never seen anyone else do that. It had always been part of him, after all.

He was not just lost in place but also in spirit. He longed for rest, for calm, for stillness. On the road one quiet day, something shiny in the distance caught his eye.

Tired but curious, he approached it. It appeared rather small, standing out against its surroundings with its strange, different shape and colour.

"Curious," he murmured. He, who had searched everywhere for his lost belongings, said to himself, "Let's have a look; perhaps I can find it here."

As he lifted the stone, a flash of light burst from beneath it, blinding him for a moment. The traveller could hardly believe his eyes. A large chasm had opened in the earth, revealing treasure glowing in a golden light: endless coins and gems.

What an enormous stroke of serendipity! The traveller had been searching for something small and had stumbled upon something infinite.

It took him a while to settle down again, to let the excitement fade and calm return. Overwhelmed, he sat beside the treasure. "What should I do with all this?" he wondered aloud. "How can I use it?"

Then he said to himself, 'How could I possibly carry such a vast treasure on my own? Besides, there are so many friends and people back home who need it too.'

Eventually, he knew what he had to do: he would return to the city and tell others about his story and the great treasure he'd found.

Of course, some would laugh and some would say he was mad, in disbelief. But surely, some would listen, some would take the path too, and along the way, they would become kind friends and fellow travellers. This huge treasure could change their entire hometown, everyone's lives. So he drew a careful map, marked with notes and signs.

Now that he knew what he wanted, and where he was going, he could finally see what was precious in his knapsack—and what was not. He threw away everything that now seemed useless, and instead filled his pouch as best he could. And then he began the journey back ..."

Soren smiled contently as he closed the book and stared out at the vast expanse of the ocean. Immersed in thoughts, he began watching the azure waves sway to the shore and then retreat gracefully. The choir of the humming birds overhead mingled with the rhythmic song of the lapping waves to create a unique symphony. Perhaps they were telling him, in their unique language, about the world that he couldn't see.

ACKNOWLEDGMENTS

The journey of creating this book would not have been possible without the support, encouragement and presence of many cherished souls who walked beside me, each in their own meaningful way. My deepest love and gratitude go to my dear daughter, Isa, whose calm presence, thoughtful reflections and tireless support accompanied me through every step of editing and revision. To my beloved son, Ryan, I owe a special thanks for the joy, inspiration and imaginative ideas that found their way into the creation of these pages.

I am also incredibly grateful to a circle of dear friends whose care, time and insightful feedback helped shape this work. A warm thank you to my beloved Sheida Shad and to Marziyeh and Abdollah Shiari, Hamid Rezaei, Karen Skinner, JoAnne Elvery, Shuaib Farahin, Neda Mirab, Hossein Sedaghat, Arezou Naderi, Peggy Alimardani, Ali Bozorgmehr, and Darya Tofighi. Thanks to Chanice Edmond, who did the initial reading and editing of the first draft. These invaluable friends' support, thoughtful engagement and encouraging words provided both clarity and courage when I needed them most.

I am especially honoured to acknowledge the influence and guidance of several remarkable thinkers and teachers: Mostafa Malekian, distinguished Iranian philosopher; Dr Hassan Mohaddesi, professor of sociology; Dr Mohammad-Reza Sargolzaei, psychiatrist and author; Dr Mohammad Hosseini-Pour, psychologist; Dr Mahmoud Masaeli, professor of law and philosophy; Masoud Zanjani, lecturer in philosophy; and Ali Omrani, celebrated actor and director.

I would also like to express my heartfelt gratitude to the wonderful team at Aurora House Publications. To Linda Lycett, the manager, for her steady presence and thoughtful coordination. To Josephine Brown, for her insightful and meticulous editing, and to Donika Mishineva, for her artistic cover design. Many thanks also to my wonderful publisher, Holly Shore, for her kind support and guidance.

I am profoundly grateful to the many others whose names may not appear here but whose kindness, insight and quiet encouragement live between the lines—I offer you my heartfelt thanks. This book carries the light of your presence.

ABOUT THE AUTHOR

Sasan Habibvand is a philosopher, counsellor and scholar of Persian literature and mysticism. Inspired by a blend of philosophical and psychological perspectives and the timeless wisdom of Rumi, Sasan offers a thought-provoking perspective on human suffering, inner conflicts and the journey towards self-realisation.

As a native Persian speaker, he brings uniquely direct and authentic access to Rumi's teachings, including Rumi's profound view of the human condition and his healing message of love and liberation.

Sasan's philosophical works emphasise the profound connection between life philosophy and human flourishing. In his debut novel, *The Tightrope Walker*, he presents this relationship in a compelling and accessible narrative that intertwines psychological insight with philosophical depth.

What is delightfully fresh about Sasan's voice is that it is enriched by both Eastern and Western cultures. Living in Australia since 2011, Sasan has lived, studied and taught across various cultural contexts, which is clearly reflected in the richness of his writings. Sasan's interdisciplinary education in psychology, philosophy and mysticism imparts a rare flavour of variety and depth to his views and works.

His forthcoming English-language books include:

- *Through the Eyes of Rumi: An Introduction to Rumi's Life, Thought and Teachings*
- *The Alien Within: Talks on Meaning, Growth and Flourishing*
- *From Pain to Liberation: Reflections on Self-Knowledge*
- *The Puzzle of Happiness: A Fresh Inquiry into the Ways and Barriers of Authentic and Lasting Happiness*

Website: www.sasanhabibvand.com.au
Instagram: @sasanhabibvandauthor
Email: info@sasanhabibvand.com.au
Facebook: Sasan Habibvand – Rumi Scholar

THE KEYWORD LIST

Note:

The following is an alphabetical list of key concepts and prominent proper names discussed throughout the book. Rather than a traditional glossary, this is better viewed as a "concept list." Many of these concepts appear across different contexts and may be referred to using varying terminology. Similarly, the same term may carry different meanings depending on the context. These distinctions are clarified within the body of the text where they appear. Because the concepts are explored in multiple places, it would be impractical to include page numbers. This list is intended to help readers identify and recall recurring themes, ideas, and influential figures central to the book's message.

- **A**buse
- Addiction
- Admiration
- Advertisement
- Alien Self
- Anger
- Anxiety
- Attention-seeking
- Authenticity
- Authentic Life
- **B**rainwashing
- Blame
- **C**aptivity
- Care
- Change
- Childraising
- Childrearing
- Climate change
- Cognition
- Cognitive errors
- Cognitive illusion
- Comparison

- Competition
- Conditioning
- Conscious
- Confidence
- Conflict (Inner)
- Consumerism
- Contentment
- Control
- Critical Thinking
- Criticism
- Culture
- **D**arwin, Charles
- Death
- Deception/Deceit
- Defence Mechanisms
- Defensiveness
- Definition
- de Montaigne, Michel
- Denial
- Depression
- Disunity
- Durant, Will
- **E**ducation
- Education System
- Ego
- Egoism
- Empathy
- Ethics
- Evolution
- Example
- **F**aithfulness

- False Language (the)
- False Values
- Fear
- Fight
- Followership
- Freedom
- Free Will (vs Pre-determination)
- **G**lobal Concerns
- Global Warming
- Government
- **H**afiz
- Happiness
- Hitler, Adolf
- Honour
- Horney, Karen
- Humiliation
- Humiliated Person
- **I**dealism
- Ideal Personality
- Ideal Self
- Identification
- Identity
- Ignorance
- Illusion
- Imitation
- Imposition
- Imposed Self
- Improvement
- Independence
- Indoctrination
- Inferiority

- Insecurity
- Insult
- Intellect
- Interpretation
- Introspection
- Intrusive Thoughts
- **J**ealousy
- Judgement
- **K**hayyam, Hakim Omar
- Knowledge
- **L**abel
- Labelling
- Language
- Liberation
- Liberty
- Life
- Life Meaning
- Life Purpose
- Life Philosophy
- Living in the Now
- Loneliness
- "Looking Glass Self"
- Love
- **M**anipulation
- Mask
- Masked Person
- *Masnavi Ma'navi*
- Meaning of life
- Mental Health
- Mindfulness
- Mysticism
- **N**afs (the)
- Nationality
- Nationalism
- Neglect
- **O**bjection
- Occupation
- Oppression
- Outwardly Person
- Over-dependence
- **P**asteur, Louis
- Patriotism
- Pavlov, Ivan
- Peer Pressure
- Perfection
- Perfectionism
- Persona
- Philosophy
- Philosophy of Life
- Political System
- Poverty
- Projection
- Praise
- Pre-determination (vs. Free Will)
- Prejudice
- Pride
- Programming
- Projection
- Pseudo-values
- Psychology
- Psychologist
- **R**eason

- Reasoning
- Relationship
- Relaxation
- Reproach
- Rumi (Jalal al-Din Mohammad)
- Rumination
- **S**elf-acceptance
- Self-actualisation
- Self-alienation
- Self-awareness
- Self-belief
- Self-care
- Self-discovery
- Self-disown
- Self-deceit
- Self-esteem
- Self-flourishing
- Self-image
- Self-knowledge
- Self-loss
- Self-lost Person
- Self-preservation
- Self-realisation
- Self-worth
- Separation
- Serenity
- Slavery

- Social Pressure
- Social Reformation
- Social Responsibility
- Society
- Spirituality
- Struggle
- Struggle for Existence
- Subconscious
- Success
- Sufism
- Suggestion
- Superiority
- Superman
- Superstition
- **T**ime
- Transformation
- **V**alues
- Value-seeking
- Value-stricken
- Validation
- Verbal Abuse
- Vicious Cycle
- **W**isdom
- Wrath
- World-image
- World War II
- Worry

www.ingramcontent.com/pod-product-compliance
Lightning Source LLC
Chambersburg PA
CBHW030102170426
43198CB00009B/463